Understanding Religious Life

THE RELIGIOUS LIFE OF MAN
Frederick J. Streng, Series Editor

Understanding Religious Life, second edition
Frederick J. Streng

The House of Islam, second edition
Kenneth Cragg

Japanese Religion: Unity and Diversity, second edition
H. Byron Earhart

Chinese Religion: An Introduction, second edition
Laurence G. Thompson

The Buddhist Religion
Richard H. Robinson

The Way of Torah: An Introduction to Judaism, second edition
Jacob Neusner

The Hindu Religious Tradition
Thomas J. Hopkins

Anthologies

The Chinese Way in Religion
Laurence G. Thompson

Religion in the Japanese Experience: Sources and Interpretations
H. Byron Earhart

The Buddhist Experience: Sources and Interpretations
Stephan Beyer

The Life of Torah: Readings in the Jewish Religious Experience
Jacob Neusner

Understanding Religious Life

Second Edition

FREDERICK J. STRENG
Southern Methodist University

DICKENSON PUBLISHING COMPANY, INC.
Encino, California, and Belmont, California

ISBN-0-8221-0168-8
Library of Congress Catalog Card Number: 75-26540

Printed in the United States of America
Printing (last digit): 9 8 7 6 5 4 3 2

Illustrations by Carol Ingram

For Elizabeth and Mark
who eventually will be confronted by some
of the issues suggested in these pages

Table of Contents

TABLE OF CONTENTS

Foreword

THE RELIGIOUS LIFE OF MAN series is intended as an introduction to a large, complex field of inquiry—man's religious experience. It seeks to present the depth and richness of religious concepts, forms of worship, spiritual practices, and social institutions found in the major religious traditions throughout the world.

As a specialist in the language and culture in which a religion is found, each author is able to illuminate the meanings of a religious perspective and practice as other human beings have experienced it. To communicate this meaning to readers who have had no special training in these cultures and religions, the authors have attempted to provide clear, nontechnical descriptions and interpretations of religious life.

Different interpretive approaches have been used, depending upon the nature of the religious data; some religious expressions, for instance lend themselves more to developmental, others more to topical studies. But this lack of a single interpretation may itself be instructive, for the experiences and practices regarded as religious in one culture may not be the most important in another.

THE RELIGIOUS LIFE OF MAN is concerned with, on the one hand, the variety of religious expressions found in different traditions and, on the other, the similarities in the structures of religious life. The various forms are interpreted in terms of their cultural context and historical continuity, demonstrating both the diverse expressions and commonalities of religious traditions. Besides the single volumes on different religions, the series offers a core book on the study of religious meaning, which describes different study approaches and examines several modes and structures of religious awareness. In addition, each book presents a list of materials for further reading, including translations of religious texts and detailed examinations of specific topics.

We hope the reader will find these volumes "introductory" in the most significant sense: an introduction to a new perspective for understanding himself and others.

Frederick J. Streng
Series Editor

Preface

This book is an expansion and clarification of *Understanding Religious Man.* Through the inclusion of some new material, more examples of religious life, and an elaboration of the different processes of ultimate transformation, the book has been considerably increased in size. The format has fundamentally remained the same, though the chapters in Part III have been rearranged and a new chapter on the religious significance of fulfilling human relationships has been added. However, much of the material has been rewritten with a concern for simplification.

The title has been changed slightly to reflect more clearly the interpretation that religious life is a complex of processes through which people are being transformed. The focus is not on a religious essence that is possessed by certain persons—as some readers inferred from the words "religious man" in the title of the first edition. Rather, the book explores with the reader different efforts to interpret religion, describes various kinds of traditional religious processes of transformation, and analyzes modes of human awareness that either can be used by traditional religious institutions or can function independently as religious forces for some people. It is hoped that the title change and the reformulation of the material will make evident the concern with different aspects of the inner dynamics of religious life.

Of course, during the past six years I have developed more fully some of the methodological implications of the approach taken in the first edition and restated in different ways for students and colleagues the interpretations that are given there. Thus, I owe a debt of gratitude to many people who have reacted with questions, alternative interpretations, suggestions for clarification, and stimulating insights. Specifically, the concerns and efforts of some persons have had a direct influence on the second edition. Two former students who are now teaching and who contributed directly and indirectly to the formulation of many statements, but especially the psychological material, are Ms. Judy Johansen and Mr. Eugene Taylor. Teachers who discussed some portions or all of the material are Drs. J. T. Allen, C. L. Lloyd, Jr., and H. N. McFarland of Southern Methodist University, and Dr. Willard Johnson of California State University at Long Beach. Professor Sho-on Hattori of Doho University in Japan raised many questions of clarification in a two-year correspondence prior to the publication of his Japanese translation of the first edition in 1974. Ms. M. W. A. Seldon was a very careful and helpful copy editor, and Ms. E. Linden of Dickenson Publishing Company saw the manuscript through production. To all of these people I want to express my thanks publicly.

Frederick J. Streng
Dallas, Texas

Preface to the First Edition

"Religious life," like "the human spirit," cannot be defined; it can only be explored. Readers who have been exposed to a variety of religious expressions and who have reflected on the meaning of their own religious commitments will be most conscious of the difficulty in exposing the meanings found in the religious life of man.

To apologize for having left out material or for slighting the contributions of some well-known scholars is somewhat pointless, since the limitation of space has dictated some nearly arbitrary choices. Nevertheless, the author feels keenly aware of the omitted material—which, for other students of religion, might have found exposure at the expense of some of the discussion here included. This includes, for example, a discussion in Part I of the attempts of Western theologians and Eastern philosophers to relate their own religious commitments to man's religious life outside their own positions; or a discussion in Part II of specialists in supernatural powers (shamans, magicians, exorcists, spiritual healers) as another form of being religious; or a chapter in Part III on psychotherapy and interpersonal relations as a mode of spiritual transformation in the contemporary scene. This is all to say that the present book is not exhaustive in its coverage; at best it is suggestive of the variety of material and concerns in the study of religion.

I want to express my thanks to Dean Joseph D. Quillian, Jr. of Perkins School of Theology for making available a research grant for the summer of 1967, when the present draft of this book was written. Also, for their secretarial help, my thanks are due Mrs. Judith Banes, Mrs. Charlie Brown, Mrs. Bonnie Jordan, and Mrs. Peggy Tate. Valuable criticism and suggestions for improvement were given to me at different stages by several colleagues at Southern Methodist University: Van A. Harvey, James C. Livingston, W. Paul McLean, and James F. White; H. Byron Earhart of Western Michigan University; and Laurence G. Thompson of the University of Southern California.

Finally, I want to express my thanks publicly to those alert and sensitive students both at the University of Southern California and at Southern Methodist University who raised significant questions about, or pressed for clarification of, this material as it was presented in their classes. Hopefully these ideas will provide the basis for other students' exploration of the meaning of religious life.

F. J. S.

"My third theory," the bishop went on hurriedly . . . "is this: there is some Eternity even in our ephemeral lives, only it is very difficult for us to discover it alone. Our daily cares lead us astray. A few people only, the flower of humanity, manage to live an eternity even in their transitory lives on this earth. Since all the others would therefore be lost, God had mercy on them and sent them religion—thus the crowd is able to live in eternity, too."

—From Nikos Kazantzakis, *Zorba the Greek*

1.

The Problem of Interpreting Religious Life

Many people today feel that what is generally called "religion" is not really a "religious" experience. Others feel that what they do with their sense of religious commitment does not fit into an accepted definition of "a religion." Still others, who reflect on religious life, suggest that studying "religion" is often not a religious activity and that "religious studies" go beyond the study of religions. This complex situation is due, in part, to the fact that different people have sometimes diverse, sometimes overlapping notions of "religion," "a religion," "religious," and "religious studies," as well as different interpretations of what it means to *understand* religious life.

These different approaches are related to a basic characteristic of religious expressions, namely that, like so much of human life, religion is an interaction of subjective and objective experiences. In order to clarify some basic concerns in the study of religion, we will respond in this first chapter, to three questions that are often asked: What is religion? Why study religion? How should (can) it be studied?

What is Religion?

While recognizing that any definition of religion combines both subjective and objective elements, we want to examine, first, three dimensions of religious life and, then, propose a working definition of religion that will help to clarify the inner dynamics of various religious expressions. The selection of three dimensions of religious life does not imply that these are the only significant elements in religious life. Many factors—economic, historical, psychological, and biophysical—contribute to the form and meaning of people's religious attitudes and actions, and religious people may take some of them for granted or wish to forget others. However, an examination of religious life will reveal three interacting dimensions that are experienced by people who consider themselves religious: the personal dimension, the cultural dimension, and the ultimate dimension.

The Personal Dimension. For the individual, the problem of interpreting religious life focuses on internal reactions, decisions, and meaning. For example, someone might ask: How should I respond to the religious claims and practices of my neighbors? Does my religion pertain only to special (sacred) activities like going to the synagogue or church, bowing before the image of the Buddha, or praying in the direction of Mecca? Can my neighbor's fanaticism for football or my friend's social and political concerns to provide justice for all be called "religious"? Does religion also have to do with the way I relate to other people, integrate new experiences with old, or generally feel and think about life? Should I pray to Jesus? Should I chant "Hare Krishna!"? Should I reserve certain times each day for solitary meditation? The idea of religion brings to mind various images for different people. A person's thoughts about religion and questions about its significance are formulated in terms of that individual's experience and culture. In a large measure the possibility, importance, and way of interpreting religious life depend on an individual's experience with what he or she labels religion.

Religious concerns are often expressed in highly personal and emotionally toned statements. Such statements reveal a sense of inner conviction, reflecting an intrinsically inexpressible aspect of one's deepest awareness. This personal aspect makes many people uneasy. They feel, perhaps, a certain anxiety or irritation when confronted by someone whose religious beliefs differ from their own. Some people feel that, because of the emotional character of religious life, there can be no fruitful discussion about the most significant aspects of a personal commitment. One might ask, for example: Can two deeply committed adherents from different traditions, say a Southern Baptist and an American devotee of Krishna Consciousness, reach a consensus? Or do they simply try to convert one another? Could an exchange of personal experiences of divine presence lead both individuals to a deepened awareness? Are all extraordinary experiences of the same value? Can two people with different kinds of religious awareness even perceive the ultimate character behind each other's religious affirmation? This personal quality and the great variety of human experience are important aspects of religion, however difficult they may be for people to discuss.

A person who tries to understand the personal character of someone else's religious life is immediately involved in a dilemma, for the observer and the believer rarely evaluate the believer's religious commitment in the same way. The devotee recognizes or establishes a pattern of meaning, and the resulting beliefs and moral decisions confirm and reinforce personal experiences of ultimate (divine, or most enhancing) reality. That reality, however, is considered to be, at best, a possible (not necessary) value by the observer. This pattern of meaning not only explains for the devotee such extraordinary events as birth and death and prescribes behavior toward friends and enemies, but it also suggests how to overcome suffering and tragedy and how to become "complete," "whole," and spiritually "free."

Those who can find value only in the patterns of past experiences are sometimes insensitive to the deepest commitments of others. Piety is the rationalization that some devotees use for failing to investigate different interpretations of scriptures within their own tradition—to say nothing of exploring the meanings of other traditions. Those who wish to explore the personal character of others' religious life must be open to new possibilities. They must also become aware of their own patterns of experience if they are to avoid a blatant projection of their unique experiences on others.

A similar dilemma confronts the scholar who tries to interpret a variety of religious data. While trying to be empathic by imaginatively recreating the depth of meaning found in religious life, a scholar will look for the key terms and practices and attempt to relate particular forms of expression, such as songs, spiritual exercises, worship, social interaction, or symbols, to a wider interpretive scheme. These and other general concepts have been derived from comparative studies of the ideas or practices of different traditions, from descriptions of the historical development of beliefs and institutions, and from logical conclusions based upon observations. An observer often uses abstract and impersonal language in an attempt to avoid judgmental statements. He or she talks about what is observed, rather than proclaiming the validity of direct personal experiences or convictions. But the scholar is also a person who will be tempted to ask: Can I learn anything new that will change my assumptions about the inner dynamics of religion? Should I allow the claims I am studying to challenge my present convictions? Do the questions that I am asking in the name of objectivity contain anything more than a personal or cultural bias?

The personal character of religious life, then, affects the life stance of the devotee; it plays a role in the devotee's attempt to learn about other people who have different deep commitments; and it concerns a scholar (as both observer and devotee) who formulates questions about religion and tries to interpret it.

The Cultural Dimension.   The cultural dimension of religious expression includes both traditional religious institutions and cultural institutions such as science, formal schooling, a language, an "accepted" classical literature, social law, political systems, and medical practices. Both types of institutions can function religiously or nonreligiously at different times and sometimes interact in a coordinated way. People live in a cultural context in which alternative values, ultimate claims, and pressures are significant influences in their lives.

The cultural dimension gives a religious expression its particular historical and cultural form. The particular form that spiritual energy takes is determined in part by biological and neurological forces as well as social, psychological, and linguistic structures. Similarly, the cumulative experiences of an individual or of a community constitute a history and condition the values, concepts, and models for self-awareness that are available in any particular time and place. Thus, a person living in a Navaho community during the sixteenth century A.D. would have a different cultural exposure than one living in first century Rome, eighth century Ch'ang-an, or second century Banaras. Language in these different cultural settings provided different options for expressing the ultimate reality as God, Tao, or Brahman. Moreover, many assumptions about life expectancy, production of food, and "natural" social relationships that were common in nonliterate societies were revised in classical traditional societies, and have again changed in modern, technological societies. The concern expressed in this book to *understand* a variety of religious expressions is itself partially a consequence of living in twentieth century America. (See Part I for a brief discussion of various recent scholarly approaches to the study of religion.)

Attitudes toward religious life, then, are mentally and emotionally conditioned by culture and habit. Such conditioning is the very fabric of our experience. On the one hand, it limits understanding, and, on the other, provides the learning processes that make it possible to transcend that limited understanding. For example, a child's relationships with parents establish a set of expectations, first in relation to other grown-ups, then peers, then their own offspring. At the same time, new experiences over several years reveal to the maturing person that parents are not only authority figures, decision makers, and providers, but also lovers, members of larger social groupings, and individuals with distinctive idiosyncracies. Similarly, those whose experience with religion has been strongly moralistic (Don't do this! Don't do that!'') will probably feel it as a restricting force. However, they may also gain a sense of security rooted in certitude and sense a transcendent expectation by foregoing some pleasures now so as to assure better rewards later.

Many other conditions structure the ways people approach the problem of understanding religious life. Even the everyday experiences that most Westerners take for granted help define their expectations and provide possibilities for new explorations: the number and variety of Christian church buildings in the United States (rather than bell-shaped Buddhist stupas and saffron-robed monks as in Sri Lanka or Thailand), the appeal to God's favor by many local and national politicians, the affirmation of mechanization and economic affluence, the positive value placed on the capacity to sell something, the belief that facts are better than intuition (and the assumption that there are such things as ''facts''). Two other assumptions commonly found in the West affect attitudes toward religion: (1) the belief that conscious choices are to some degree possible, and (2) the notion that an awareness of the unconscious and conscious forces in our lives can give us—at least partially—a liberating perspective.

A prominent Western cultural assumption has regarded religion as a special institutional activity. A person who was ''religious'' was expected to be a member of a special organization and of only one religious institution at a time. For most Westerners, ''revelation'' was expressed in a sacred book (or collection of writings), which was protected by special authorities, such as priests, jurists, or theologians from profanity, and preserved by a community of like-minded people. This perspective has led many to divide the world into ''sacred'' and ''secular'' spheres. Such a view has been the basis for much tension in the Western world during the past three centuries, because many people who affirm that the physical, social, and historical sciences and the use of reason are valid techniques for self-understanding place themselves in the ''secular''—and thus ''nonreligious''—category. From the standpoint of these sciences, traditional religion is seen at best as only one authoritative cultural element that contributes to self-awareness, and at worst as a superstition that is no longer useful as a controlling social authority.

Today those living in a modern society can decide whether or not to participate overtly in the religious forms of their culture; they have greater latitude than ever before in the expression of ultimate values. Likewise, interpreters of religion today are redefining religion to ask new questions about its nature and to perceive new forms that express the expansive and multidirectional character of people's ultimate hope, trust, and love. Nevertheless, these forms will be part of the cultural fabric of particular people as they live in a specific historical situation.

To the extent, then, that religion is expressed in institutional and cultural forms, it can be understood as a social expression of particular hopes, problems and models for living. Many religious people and scholars recognize that religion, like any other human expression, is conditioned by historical, social, economic, and political forces. They also realize that these forces contribute to the character of any particular religious expression.

The Ultimate Dimension. People today are often conscious of their "conditionedness"; that is, they are aware of their limits and recognize that they must make decisions that can bring important changes in their lives. Within this consciousness, they wrestle with the larger questions of truth, reality, meaning, and the problems involved in living a full life. Many ask what is really true, and what is the purpose of life, thereby pondering in the most comprehensive way what it means to *be*. When people make demands on themselves and others in the name of a transpersonal and transcultural force (or forces), when they perceive facets and images of life that expose the source of life, wisdom and joy, or when they become aware of modes of consciousness that transform common events into moments of extraordinary significance, they are probing the ultimate dimension. The fact that these perceptions may occur outside of traditional religious life makes them no less "ultimate" for those who experience them.

The last section suggested that the ultimate dimension of life takes many forms within individual awareness. It is communicated and preserved in different cultural symbols and social patterns. It is woven into the personal and cultural aspects of human life. Yet, the ultimate dimension is what distinguishes religious expressions from nonreligious personal or cultural expressions. For example, there are various answers to the question: Why read this book? One response, "It is assigned reading for a class," would answer the question within the context of an educational system, with a value placed on an academic degree. Another response, "I am curious to see how someone in the last third of the twentieth century makes sense out of a world characterized by religious pluralism," would answer in the context of Western intellectual history. A third reply, "I am trying to understand who I am so as to gain some insight into the ways that the ultimate nature of existence is expressed through me," would raise a "religious" or ultimate question. A religious answer relates to the most profound meaning of one's existence. It responds to the question of whether ultimate truth can even be expressed or ultimate reality known through words, reflections, and symbolic images.

The ultimate dimension is that to which one gives one's loyalty as the pervading character of life. Thus, the dynamics of religious life expresses not only subjective feelings and cultural forms, but the reality or value that an individual or group recognizes as the source of happiness and the fullest possible expression of reality. This ultimate dimension is the limit that confronts human sensitivity and the limitless power that makes possible the transcendence of a prior limitation. As the pervading character of life it exists prior to any particular sensitivity or knowledge of it, while at the same time it is the fullest possible expression of joy, goodness, equanimity, or power. In short, it is what is most fully real. A fuller definition would be fruitless, because that would require an elaboration of a view of reality—and there are several basically different views in the history of religions. The point here is simply that the ultimate dimension differs from both the personal and cultural dimensions, though it is expressed through them.

One practical expression of the ultimate dimension is its force in establishing values—including finally the most pervading, or ultimate, value according to which people live. The impact of an evaluating process is seen in the common experience of deciding what is real and what is significant. Not everything people experience is equally real. For example, holding a silver dollar in your hand is not the same as remembering that you held one yesterday, dreaming that you hold one, or mistaking a piece of aluminum foil on the ground for a silver dollar. Likewise, there are important differences in the ways people evaluate similar experiences or the values they place on physical objects, such as food, clothes, status symbols, and art. Everyone's personal history has moments that are more "real" than others—moments that define a person, such as a birthday party, a first date, graduation, or some unusual state of consciousness. Thus, individuals make judgments consciously or unconsciously about their experiences, forming them into patterns that together constitute "existence." Some people's experiences seem alien, some do not. The fact that human beings can and must make choices is both exciting and troublesome. There is something awesome about the power to choose, for people's choices—saying "yes" to some things and "no" to others—shape their character and give them a sense of direction. The world provides no automatic sense of identity; each individual must forge his or her own within the context of a particular society. Nor are the reasons for individual behavior self-evident. Life is filled with confusion, decision, and possibility.

A person who lives in an ultimate frame of reference claims the power and insight to distinguish what is real or true from what is secondary, derivative, or even false. This insight, which has been called "revelation" or "wisdom," opens new horizons for self-realization. To know the truth, then, is to live an authentic life, to grow beyond both habits and fantasies, since truth is an exposure of the nature of things. The discovery of reality is experienced, on the one hand, as the most natural awareness, because this reality is both the ground of one's present existence, and at the same time the ultimate goal of one's life. On the other hand, ultimate reality is sometimes experienced as something strange, awesome, even bizarre, since it differs from familiar, everyday experience. As individuals realize who they really are, they lose the marks of "secondary existence": destructive tension, limitations, and biases that prevent joyful living. At the same time, for those who live authentically, this "secondary existence" is transformed; such people participate in the structures and activity of human existence, but with a different purpose.

To express a religious concern is to be conscious of the question: How am I to be "real"?—rather than "fake" or "phony," or "less than what I could be." In general, to have a sense that one is "real" means to know what is true and right, translate this knowledge into *aims* (or decide what one ought to do), and then have the means to accomplish these aims. From the standpoint of "conditionedness," the ultimate reality is what appears as the ideal. Thus, questions about the nature of freedom or a right action in a particular situation are vital questions in the effort to make sense out of existence. Some practical ultimate questions might be: How can I experience ultimate happiness when I can't even do simple things that others seem to do easily? How do I know when I am living in truth and not in illusion? Is there any way to test the assertions of others who claim to know what life is all about? When does my personal experience give a true picture of reality? If I admit that I make a single mistake in judging life, how do I know that the "correction" is not also a mistake? Maybe my experience is only a facade; perhaps there is something greater or more profound that is escaping my view? With such questions, people "lift off" from everyday life into the rarified atmosphere of religious awareness. The ultimate dimension of religious expression, then, refers to the reality that emerges or appears when a person lives within an extraordinarily deep sensitivity to life or a very profound strategy for action.

Religious life—to sum up—involves a personal subjective element, takes specific cultural forms (for example, in ideas, art, and institutions) and expresses an ultimate, supreme, or comprehensive reality. The interaction of these three dimensions of religious phenomena, makes the study of religious life a complex effort, because it requires the interpretation of a variety of particular cultural expressions in relation to a general notion of ultimate value. This effort is necessary whenever investigators of religion seek to understand those aspects of religious meaning and intention that go beyond the social, psychological, economic, or biochemical functions of physical existence. Two basic assumptions of this book are that it is—to some extent—possible to study more than the external aspects of religious life, and that such a study is most fruitful from a perspective that grants that others' ultimate dimension is more than a product of their physical and social environment.

A Working Definition of Religion.   While interpreters may keep in mind the complexity of the interaction between the three dimensions of religious life given above, they also use the term "religion" or "religious life" in a general way. This is a practical necessity for distinguishing what is "religious" from what is "not religious" and for relating one religious expression to another. Such an image is a composite of several types of religious expressions and is useful when it raises questions regarding the meaning of specific, concrete religious forms, instead of providing a final definition of religion. The general definition of religion used in this book is not a substantive one; it has no historically specific content. Instead, it is a functional definition focusing on the role of various types of processes of change through which people actualize a perceived ultimate value. The formal definition used in this analysis of religious life is: Religion is a *means of ultimate transformation*. In this definition, the focus is on the character and function of human life as consciously expressed by people in the past and present when they described or acted upon an extraordinarily significant and comprehensive awareness; it includes at least two elements: ultimacy and effective power.

Ultimacy, as noted above, is one of the dimensions of religious life. Religious awareness brings people to the most comprehensive awareness possible in any given moment. A common assumption of religious people is that life evokes higher sensitivities than can be expressed in solutions to short-term problems alone, or in the self-identity people achieve by acting merely in terms of cultural habits. It is this "higher than" character to which the term "ultimate" points.

Effective power is expressed in a variety of ways. For example, it may be a deep feeling, a participation in a sacred rite, an ethical act that establishes a cosmic order or that expresses divine will, or it may be experiences of a transcendent state of consciousness. In all these cases, ultimate reality is experienced and expressed as a transforming power, for in realizing the nature of his or her being, a person becomes "spiritually whole." In this context, religion is an ultimate, dynamic process in which people participate. The process of transformation may occur in symbols, social relationships, feelings, and states of consciousness, but these are not simply objects of observation or bits of information. When imbued with an ultimate dynamic, the concrete personal and cultural forms (whether traditional or not) are significant because they provide the means to communicate a spiritual power that is not confined to "the letter of the law" or to the self-serving demands of individuals or institutions that use religious symbols. When the ultimate dimension motivates human self-awareness, it starts a total process in which a person or a community extends and grows beyond former limitations.

The focus on religion as effective power, then, stresses the recognition by religious adherents that their symbols, techniques, and social expressions are not just wishes, hopes, or fantasies; rather, these are practical means of transforming life from unreality to reality. The practical character of religious forms is found in devotees' assertions that the power of transformation is inherent in their method of ultimate realization. Such ultimate power can be felt as coming from outside of human existence, or from within it. In either case, the believer is not destroyed by the problems and frustrations of daily existence, for a person participating in a religious process of transformation exposes the ultimate nature of things. Sometimes there is a stress on personal transformation and sometimes on social interrelationships of a religious community. At times, the personal and social aspects are at odds with each other. However, if a personal new religious awareness is to be preserved and become part of the history of religions, it must be validated by other people. It will be corroborated either in a communal consensus, as in a devotional expression, or by a small, religiously sophisticated group, such as a monastic community.

The practical power of religion, thus, provides a set of religious activities or an insight whereby a person is able to attain ultimate goals. The final justification for the power of transformation, however, is not an appeal to a particular institutional or cultural identity, nor is it a specific practice or discipline as such. The life of the spirit is not, for example, merely a product of the social or political power of a church or religious community. Rather, the validation is found in the "total experience-affirming" character of religion, so that anywhere and in any circumstance, whether for a family person or a solitary recluse, the entire surroundings confirm and are confirmed by the power of ultimate reality.

Why Study Religion?

The notions with which people begin their investigation of religion become a part of their interpretation of religious life. Some people are merely curious to explore some idea or experience that seems different from their own. Others study unfamiliar religious expressions in order to find "weaknesses" based on a personal religious commitment. In both cases, the notion of "religion" is often an explicit extension of a person's cultural experience. A Western person usually identifies religion with beliefs about God, tries to find the sacred writings (scriptures) of a community, and looks for sacred rituals and symbols. While these are indeed important elements in some religious traditions, they need not be the most important aspects of all religious life. At least, students of religion will find it useful to examine whether or not all people regard them as equally important. The first object of studying religion, then, is to gain some specific information about other people's religious activities and about the variety found in one's own religious-cultural tradition. The data for a cross-cultural study of religion are in the acts, feelings, and attitudes about the ultimate meaning of life that are recorded in epics, songs, drama, philosophy, and architecture throughout the world. Therefore, to understand religious life means to comprehend the feelings, activities, ideas, and social forms of people as they express the ultimate dimension of their lives.

The second reason for studying religion is to place one's own religious life within a universal perspective. A study of religious experience throughout history offers insights into the temper of one's age, which is all too often taken for granted as the only, or even more egotistically, the best, form of existence. A study of previous religious life brings elements of the past to one's awareness and may reveal the latent possibilities of previously unexpressed religious impulses. An awareness of new possibilities may free a person to choose other options; at the same time, this self-consciousness of choice entails the acceptance of a wider framework of responsibilities. To understand religious life, then, means to go beyond acquiring bits of inert information; it means acquiring the skills and sensitivities that can organize concrete data into a larger understanding of humanity. A knowledge of the history and culture of other traditions as well as one's own provides an understanding of oneself in relation to others that is superior to an interpretation of life that is based primarily on a provincial perspective or mere wishes and hopes. Also, a general interpretation of religion grounded in concrete facts should be taken from a variety of cultural expressions if it is to have more than regional importance. The inclusion of data from "the other side" of the world shows recognition of the fact that the world is "round."

A third reason for studying religion is to examine its relation to other cultural forms. Many scholars analyze various facets of religious beliefs, institutions, and ethical expressions in hopes of finding answers to questions about cultural life. Do certain beliefs lead to economically discriminatory practices, for example, or does a doctrine about nature promote or hinder the development of technology? Other scholars may want to investigate the social, psychological, political, economic, or linguistic determinants of particular religious forms. Thus, a historian might ask about the impact of political forces on the development of the Christian church in the third century A.D., or a sociologist might study the relationship between family life and religious affiliation in post-World War II Japan. Such scholars would examine historical changes in religious claims or institutional forms to identify constant elements, differences in content or function, and repeated patterns of change.

Finally, a fourth reason for studying religion is to gain a new awareness of oneself as a religious person. While not every academic study of religion is intended to transform the researcher, many investigators indicate that learning about different religious options and gaining a cross-cultural perspective of humanity can lead to a new self-understanding. To listen with an open mind to others means to engage in a meaningful dialogue with an ''other''—another person—and the otherness found there helps to define one's own self-awareness. In considering the religious self-awareness of other people the investigator must reflect on his or her own presuppositions about humanity, existence, and the nature of truth. Everyone does, in practice, act on the basis of attitudes and presuppositions. Unless people are conscious of their attitudes and presuppositions—especially in regard to religious transformation—they are unknowingly bound to them.

A dialogue with another person regarding ultimate values has all the possibilities and dangers that are inherent in any real communication. It can extend and deepen one's religious sensitivities, enabling one to become more fully human, that is, more aware of a wider range of possibilities for realizing the meaning of human life. On the other hand, learning about another value system may produce great discomfort by causing a person to judge past attitudes and ideas as irrelevant and to develop a new orientation toward what it means to be human. To understand another person's different orientation makes possible a comparison and, eventually, an integration of or decision between two or more value orientations. A person may be forced to ask: Which elements in my orientation are so intrinsic to my being that to lose them means spiritual death? A real encounter with another life orientation may finally mean that a person judges that, though the death of a particular orientation may be painful, it is good to grow beyond it. One meaning-orientation may have to disintegrate so that a new one can emerge.

These processes of change—maturing, death, and rebirth—are not separate segments of a serial process. The thrust toward maturity is simultaneous with release from the old and building of the new. In discovering the variety of possibilities for becoming human, people can discover and rediscover who they are. Unconscious urges as well as conscious images of life influence one's basic decisions every day. What a person does in relation to other people either individually (e.g., ''my mother'') or collectively (e.g., ''the Chinese'') depends on how he or she conceives of these people. Images are derived in part from personal and intellectual experiences. To really engage another person means, in part, to achieve release from those limitations by which one previously defined existence; such release means that individuals are more free because they are more self-conscious and can choose from a wider range of possibilities. In this way, some students of religion seek to become more fully human by transcending their individual culturally-bound selves.

How Should Religion Be Studied?

How are we to study religion—that transforming power in the recesses of consciousness that draws people beyond their empirical selves? What methods can be used to describe and display the nature and forms of ultimate value and meaning?

The Variety of Forms and Processes of Religious Life.   Religious life includes an immense range of phenomena—religious dances of American Indians, Shinto shrines of Japan, and records of ancient China; burial customs of the ancient Egyptians, Hindu cremation rites, and American embalming practices; images of God in certain religious traditions (such as the Christian and Hindu) and the injunction in others against pictures or statues of the Creator of Life (such as Islam and Judaism); the expression of yearning for Allah by the Muslim Sufi, the passionate desire to experience the presence of Jesus or Krishna, the crying for a vision by a Sioux lad, and the patient emergence of full awareness in Buddhist meditation. Religious life may also include a new sense of identity found in reintegration of one's past and present through psychoanalysis, in becoming ''turned on'' through the pleasures of touching something or someone, in clearly formulating an intellectual concept, or in organizing people to work for political freedom and economic and social justice.

Clearly, human religious goals and practices are not limited to those found in one's own value orientation or to the theological concerns of one historical religious tradition such as Judaism or Christianity. The most important questions found in any religious tradition are not necessarily those of other religions. To understand the variety of religious experience, one must first admit the existence of *various possibilities* for religious awareness. Christians or Jews may have to rephrase their traditional religious questions in order to perceive the significance of the experience of non-Western religious traditions or to understand some contemporary nontraditional religious attitudes, actions, and ideologies. Likewise, Hindus or Buddhists would have to become sensitive to other's religious assumptions and claims in order to understand them.

Not only do different religious symbols provide different understandings of human experience, but the variety also suggests that different dimensions of human life (for example, reason or aesthetic awareness) become avenues for attaining different sorts of religious meaning. There are not only different religious views but different ''processes'' whereby people become aware of, and realize, their ultimate values. Thus, a concept such as "God" or "goodness" not only means different things to different people, it also functions in different ways. This difference may be partially accounted for by the fact that people speak different languages and have had different personal experiences. To say this, however, does not exhaust the significance of religious differences. Indeed, the most significant religious difference may be that the same term is used differently in various types of religious processes of ultimate transformation. For example, the meaning of the term "God" in a Roman Catholic mass is expressed through a sacred act in which God's presence is directly available in the bread and wine consumed by the believer, while in the Hindu yogic discipline the meaning of "God" is communicated when all symbolic forms are perceived to be illusory and the yogi realizes his original undifferentiated oneness with divine power. Likewise, conflicting claims of different adherents that each has the final divine revelation, as found in Islam and Christianity, can be seen to participate in the same type of religious process (see Chapter 6 below).

Thus, "religion" is not so much the expression of a single human experience or activity; rather, it is a term for a *cluster of different but partially overlapping processes of religious life.* Many processes of change contribute to religious transformation. Some are linguistic, biological, and psychological. More important for the analysis in this book, however, is the religious process of ultimate transformation. This process of change integrates ultimate value with one or more modes of human self-awareness through which people apprehend and express their true being. Religious transformation can take symbolic, social, and psychological forms, but its religious significance is that it expresses the nature of existence, the way things are; it is an ontological (*ontos* means "being") transformation. Each of the four chapters in Part II describes a different process of ultimate transformation found in a traditional "way of being religious." Part III then examines processes inherent in various modes of human awareness that are used by some people as a means of ultimate transformation outside traditional religions.

Central to each process is a pattern of elements that expresses a means of ultimate transformation. The elements include the use of symbols; assumptions about the basic problem(s) of life; the function of feelings, reason, unusual states of consciousness or social obligations; and different kinds of authority. These elements appear in a particular pattern because of a hidden "structure" of interaction among the elements. The structure is the decisive ordering of the aim, assumptions about the nature of existence, and means of ultimate transformation within a particular process. Different structures have different "inner logics" of religious meaning that are expressed in ultimate moral acts, symbols, claims, and states of consciousness.

Each religious process emphasizes a particular mode of human awareness, such as the human capacity to symbolize, or to create social forces, or to experience deep emotion. Each process, therefore, focuses on a certain human capacity for stating value and meaning; and it, in turn, becomes a medium for experiencing the depth or height of life. For example, the capacity to experience deep emotion makes it possible for devotees of various faiths to experience a holy presence—the prophet Isaiah in ancient Judaism, the "baptism" of the Holy Spirit contemporary Christian Pentecostals, or the Krishna Consciousness of the sixteenth century Hindu Vaishnava reformer Caitanya. Each of these examples participates in a type of religious process that we label below as "personal apprehension of a holy presence." A different type of process is found in the human capacity to symbolize, the ability to represent the ultimate nature of existence in religious myth and ritual.

In the past, scholars have sometimes defined "religion" as the awareness of a holy presence, other times as the symbolic value of religious ritual, as mystical union with infinite reality, or as living according to a cosmic rhythm in the ordering of social relationships according to a sense of obligation and morality. In the approach used here, each of these is only one type of religious process. While each of these processes has been regarded as the "purest" religious form *by its adherents,* comparative students of religion can question whether any one process can express the religious meaning found in the variety of religious life. The interpretation of all religion in terms of only one process, whether it is the feeling of awe and fascination before a holy presence or the symbolic acts of sacred rituals, oversimplifies and overlooks the distinctive character of other forms of religious life.

Objective Data and Subjective Experience.   The central problem in understanding religious phenomena is how to balance the competing claims of objective data and subjective awareness. While social scientists attempt to collect empirical facts and historians seek to base their interpretations on documents, artifacts, or other observable data, the worshipper or mystic maintains that an objective observer can only scrape the outer surface of human religious expression. Similarly, the more the psychologists speak of the "psyche" or the "unconscious," the more they are regarded as moving out of the empirical realm. The philosopher and the theologian are also aware that certain subjective presuppositions inform their understanding and limit their interpretations. The concepts we use and the self-imposed limitations of empirical methods are the barriers, as well as the vehicles, for understanding. Since we cannot stand outside this conditioned situation, the best we can do is to become self-conscious about our personal and cultural presuppositions.

Let us first consider the question of personal religious belief. Can a Christian really understand Buddhism? Some people hold that religions are closed systems of propositions, which a person either accepts or rejects. But there is a difference between "understanding" and "believing"; a person can understand another religious form without believing it and thus "entering" it. "To understand" means to appreciate how it is possible for others to believe what they do given the presuppositions they hold. "To believe" means to accept certain presuppositions about life and to live according to them. Understanding a religious claim or act calls for the same sort of effort as understanding any human claim or act. It may not be easy to listen to another person expound a religious view different from one's own. Understanding requires a conscious attempt to identify with the thought patterns and emotional tone of another person's convictions. Because it is often more difficult to identify with the emotional tone than the thought patterns, two religious people of different faiths may be able to communicate better with each other than with a non-religious person. The attempt to empathize, however, is fraught with problems. The danger of projecting one's own symbol system or type of religious awareness onto the beliefs and sensitivities of the other person is always present.

In seeking to avoid a sectarian or a dogmatic interpretation of religion, we must also beware of reducing human events to mechanistic changes or natural principles. This danger arises with any assumption that one single, universal, "scientific method" can be applied in the same way to every phenomenon. Different objects of study require varying kinds of "objective analysis" because they have different basic characteristics or qualities. For example, both human beings and stones have physical properties, but to reduce human beings to physical properties is to miss a large part of what it means to be human. Similarly, historical events and philosophical principles have a different relevance for human beings. The human past, which is the object of historical study, is different from both laws of physics and rational deduction. Knowledge of the meaning of human life, especially as it is expressed in ultimate hopes and fears, desires, and wisdom, is often indirect and inferred. Such knowledge is always founded on an interpretation.

Religion is not merely some external "thing" to be found and then analyzed. There is nothing that is purely religious as such. On the other hand, anything may serve as a source for the person who knows how to use the evidence. To recognize what is religious, a person must ask about the religious meaning of some human expression. Of course, some human expressions, such as prayers, religious rituals, or mystical experiences, have been used to expose self-consciously the ultimate dimension of life more clearly than others, such as economic theories or a parts description of an electrical appliance. However, prayers and rituals may be interpreted purely from a psychological or a sociological perspective, which does not expose their *religious* significance. At the same time, economic theories or mechanical drawings can express the creative spirit in life. The evidence gives answers only when the questions proper to religious meaning are asked, and many questions that would reveal the meaning of religion for contemporary people have not yet been asked.

In sum, the person who develops a sensitivity for the religious dimension in life will learn to "think and feel with" those people in the past and present whose intellectual and artistic commitment and social behavior reveal the ultimate dimension of life. The person who does not develop this sensitivity will miss the problems that give rise to religious expression. Without this sensitivity, which can be developed with training and practice, a person will overlook the hopes, frustrations, and perseverance of people who yearn for what is true. If students of religion have no concerns of their own, how can they be responsive to the religious life of others? Thus, the effort to overcome a sectarian interpretation is never the same as a lack of concern for the problem of religious meaning.

Understanding requires the examination of specific, concrete data, such as ideas in literature and descriptions of rituals, social institutions, historical developments, lives of great personalities, and political and social conditions. But this does not mean the mere recording of unrelated facts. To understand means to be aware of a principle of selectivity that serves as a filter for interpretation. To understand means to integrate data within a context that does not give equal weight to every element in an experience but provides the concepts and questions that permit one to understand the data in a certain way. The basic interpretive principle of this book is the identification of elements in processes of ultimate transformation.

Finally, to understand means to remain open to the development of further possibilities, to resist the temptation to close one's mind to other value orientations. It means to examine seriously all aspects of the data, however unfamiliar some may be. It also means to rise above the conflict sometimes generated by the dichotomy between religious belief and objective study. Understanding requires an awareness that the presuppositions of both positions are important.

Interplay of Religious Intention and Cultural Forms.   In recorded human experience, only rarely has the "religious dimension" in life been developed to a high point. Although many people are partially aware of ultimate truth in their lives, seldom has religious reality become an example or model for future generations, and thus a dramatic force in social awareness. Among the exceptional cases are the founders and leaders of institutionalized mass religions, such as Christianity, Buddhism, or Confucianism. These forms provide the clearest data for studying human experience that is self-consciously religious. However, religious people do not regard the forms as synonymous with the most profound human awareness; for them, religious experience and expression differ from, and transcend, their physical, historical, cultural, or institutional elements. The power of religion as the most authentic human experience, as the awareness of what is true or real, breaks the institutional forms while still being expressed through them. Thus, students of religion must be aware not only of the concrete data, the forms of religious expression, but also of the intention of these forms, which is to point beyond themselves.

A person who is aware that religion is not simply an idea, ritual, or a social form, but a force that establishes a person's very being and opens consciousness to insight, will perceive the intention of religious concern and will be better able to understand religious problems. This dimension of human experience, which sometimes provides the basis for cultural forms and interpersonal relations and sometimes destroys them, is the power with which people wrestle when they are self-consciously religious. The conceptual formulations, ethical practices, and social institutions that are generally labeled religious data are not in themselves the sum of that reality with which the student of religion must deal. The historical forms and patterns are, however, regarded as crucial by those who, transformed by the power inherent in them, thereby fulfill their life and purpose. Such formulations, practices, and institutions are therefore important in any consideration of religious experience that seeks to go beyond personal experience.

Thus, religion encompasses both (1) the power of transformation and (2) the cultural forms that express and release this power. To speak of the former without the latter is impossible; to speak of the latter without the former is to ignore the very "mode of being," the ultimate quality, the depth perspective of religious life. These two aspects mean that religious life is not simply some petrified shape of past human experience, an interesting but irrelevant impression left in culture by prescientific society; rather, it is the creative force in human experience that has emerged and is emerging, in particular forms.

This book will examine different ways in which human beings have answered religious questions but will not judge the rightness or wrongness of the answers. The effort to learn "objectively" about religion follows a century-long tradition of scholarship dedicated to the examination of the nature, forms, and meaning of religious life. The goal of an objective study of religion is quite different from the goal of religious practice or belief. The methods employed in seeking to understand the meaning of religious symbols and institutions are comparable to those used in any other academic study of human life.

Any attempt to understand human expression starts from an assumption about what constitutes *human* life. The basic assumption here is that people are symbolizing creatures. A person's self-understanding—in poetry, science, history— requires the use of imagery, concepts, and patterns of thought that force that individual to experience life in conformity with the limitations inherent in them. This assumption has two direct implications. The first relates to the investigator of religion, and the second concerns the notion that every human expression tells something about those involved in it.

First, the perceptions of all interpreters are limited by the assumptions and terms of their analysis. It is entirely possible that the analyst's ideas, perceptions, and awareness may be inappropriate to another person's concerns and sensitivities. Likewise, investigators of religion must consider whether their ideas, procedures and empirical measurements correspond to the actual dynamics and internal characteristics of religious life. The questions asked about religion determine, in part, the answers received. The limitations in language and in personal and cultural perspectives, however, are balanced by the possibilities in the second implication.

Second, the assumption that people are symbolizing creatures means that every human expression tells something about humanity. The symbols we use to express ourselves are part of the reality we find. Our sensitivity to the limitations of every analysis should not lead to the conclusion that symbols are superficial expressions of some untouched inner reality. Rather, they are part of the dynamics, the changing and living character of human self-awareness. Thus, the ultimate symbols, ethical actions, transcendental experiences, and perfection of insight examined in this study are not mere exterior forms behind which there is a more "real" religious reality. Instead, concrete religious expressions, as well as the inner dynamics and structures of the specific forms, are real forces through which individuals know themselves, relate to other people, and leave impressions for posterity. The things people do and make, their laughter and tears, their feelings of ecstasy and depression—all are threads woven into the fabric of existence.

In sum, religious life is a complex process that includes at least three dimensions: personal, cultural, and ultimate. Any person attempting to understand and interpret religious experiences is also participating in them as a human being. Thus, it is important to become self-conscious about one's assumptions and attitudes about religion.

Second, religion is defined in this book as a means of ultimate transformation. This definition focuses on the dynamic process of change in religious life, a change from a disharmonious, illusory, evil, or destructive state of existence to ultimate harmony, enlightenment, purity, or creative power.

Third, the reasons for studying religion are varied and depend on the investigator's attitude and definition of religion. One reason is to collect data on religious life in order to explain changes that occur over time and to account for variations in form. Another is to understand an individual's particular religious expression in light of a transcultural perspective. This provides a way to understand comparable and distinctive elements within diverse cultural forms. A third is to examine the relation of religion to other cultural forms. Finally, a purpose not accepted by all students of religion, but which is affirmed in this book, is to develop a new self-awareness whereby the investigator continually examines his or her ultimate stance. Different religious dynamics permit people to rediscover latent resources for meaning, to probe their basic presuppositions and sensitivities of ultimate value, and to gain perspective on the options for religious commitment in a time of rapid social change. The purpose, then, of understanding religious life is neither to judge whether one or another religious answer is right or wrong, nor to convince the reader of the ultimate truth of any one religious expression, tradition, or type of religious process. Rather, it is to point out various possibilities for religious awareness, each of which is recognized by its adherents as having the power to transform a person ultimately.

Fourth, the differences among religious expressions are as important as the similarities. The traditional religious data examined in Part II are organized under headings that express different types of religious processes. The differences among these processes are important in accounting for the sometimes basically different orientations of religious life within any one tradition or between different historical traditions. The types of religious processes express the interaction of ultimate value with processes of human awareness that are not regarded as ultimate by adherents to traditional religions. However, these processes—which form different modes of human awareness—are sometimes regarded by others as ultimate. Part III of this book describes how processes of human awareness can also be used as non-traditional "means of ultimate transformation."

Fifth, some basic methodological assumptions contribute to the analysis in this book. One is that a wide range of objective data are necessary for gaining a general view of religion. A complementary assumption is that empathy is required to understand both the subjective aspects of other people's religious experiences and to describe accurately and analyze the objective factors of an ultimately transforming process (i.e., religion). Another methodological assumption is that all human beings are self-conscious, symbolizing, and value-forming creatures who are, on the one hand, limited by their culture and, on the other hand, capable of using culture as a means of ultimate transformation. Thus, religious data express dynamic forces in the lives of human beings and reveal not only the historical-cultural conditioning of any human form but also the religious intention of the dynamic forces that make transformation possible.

SELECTED READINGS

Paperback editions in this and subsequent sections are marked with an asterisk.

*W. H. Capps, *Ways of Understanding Religion* (New York: Macmillan, 1972). This book of readings covering seven basic problem areas in the Western study of religion organizes the systematic understanding of religion in a fresh way.

*M. Eliade, *The Sacred and the Profane: The Nature of Religion.* (New York: Harcourt, 1959). Focusing on myth, ritual, and symbolism, this well-known religious historian explores the nature of religion as the manifestation of a wholly different reality—the sacred.

*G. van der Leeuw, *Religion in Essence and Manifestation: A Study in Phenomenology* (New York: Harper, 1963, first published 1933). The entire work is an exposition of religion as the expression of man's relationship with God. Chapter 108, "Religion", is a brief but weighty summary of the object of religion and the nature of man's awareness.

*A. H. Maslow, *Toward a Psychology of Being,* 2d ed. (Princeton, N.J.: Van Nostrand, 1962) Basing his views on psychological inquiries, this famous psychologist calls for an understanding of the human awareness of being, which is traditionally called religious, is known in peak experiences, and leads to self-actualization.

H. Nakamura, *Ways of Thinking of Eastern Peoples: India-China-Tibet-Japan,* rev. ed. (Honolulu: East-West Center Press, 1964). An analysis of the ways that different cultures in Asia interpret key Buddhist values and ideas.

*M. Novak, *Ascent of the Mountain, Flight of the Dove* (New York: Harper, 1971). This personal statement of religion as the "ultimate drive" of humanity sees religious studies essentially as a series of conversions in one's experience of life.

*R. Otto, *The Idea of the Holy* (Oxford: Oxford University Press, 1958, first published 1932). One of the classic analyses of religious life; religion is discussed as the irrational awareness of the "numinous."

*S. Radhakrishnan, *An Idealist View of Life* (London: George Allen & Unwin, 1932). A famous Indian philosopher analyzes the universal nature of religion through an appeal to both Eastern and Western thinkers.

N. Smart, *The Phenomenon of Religion* (New York: Herder and Herder, 1973). In Chapter 2, "Religion as a Phenomenon," this British philosopher of religion presents an incisive discussion of the basic elements in a descriptive phenomenology of particular religious expressions.

*W. C. Smith, *The Meaning and End of Religion* (New York: Macmillan, 1962). A noted scholar argues that man's religious life can be properly understood only if the notion of "religion" as an abstraction is eliminated. The concept "religion" is to be replaced by the two separate concepts of "a cumulative tradition" and "a personal faith."

*P. Tillich, "Religion as a Dimension in Man's Spiritual Life," in *Theology of Culture,* edited by R. C. Kimball (Oxford: Oxford University Press, 1959). In a short essay, this well-known Protestant theologian argues that religion is not limited to a special kind of human expression, but provides the dimension of depth in all human life.

*J. Wach, *The Comparative Study of Religions* (New York: Columbia University Press, 1958). In Chapter 2, "The Nature of Religious Experience," this scholar of religion explains what the description of religion as man's apprehension of ultimate reality means to him.

Part I

METHODS
USED TO UNDERSTAND
RELIGIOUS LIFE

During the past century, scientific investigation has been one of the most important influences on the study of religion. It developed first in Western Europe and then extended to academic centers throughout the world. Scientific procedure emphasizes rational inquiry and empirical analysis. No subject matter is excluded as too sacred. In the second half of the nineteenth century, the study of religion, together with anthropology, sociology, and psychology, became an academic discipline; all these disciplines had human existence as an object of study. This concern to discover new data for an ''objective'' understanding of life had been stimulated by the eighteenth-century European Enlightenment.

For the Enlightenment mind, reason was not just a body of principles or truths; it was a force by which humanity could unlock all the doors of meaning and mystery. Ernst Cassirer summarized the significance of reason in *The Philosophy of the Enlightenment:* ''The power of reason does not consist in enabling us to transcend the empirical world but rather in teaching us to feel at home in it.''[1] The center of Enlightenment rationalism was its claim for a basic unity of all creation, which was to be found in the processes of understanding as well as in the inherent order of physical existence. Reason provided the principle of unification. If people wanted to ''know'' something, they would analyze its component parts and place them into a relationship with each other that was defined according to one consistent and universal rule.

In such a scientific understanding, human beings were defined in terms of environmental conditions that were analyzed objectively. The meaning of religious practices was defined primarily in terms of *causes* which *produce* the beliefs, prac-

20

tices, and values. This approach to religious life was intended to be radically different from a theological concern to interpret life in order to bring a person to salvation. The advocates of objective study also rejected the claim that revelation was an absolute mode of knowledge. The "sacred" in human life was brought under the scrutiny of objective investigation. Religious conviction was not viewed as the result of divine grace or supernatural power, but religious beliefs and symbols were interpreted in the context of human forces and institutions. In scientific study, the investigator's personal attitudes toward religion were supposed to be excluded. The personal attitude held by many investigators that religious life was simply a product of empirically discoverable historical-cultural, linguistic, and social-economic forces was not regarded by them as a value judgment. Most "scientists" of religion assumed that there were natural and universal explanations for religious behavior that could be learned through empirical study.

In contrast to the effort to explain human events by investigating universal and natural forces, however, some scholars focused on the uniqueness of every historical event and the creative character peculiar to human life. By emphasizing the importance of the individual in history, they suggested that the meaning of human existence was not to be found simply in universal laws of reason but in a unique historical situation. This shifted the focus in interpreting existence from the physical world to people. People were regarded as creative agents who formed—not only found—the reality they knew. Religion was seen as part of the creative activity of human existence and could not be reduced to mere physical laws. Every historical expression of religion was to be interpreted in relation to its cultural and temporal context. A general understanding of human religiousness required the comparison of concrete historical religious expressions.

In presenting some of the basic tasks, procedures, and assumptions of "the scientific study of religion," we should keep in mind that these understandings of religious phenomena are based on cultural assumptions and presuppositions of Western religious scholarship. One of the most prominent characteristics of this effort has been the accumulation of a large body of descriptive information about what people throughout the world think and do. Because many believe that the best scholarship is based on first-hand information, field research and language study have been emphasized to bring about direct communication with the sources. A major assumption is that somehow all bits and pieces of human experience and physical existence are integrated. The accumulation of information can thus stimulate comparisons that may reveal broad human patterns. Ideally, a wide range of information about human behavior elsewhere—from the eating habits of a people thousands of miles away, to the art of an ancient civilization, or an unfamiliar vision of life-after-death—will enrich people's understanding of their own humanity.

As important as it is to point out the cultural roots of scientific thinking, it is just as important to recognize that different scientific disciplines have emphasized different aspects of life and interpretive directions. Within the "science of religion" scholars have undertaken various tasks in the effort to understand religious experience and behavior. Several of these tasks are: (1) to explain the fact of religious life by analyzing its earliest formative expression, (2) to explain the significance of religious life in terms of its social and psychological functions, (3) to describe the historical forces that would account for change and variety in religious forms, and (4) to describe the religious intention of religious expressions through an intuitive grasp of their inner structures. One of the continuing problems is to decide *which* tasks will lead to the most fruitful results. The solution depends, of course, on what kind of result is considered most useful. For instance, those desiring to predict future behavior will not ask the same questions as those seeking to explain past behavior. Combinations of questions may also elicit answers with varying implications. For example, some studies may explain past behavior and provide a religious insight—as might be the case with some studies of the resurrection of Jesus, or of the Buddha's insight into the arising and dissolution of existence.

There are two reasons for reviewing here a few key researchers and problems of interpretation and for indicating some of the difficulties inherent in their approaches. First, it is important to be aware of the academic context out of which this book emerges, and second, it is helpful to know what questions have been asked about religion and the range of answers given. Some questions have been based on faulty assumptions; some answers are limited. Further explorations may reveal new perspectives. Part I will briefly summarize various scholars' ideas within a wide spectrum of approaches, without focusing exclusively on the work of any one person. Rather, their interpretations are grouped under three general headings, which suggest different methods and presuppositions. Chapter 2 focuses on the effort made to find the origins of religion. Chapter 3 then points out some of the insights into the social functions of religion provided by the social sciences. Finally, Chapter 4 describes the efforts of the historian of religion and the descriptive phenomenologist of religion to ''understand'' religion by assuming that the nature of the data requires the observer to empathize with religious assumptions and not reduce religious data to something else.

2.

The Origins of Religious Expression

One of the major efforts in the scientific study of religion was the attempt to find the beginning of religion, while more recent religious expressions were seen as only derivatives of this primordial event. In the second half of the nineteenth century, especially, some scholars sought to understand the nature of religion by investigating the earliest religious expressions then known. They felt that if they could find the origin of religion, they could understand its nature and properly interpret the subsequent changes in religious history.

When looking for the beginning of religion, the scientific investigator considered only those sources that were objectively measureable. Therefore, traditional religious descriptions of the origin of the world and humanity, as found, for instance, in the biblical account of Adam and Eve, or the creation stories in the Muslim *Qur'an,* the Hindu *Veda,* or the Japanese *Kojiki,* were rejected as inadequate bases for explaining how religion began historically. God, as revealed in any of the sacred scriptures, could not be regarded as the actual source of man's religious reflection or worship. While religious mythologies were indeed studied, they were not regarded as describing actual happenings. They were studied as evidence from which the historical and empirical truth could be reconstructed according to the "objective criteria" of the investigators within the framework of evolution. For these investigators, the myths and rituals did not accurately explain the nature of personhood, the development of life, or the source and conditions of the deepest meaning, joy, and wholeness in human experience. Rather, the material presented the investigator with data that could be interpreted according to logical criteria and evolutionary theory in explaining the linguistic, psychological, and social causes for religion. The revered documents or oral myths of any religious tradition, either singly or taken together, were not accepted as an unquestioned norm for learning about the causes of religious life.

The concern of the investigators to avoid a sectarian or doctrinal interpretation of religion did not preclude their having assumptions that helped determine the results of their investigations. Central to their effort was the assumption that there was *one* beginning point, with its corollary that all religious expressions are essentially the same, having been derived from an original. Connected to this was the working hypothesis of an evolutionary development from a simple religious form to later complex expressions. The image of religion that dominated early scholarship arose from the study of material primarily from the ancient Near East and primitive societies, and the problems of interpretation centered on the worship of a deity or some supernatural force and the image of man in relation to nature. A methodological assumption, especially at the beginning of these studies, was that the most perfect meaning of human life was to be found today; thus, whatever was strange to the investigator was interpreted as less mature than his or her own thinking. One further assumption, based on evolutionary reasoning, was that the basic *causes* of religion were to be found by the study of contemporary living nonliterate (or "primitive") societies. If one could observe the activities and learn the ideas of living nonliterate cultures and compare them with those found in the contemporary West, one could reconstruct the formation of religious life. Religion was studied, then, insofar as it could be regarded as a product of the physical and psychological traits common to all mankind. Thus, by a comprehensive comparison of data within an evolutionary scheme, "objective" nineteenth-century scholars of religion proceeded to understand the origin and development of religion from the most "primitive" to the most "advanced."

Religion as a Product of Faulty Thinking

A fairly common approach to understanding myths during the last half of the nineteenth century was to view gods as personifications of natural phenomena. During this time, the accepted scholarly opinion was that the worship of many gods (polytheism) was earlier, or "more primitive," than the exclusive worship of one god (monotheism). This was based on an assumption that before people developed clarity of thought—which found its highest expression in modern times, according to the advocates of mental evolution—their expression was dominated by intense feelings. This view had important implications for an investigation of the language of religious myths. For example, F. Max Mueller (who is sometimes called the father of the science of religion) explained the origin of religion as a mental slip in thinking that the natural *objects* of our senses were "acting *subjects*." In his early work *Essays in Comparative Mythology* (1856), Mueller held that natural objects, in their extraordinary expression (lightning or tornados) or in their regularity and inevitability (sun or mountains), were objects that incited terror, wonder, trust, and security. Religion was first experienced as rapture before natural phenomena, for example in the experience of daybreak. The earliest human expression of this experience of joy at dawn, or terror of lightning, took the form of a "primal language" that was visual rather than abstract. To say, "The sun follows dawn," was directly apprehended as true, but the formulation tended to include the notion that the sun was an active agent doing something—in this case "following." The characteristics of natural phenomena were mistakenly compared with human acts, and emotions, feelings, and activities that were normally used to express human activity were applied to natural objects. A thunderbolt, for example, was called "something that tears up the soil," or the wind, "the whistler." In this way, spirits or personal agents were invented as the actors of these phenomena. So arose the various dieties. The expression of religion, then, was a "disease of language" by which people mistook a way of speaking for an indication of a reality.

Mueller's reconstruction of the origin and growth of religion is essentially that when man perceives the infinite, he gives this experience a name, and the name can be passed on in a literalistic fashion so that the object of religious awe becomes a personified caricature. This process of being aware of the infinite, of naming the infinite, of passing on the name, of the degeneracy of the name without the original meaning, and ultimately of rejecting the name was for Mueller the "dialectical growth and decay" of religion. By making a comparative study of the language about God, that is, the naming of the infinite, a scholar could trace the history of religions. The material Mueller used is recognized today as a relatively late development in culture, so his theory is not commonly accepted as an explanation of the origin of religion. However, the effort to compare the names and forms of gods led to detailed linguistic studies; the recognition that religious belief is closely related to, if not an extension of, human symbolizing capacity is still prominent today.

Another attempt to find the origin of religion in faulty thinking was made by E. B. Tylor in his *Religion in Primitive Culture* (1871). Here he claimed that the earliest form of religion was animism—the belief that all of life was full of spirits or powers (*anima*). For Tylor, the rational nature of humanity is the clue to understanding how religion was produced. People in nonliterate cultures, he felt, had the same kind of mental faculty as modern man—though in an inferior stage of development. While they recognized spirits as invisible forces of life, they did not clearly express the idea of a single deity.

Tylor felt that religious ideas came about because thinking people in a low level of culture were deeply impressed by two groups of biological problems: first, the difference between death and life, and, second, the appearance of human shapes in dreams and visions. He maintained that as primordial people looked at these two phenomena they made the logical inference that everything is composed of two aspects—the physical and a spirit or soul. By positing a spirit, they could explain the apparent similarity between a live body and a body in death or in an unconscious state and at the same time explain how dreams and visions are possible. Once the reality of human experience had been divided into physical life and spirit life, it was only a short logical step to the doctrine of transmigration of souls or the existence of a personal soul in a future spiritual life, or to the belief that very powerful spirits lived in other (heavenly or nether) realms. For the rest of the nineteenth century, this theory of animisn dominated scholarly thinking on the earliest expression of religion.

Prelogical Sources of Religion: The Emotion of Awe

While the theory of animism was widely accepted, it did not go unchallenged. There were several scholarly attempts to show that the cause of religious phenomena is something prior to the logical inferences that were at the center of Tylor's theory. The most persuasive arguments came from men who had done field work among the primitives themselves. R. H. Codrington, in his work *The Melanesians* (1891), described the religion in Melanesia as based upon ancestor worship, magical practices, and *mana*. *Mana* was a force that existed everywhere and could act for the good or evil of man. The possession and control of *mana* was seen as a type of religious experience that preceded mythology and belief in spirits. Other terms such as *wakan, orenda,* and a type of Polynesian *mana* were soon discovered as expressions of this impersonal supernatural power in various peoples throughout the primitive world. In 1900, R. R. Marett published an article entitled, "Preanimistic Religion."[2] This article became one of the most famous expositions of the theory that the first stage of religion was not in naming the gods or in asserting the existence of nonphysical spirits, but rather it was an emotion of awe evoked by a feeling of personal relationship with an impersonal supernatural power *(mana).* This theory has played a very important role in understanding preliterate religious phenomena, and it is still assumed by many people to be the best explanation of religious origins—despite criticism by students of ethnology.

The concern to emphasize the direct feeling of awesome power among primitives, which cannot be put into Western religious categories, was championed by Lucien Levy-Brühl, who in *Primitives and the Supernatural* (1935) also opposed the view that religion resulted from a faulty reasoning. He pictures the primitive's "irrational mental life" as a capricious world of ancestral spirits, witchcraft, omens, pollution, and purification. Such notions as "supreme God" or even "a religion," he maintains, correspond to nothing in the minds of the primitives. Instead of conceptualizing man's experience, he goes on to say, the primitive is sensitive to the presence and action of invisible powers that have greater or lesser influence throughout his existence. These invisible powers, or indefinable influences, are always present, and the primitive man, woman, and child learn to cope with these powers by following various rules and traditional precepts. A sensitivity to the nonconceptual aspects of religious behavior, then, forms the basis for a true understanding of primitive religion.

Religion as an Outgrowth of Magic

Another theory that has influenced the study of religion is James G. Frazer's notion that religion was an appeal to supernatural beings for solutions to problems not satisfactorily solved by magic. Magic was regarded as primitive science. This perspective is found in Frazer's *The Magic Art,* which is part of the twelve-volume work entitled *The Golden Bough: A Study in Comparative Religion* (1911–1919). While partially successful, magic was deficient in its approach to cause and effect. The principles on which magic is based are (1) like produces like, or an effect resembles cause; and (2) things once in contact with each other continue to act on each other at a distance. These two principles of magic are based on the assumption that things act on each other through an invisible or secret sympathy. The idea of the operation of supernatural agents is a more complex idea, claimed Frazer, and thus it appeared later than did sympathetic magic, since even animals associate the ideas of things that are like each other or have been found together in their experience.

METHODS USED TO UNDERSTAND RELIGIOUS LIFE

For Frazer, knowledge of the supernatural began when men experienced certain extraordinary emotions and conceived extraordinary ideas for which they could not account in ordinary forms of experience. The solution was to designate these forces as the actions of a powerful spirit or deity. Once religion is achieved, says Frazer, it assumes one of two forms; however, both forms are often found simultaneously. These are (1) the worship of nature (animism) and (2) the worship of the dead. It is hard to say which form came first, but the belief in spirits soon evolved into totemism (see below.) as human social structures took form. The tribal totem, in turn, became a god with human form. This completes the evolutionary process to the present time, according to Frazer, and the distinction between magic and religion provides a means to handle those aspects of life moved by nonmaterial forces while keeping religion in terms of living, powerful, supernatural beings.

To document this theory, Frazer argued that the most primitive evidence of religious life comes from the aborigines of Australia, where magic is universally practiced—he said—and the propitiation of higher power is nearly unknown. During the past fifty years, Frazer's theory has influenced students of archaic religions, but he has been severely criticized for not interpreting his religious data in relation to levels of cultural development. For example, a group of people drinking wine together, or worshipping a corn goddess, can have certain cultural meanings in an agriculture-dominated village and others in an urban, commerce-dominated setting.

Many anthropologists since the time of Frazer have followed his distinction between magic, as the understanding of natural forces, and religion, as the understanding of supernatural forces, among primitives. Not all, however, have separated magic and religion in the way Frazer did. For instance, Bronislaw Malinowski rejected Frazer's assertion that magic is an inferior science. Malinowski claimed that the primitives clearly were aware of the difference between magic and naturalistic laws. Magic was the spontaneous activity in human situations of stress when recourse to all naturalistic laws had failed. Magical force was generated and transferred in the atmosphere of the supernatural—not the natural world. The distinction Malinowski saw between magic and religion, then, was that religion creates values and poses ultimate ends directly, whereas magic simply has practical, utilitarian purposes and is understood to be only a means to an end.

Various scholars in recent years have had different specific notions and descriptions of magic. However, the dominant notion, as expressed by Ruth Benedict and Claude Levi-Strauss, is that magic and religion are not two alternatives or stages in evolution; rather they are two components in human self-awareness reflecting two ways of interpreting the outside universe. Here we cannot go into a description of the place of magic in primitive or modern thinking (nor of the notion of *taboo*).[3] The issue here, in locating the earliest form of religion, is whether the notion of religion as an awareness of a supernatural being or beings is an adequate description of the kind of self-consciousness in primitive cultures. The distinction between magic and religion is one attempt to deal with this problem.

The Origins of Religious Expression 29

Totemism

A scholar's image or concept of religion cannot help but influence his other investigation of the origins of religion. This is true also for the sociologist Emile Durkheim, who in his famous book *The Elementary Forms of the Religious Life* (1912) sought to locate the causes of the basic forms of religious acts and notions. For him the purpose of religion was to regulate human relations with spiritual beings. Thus, the study of religion could not take place in a social environment where there was no prayer, sacrifices, rites, or other such outward actions. In contrast to the scholars who saw the beginning of religion as an incorrect understanding of life, Durkheim held that religion was created by pressures of social obligation related to the supernatural realm.

Religious forces, said Durkheim, are human forces that add a new dimension (the realm of the sacred) to natural perception. This religious force becomes manifest in social interaction because the collective life "brings about a state of effervescence which changes the condition of psychic activity."[4] The formation of the sacred realm is identical to the ideal self-understanding that a society has of itself—when a group of people who think together produce a unique orientation. A "society" is not made up of a mass of individuals in a particular geographical location; rather it is the result of the idea the people form of their group. Such a construction of the society's self-awareness is not, says Durkheim, a luxury or pastime but a condition of its existence.

Seeing the origin of self-awareness in group interaction, Durkheim sought for the earliest expression of religion in the symbolism of natural phenomena whereby a group of people identified themselves. This was found in the practice of totemism, which expresses the idea that there is some magical affinity between a society and a plant or lower animal form. The totem is the object of awe and reverence (a particular tree, a crab, or a particular stone) and has a special relationship to the group that identifies itself in terms of this object. The totem is not merely an idea, it is a symbol for the sacred whereby the primitive individual becomes one with the sacred. For empirical evidence, Durkheim appealed to the totem found among the Australian aborigines. He noted that the totem symbolized sacredness and the clan at the same time. He argued that the clan could not exist without the totem because there was no other way for the members to be united; therefore, totemism must be the primitive religion.

The High Being

During the first quarter of the twentieth century, while Marett, Frazer, and Durkheim were propounding their notions of *mana,* magic, and totemism, respectively, students of ethnology were criticizing them for not differentiating the evidence found at various levels of social and cultural development. One of the leading ethnologists, Wilhelm Schmidt, claimed that the origin of man's idea of God cannot be found without using a scientifically based historical method to distinguish and clarify various levels of development within nonliterate societies. Schmidt thought that, by identifying levels of development in the living remnants of the oldest civilization and arranging these in a genetic succession, a scholar could establish a historical line of "before and after." While he recognized that no living culture represents the earliest human life, he held that one could reconstruct the primordial religion by projecting backward from the available evidence.

Schmidt's cultural-historical approach to ethnology served to establish some widely accepted principles for reconstructing the development of culture. The principle of cultural diffusion, for example, has placed the Pygmies within the lowest level of technological development and generally located the areas of the earliest living cultures of nonliterate societies at the extremities of the Asian and American continents. An important element in Schmidt's methodology is that the latest or youngest element in a culture complex is that which appears to be the strongest. Thus, the most prominent elements among the nonliterate societies living today (for example, *mana*, totem, magic) are only later modifications of an original religious phenomenon.

In the first volume of his large work *The Origin of the Idea of God* (1912), Schmidt argues that the least technologically developed tribes indicate through their beliefs and cultic practices a distorted but positive reflection of the earliest religious experience—the worship of a "high being." While some scholars today reject Schmidt's thesis outright, others conclude from his evidence that a high being is recorded in the myths of the least technologically developed cultures alive today. For those scholars, the problem of an "original monotheism" or of the nature of a high being remains a live issue in discussing the earliest expression of religion.

One scholar who has made detailed studies of nonliterate peoples and has helped to define the contemporary discussion of early religious forms is Raffaele Pettazzoni. In his *The All-Knowing God* (1955) he discussed the problem of primordial monotheism. He denies the presence among nonliterate societies of monotheism, as it is historically defined, since this term suggests a denial of all other gods and as such presupposes polytheism. While he affirms the existence of a high being in the most primitive tribes, he does not wish to approach the study of religious phenomena with preconceived notions of the attributes of a supreme being—notions that have been formed in a comparatively late stage of philosophical development. Rather, in discussing one of the attributes of God, omniscience, he attempts to see how cultural influences affected its cultic expression. The form of deity changes according to the ethos of the group. A religious myth, Pettazzoni maintains, is not just a pleasant contemplation nor a result of logic; rather, it is the mental and spiritual orientation by which man knows himself. A myth of creation, for instance, is not meant to be a means for primordial man to find a primal cause; rather, it expresses a vital need—a guarantee for the existence of man and the universe as given in symbolic formulation.

A contemporary scholar of archaic religious symbols is Mircea Eliade, who holds that, while we cannot find the earliest religion, the evidence reflects a complex situation including "elevated" ideas that have coexisted with "lower" forms of worship and belief. In his article "Structures and Changes in the History of Religion,"[5] Eliade states that the most archaic living societies affirm belief in a supreme being of a celestial structure, but that this supreme being does not play a central role in religious life. This is not meant to imply a confirmation of Schmidt's thesis of an original monotheism, for other religious forms are found in primitive cultures in addition to a belief in a supreme being. Eliade acknowledges the ethnological distinctions between various levels or developments of religious life according to the cultural development of humanity and thereby finds different religious expressions reflecting different economic and cultural needs. The symbolism, the imagery, and the rites of different people reflect their particular needs and orientation to existence. Nevertheless, despite the cultural differences, says Eliade, religious symbols emerge from the human need to live in a paradigmatic world—a "cosmos." Religious people realize that this world is derived from eternal and infinite reality.

Can the First Religious Expression Be Found?

The attempt to define the original religious experience through a study of nonliterate societies assumes continuity between them and prehistorical religious life and between them and modern, science-oriented cultures. If the judgment is made that present ideas and life activities are dependent on those of the past, and the past is significantly related to present personal and cultural awareness, then it is important to look into the earliest expressions of religion to understand ourselves and the contemporary scene. As indicated above, however, the study of nonliterate cultures has produced evidence of *different* expressions of supernatural power. We even find that a contemporary notion of a "supernatural being" *may* not apply exactly to the earliest awareness. Thus, an investigator must be open to several possible meanings and images of religion. There is a strong possibility that the earliest religious experiences were quite diverse and that the history of development cannot be formulated in a simple, general evolutionary scheme in which the variety of religious expressions is regarded as derivations from a single source. If we are willing to allow for a variety of religious experiences as the very condition of what it means to be human, then we can see that what we abstractly term "religion" may find its source in a variety of circumstances that reflect individual and local cultural differences.

The study of origins has seldom resulted in positive conclusions—other than the recognition of the complexity of the problem. The general trend of inquiry into religion by social scientists is the investigation of the socio-cultural role of religion, which will be discussed in Chapter 3. The subject of the origin of religion is usually omitted entirely. The present concern in contemporary studies of nonliterate societies is to record data as accurately as possible and to define the type or structure of religious beliefs, rites, and religious institutions.

The effort to locate the earliest expressions of religion has shifted from a study of living nonliterate cultures to prehistoric archeological discoveries. Some scholars, for example E. O. James in his *Prehistoric Religion,* used both archeological data and studies of contemporary nonliterates to interpret archaic religion. However, during the past three decades the discoveries of evidence of prehistoric religion in archeological sites has generally been limited to getting clear and specific data rather than formulating these data in defense of a theory about the earliest form of religion.

This archeological evidence suggests that we can classify the artifacts that have been interpreted by some scholars as religious into three periods: "the Old World" (Upper Paleolithic), 100,000 to 25,000 B.C.; the Late Stone Age (Mesolithic), 25,000 to 8,000 B.C.; and Neolithic, 8,000 to 3,000 B.C. In the first period, we find no art, but we do find careful burial with various cultural implements buried with the corpse. In the next period, we find *Homo sapiens* (or Cro-Magnon man) and evidence of deliberate and careful burial in which the dead bodies were decorated with red ochre and shells; alongside the bodies are various cultural implements. The art during this period includes painting, engravings, carvings in relief, and models of animals in clay, *suggesting* the practice of magical rites to ensure productivity and success in hunting. The Neolithic period is said to have begun with the discovery of agriculture and the domestication of animals, and there is much evidence of agricultural rites and worship of a fertility goddess as well as the goddess' male partner, a cult of the spirits of the dead or ancestors, and a cult of the powers in the earth.

Such a brief summary of the conceptual framework into which archeological findings are placed merely indicates the present recognition that, because of a lack of sufficient evidence and serious methodological problems in interpreting the limited evidence we have, any explanation of religion in prehistoric periods is very problematical. At present, many social scientists and historians feel the effort to find "the first expression of religion" is not only a frustrating problem but a false one.

SELECTED READINGS

A selection of ten readings by leading social scientists on the origin and development of religion is found in W. A. Lessa and E. Z. Vogt, eds, *Reader in Comparative Religion: An Anthropological Approach*, 2d ed. (New York: Harper, 1965), Section I, "The Origin and Development of Religion." These readings provide a basic introduction to the problem of locating the earliest form of religion.

Paperback reprints of some early studies of the origin of religion are available. Among these are: E. B. Tylor, *Religion in Primitive Culture* (New York: Harper, 1958); S. Freud, *Totem and Taboo* (New York: Random, 1946); J. G. Frazer, *New Golden Bough,* abridged, edited by T. H. Gaster, (New York: Macmillan, 1959); E. Durkheim, *The Elementary Forms of the Religious Life* (New York: Collier, 1961); P. Radin, *Primitive Religion* (New York: Dover, 1957).

A. Goldenweiser, *Early Civilization: An Introduction to Anthropology* (New York: Knopf, 1922). An example of the approach to the origins of religion among many anthropologists of the time.

*E. O. James, *Prehistoric Religion: A Study in Prehistoric Archeology* (New York: Barnes & Noble, 1957). Here a renowned historian of religion brings together archeological information and anthropological studies of living nonliterate cultures to present an overall picture of prehistoric religion.

The Origins of Religious Expression

A. E. Jensen, *Myth and Cult Among Primitive People* (Chicago: University of Chicago Press, 1963, first published 1951). An interpretation by a leading ethnologist of the religious configurations found in primitive culture.

J. Maringer, *The Gods of Prehistoric Man* (New York: Knopf, 1960, first published 1952). A description of the evidence in an interpretation meant for the general reader. Pictures and diagrams are included. A clear exposition of the present state of knowledge on the subject.

E. Norbeck, *Religion in Primitive Society* (New York: Harper, 1961). An anthropologist's statement on the role of religion in primitive society. Chapters 2 and 3, "Origins" and "Conceptions of the Supernatural," are clear summaries of the problems in trying to find the "original" expression of religion.

3.

The Religious Factor in People's Lives

When scholars of the past century, in their restless pursuit of human self-discovery, were unable to find the basic character of religion in its "origin," they shifted their focus to the *continuing* formation of religious expression. This study concentrated on the role, or function, of religion in social interaction, personal responses, and cultural patterns. Both the *fact* of religiousness and the *variety* of religious forms were understood as the products of cultural, psychological, and social conditions.

From the traditional standpoint of the social scientist, human life is distinguished from that of other animals primarily by the fact that people create, preserve, and transform culture. Not only do human beings use tools to modify their environment, but their sense of themselves is determined, in part, through the creation of symbols and systems of symbols (ideologies). Human contact, then, is held to be regulated not only by "instinct" or physical limitations; it is also conditioned by "values," patterns of judgment and expression that indicate one's place in an *order*. People seek meaning in their experience; they place hopes, frustrations, sense observations, likes, and dislikes into a world view, an outlook on life. An integrated pattern of awareness, which we might call social values, is, by definition, selective; any ordering of experience requires elevating some elements of experience and repressing others. Thus, value systems produce opposite pulls of "good" and "bad"; and society rewards and punishes in relation to these value patterns.

While contemporary trends indicate an interest in the importance of the inner dynamics of a person's religious experiences, and their subsequent influence on outward functioning, the traditional approach has been mainly an attempt to describe cultural religious forms and processes of change. In traditional interpretations, religious activities, ideas, and institutions are understood as part of a more comprehensive and fundamental context of human existence: society, psychological needs, and culture. For example, religious rites may be examined in terms of their ability to allay anxiety in face of threat, such as death, or belief systems may be studied as either causes or results (or both) of racial identification and prejudice; or ecstatic personal religious experience may be analyzed as an effort by relatively powerless and poor people to achieve self-affirmation; or membership in various church denominations may be correlated with parishioners' social, educational, and economic patterns.

While various studies in the social sciences have limited goals of description or clarification of specific data, the general goal has often been defined as the ability to test theories of social interaction by empirical study. For instance, an assumption that human beings are the sum of their social roles implies that religion can be studied as a function of human role playing. An interpretation of religious rituals and morals in terms of their social function, then, requires some theory of socialization. In such a theory, there is a general assumption that all people throughout the world in the past and present use similar processes to internalize the values of their society. A related assumption is that all people have certain invariable traits (biological, psychological, social) that condition the human maturing processes.

This chapter will describe the functional approach to the "scientific study of religion." While it is not the only one found in the social sciences, it has been very important during the past century and is felt still to provide a significant method of interpretation today. Such an approach has assumed, at least as a working principle, that societies are systems of interdependent parts and forces. Religion is regarded as both a product of and a contributing factor to society. Religious institutions are seen as an important force in the personal development of individuals; along with other social institutions like the family, educational system, and government, they help make up a total cultural system. Functionalists, then, define culture as a complex set of symbolic, institutional, and physical systems that interact with each other to structure human life. These systems together shape a person's values, goals, and capacities for fulfilling these goals.

The fact that some systems have more importance for some people than others means that different individuals may stress such different values as physical comfort, sensitivity to other people, moral obligations to a community, or political power. In the functionalist view, traditional religious institutions, such as church denominations, rites, or belief systems, are regarded as but one form of value-system in the whole culture. As a result, many studies have tried to answer the general question: What is the function of traditional forms in maintaining or shifting the equilibrium of individual personality structure and the social system as a whole? Until recently, studies of religious life have taken one of two general directions: the study of the emotional, irrational character of religion or the analysis of the social-cultural forces that structure the individual. Following these two general orientations, this chapter will first discuss some psychological interpretations of the key issues in understanding religion as part of a cultural system and will then focus on the social-cultural interpretations of sociologists and anthropologists.

Religion as a Means of Personal Adjustment and Self-Fulfillment

The term "religion" is used in at least two basic senses in psychological studies. One is the definition of religion as a set of "accepted forms" (prayer, worship, mystical experiences) that are set off from, but related to, other forms of personality expression. In this context, religion has only limited significance for the human personality, since it is one of several organizing factors—and not even the most important of these. Religion here is seen as a certain kind of social conditioning that can have either beneficial or detrimental effects on the person who is trying to adjust. On the other hand, the term "religion" is sometimes used to indicate the whole field of self-fulfillment. This is a definition of the function of religion in terms of personality integration, spiritual wholeness, and self-actualization. Of course, such a use does not require that the investigator accept theological propositions—for instance, about the reality of God as the object of worship. It only assumes that the human personality, as we experience it in ourselves and others, requires "moral and spiritual values."

The psychological studies based on these definitions have developed into a theoretical and historical schism within traditional psychology as a whole. The former is used by many researchers who follow experimental behaviorism (an approach that stresses the use of repeated experiments and interprets human behavior as the sole result of a stimulus-response mechanism) and the more clinical, although no less deterministic, position of Sigmund Freud. The latter definition is found in the work of Gordon Allport, Carl Jung, and some of the more contemporary approaches in the humanistic and transpersonal movements in American psychology.

Elements of both approaches to the psychological study of religion appear in the work of the founder of American psychology, William James. As early as 1874, James set up the first psychological laboratory; by 1890, he had published his famous *Principles of Psychology*. In this volume he introduced, among other concepts, the notion of a stream of consciousness in mental life and the concept of self, which included a spiritual self as an aspect of personality development. Then, in *The Varieties of Religious Experience* (1902), James excited the general public with his interpretations of the psychological meaning of religion and his analysis of different forms of personal religious experience. In applying scholarly investigation and scientific method to the study of religion, James demonstrated the benefits of objective analysis of observable phenomena and his sensitivity to the very personal and private nature of religious experience and its importance in personality growth.

The experimental behavioristic position influenced a late nineteenth-century movement that attempted to pattern psychology on the natural sciences. A major exponent was the German psychologist, Wilhelm Wundt, who founded his experimental laboratory in 1879. So great was the influence of this school on American psychological studies that the domain of psychology was seen only as that which could be observed and measured. Psychology thereby developed into the scientific study of behavior. "Religion" was defined as conventional institutional activity, which was one among many sets of definable stimuli that conditioned people's observable and measurable social behavior. Thus, notions of a religious consciousness or awareness that was different from other cultural components were regarded as inappropriate explanatory concepts; they were judged to be unscientific and therefore not properly psychological.

This attitude originally attempted to relegate "religion" to the status of observable emotional behavior. More recently, it has fostered a number of studies that regard religion simply as the internalization of cultic forms available in one's culture. The attitude is often found in questionnaires for mental and personality testing. Religiousness is implicitly defined by a set of test questions limited to traditional, conventional, Western cultural experiences, beliefs, and practices which can be generalized for short interviews or multiple-choice questionnaires. A built-in bias in many questionnaires equates intellectual activity with scientific interests, and emotional expression with religious fervor and belief. Many people taking such tests are led to feel that intellectual activity is superior to emotional activity.

Some scholars have pointed out that the measures of "religiosity" in religious-preference questionnaires are designed (either consciously or unconsciously) to indicate how close a person is to certain traditional religious practices, rather than the nature of his or her religiosity. Thus, responses to questions like "Is there a life after death? Is the Bible inspired? Does the devil exist?" indicate only whether or not an individual subscribes to certain traditional views. A person who has dropped out of a fundamentalist sect to work for peace, civil liberties, and open housing in nonchurch related organizations might get a low score on such a religiosity test, although members of social action associations would probably give him or her a high score for such activities. There are many difficulties in drawing up a questionnaire that will reveal the deepest values of a person or of a significant sample of the population. Unless questionnaires can be designed to explore both traditional and nontraditional religious data, they lead to invalid conclusions about religious life in a modern world.

Sigmund Freud's attitude—that religion is part of a learned mechanism to control a basic biological energy while releasing tension and frustration—also influenced studies of the psychology of religion. Freud held that religion was a product of people's helplessness and fear of aggression and sexual energies. A person's conscience was seen as an internalized control mechanism—the civilizing force learned from one's family and culture—which, when violated, produces psychic pain or guilt. Corporate religion was regarded as a fantasy designed to recover a lost image of childlike intimacy with parents. Freud's theory about the origin of religion—that it arose through a corporate guilt derived from the sons' primeval murder of their tribal father—has been discredited. Nevertheless, his effort to locate psychic powers and forces below the level of consciousness constituted a major contribution to the psychological study of religion. He saw that human actions (rituals and symbols) communicate patterns of self-awareness even if they are not expressed in conscious conceptual propositions. In this view, religion is socially significant because it regulates life, but psychologically it functions like the obsessive acts of a neurotic person in expressing unfulfilled goals and avoiding the guilt acquired from falling short of these goals.

For Freud, religion (by which term he meant Jewish and Christian moralism of the late nineteenth century) was the social control over the individual libido, or inner energy of the psyche for creative self-expression. When this psychic energy is repressed, he claimed, its natural forms of expression are sublimated into socially acceptable religious and artistic forms. Such expressions alleviate the anxieties caused by the repression. Sometimes, however, the psychic energy is so strong that it bursts the conventional modes of regulation; this is called neurosis. Religion as a defense against instinctual drives and irrational forces was satisfactory in an earlier nonscientific culture in which myth was alive and ritual actually controlled human self-awarenesses, but, Freud warned, in an intellectual and rational age religion is only an infantile attempt to use the psychic force creatively.

A closely related interpretation, which places a higher functional value on religious activity, argues that religion gives people "something to hold on to" in periods of personal crisis. This view, expressed by such scholars as Clyde Kluckhohn and E. O. James, emphasizes the fact that human beings live in a precarious environment full of dangers and hazards. Religion serves as means whereby people preserve their personal integrity and a sense of meaning in the face of biological, physical, social, and psychological threats—the most profound of which is death. Religious rituals are social forces that give stability and reinforcement to the person and to society in the face of disaster and provide more significant rewards (for example, heaven) than those achieved through mere biological maintenance and reproduction. Through religious beliefs and rituals, men anticipate potential threats and are thereby better able to handle them when they actually come. Similarly, they are better able to accommodate unfulfilled wishes by placing them in a transcendent, universal context whose ultimate purpose is beyond human comprehension. Not all psychologists and psychiatrists, however, define religion as corporate cultic and moral practice, or interpret its basic significance as control of fear and irrational drives. To some, religion represents the most complete human awareness and means of achieving self-fulfillment. It is the most profound expression of personhood whether through "normal," socially acceptable religious practices or through "abnormal" attempts to preserve self-integrity.

Here "abnormal" can mean either neurotic responses to fear and anxiety, or healthy, religious expression that rises above the do's and don'ts of one's culture. Religious institutions can sometimes meet the religious needs for completeness, self-fulfillment, and creative freedom but at other times may block them. Among those who stress the life-enhancing powers of religion are Gordon Allport, Carl Jung, and others representing the more recent trends within existential-humanistic and transpersonal psychology.

Allport's classic statement is *The Individual and His Religion* (1950). He argues from the standpoint of a scientist interested in the ultimate uniqueness of each individual's expression of religious sentiment, particularly the function of this sentiment in the mature personality. For Allport, the religious quest begins with the introduction of outward religious forms, which the individual then subjectively, or personally, interprets. However similar the outward forms may be, the infinite variety of ways in which people can combine them internally makes the religious response of each individual unique. Indeed, there are as many varieties of religious experience as there are religious people.

An individual's religious development is affected by such diverse factors as bodily needs, intelligence, interests, curiosity, and cultural symbols. The synthesis of these factors, Allport feels, engenders a religious sentiment. He defines sentiment as an organized system of thoughts and feelings directed toward some identifiable object of value. In the case of religion, the object of value has such ultimate importance that an individual's original, culturally conditioned responses take on an autonomous character, often becoming independent of their origins. An individual has formed a mature religious sentiment when he or she has succeeded in integrating such influences as parental hopes, legal restraints, personal relations with others, and body sensations into a feeling of individual responsibility and a sense of meaning in life. A religious sentiment is mature when it develops along avenues of widening interest, detachment insight, and self-unification; it creates a discriminating, dynamic attitude that is capable of producing consistent morality; and it provides a comprehensive, integral, and interpretive picture of existence for the individual.

Carl Jung also offered psychological insights into the meaning of religion while seeing religion as the greatest and strongest value within the organizing process of the human psyche. "That psychological fact," he said, "which is the greatest power in your system is the god, since it is always the overwhelming psychic factor which is called god. As soon as a god ceases to be an overwhelming factor, he becomes a mere name."[6]

Jung understood "man" not simply as a combination of biological and chemical forces, but as a totality formulated symbolically into an image of the self. This totality, of course, includes both "unconscious" and "conscious" existence. The integration of these two spheres of mental life constitutes the highest point in the evolution of the unique and spiritualized possibilities of the human personality. However, the integration of the personality can only be achieved through discovery of and struggles with the depths of the unconscious. For Jung, the forces and patterns at the unconscious level are always religious, for they are the most profound determinants of people as they create their own humanity. Jung's contribution has been amplified by other psychiatrists who point out that the thwarting of this basic psychic urge for self-realization by parental, societal, or church authority can destroy the basic "religious" potential for self-actualization and result in neurosis and psychosis.

If an investigator assumes a human need to find and express full human potential, it is not surprising that both the neurotic personality and the religious convert express a common conflict within their personalities. Both use the means available to preserve their center, their own existence. In this context, Rollo May and other scholars of "existential psychology" affirm the basic need for self-affirmation. This position suggests that neurosis cannot be identified with a failure to adjust to social standards; human social and religious conduct cannot be defined simply as "adaptive behavior in reaction to appropriate stimuli." Rather, both neurosis and religion express a much more profound condition of human existence. People require a goal or purpose that transcends them; yet they achieve that goal through the uniqueness of their individual personalities. The definition of religion as socialized adjustment ignores this larger dimension.

Some nontraditional, but contemporary trends in the areas of humanistic and transpersonal psychology are exploring this larger dimension. While the humanistic movement emphasizes meaning and values in science and focuses on the development of healthy relationships *between* people, representatives of the transpersonal movement emphasize the psychology of spiritual growth *within* the evolving personality. While the first group is concerned with, for example, the role of religious values in mental health, the second emphasizes techniques and states of consciousness associated with the actualization of those values, inside or outside of organized religious institutions. Thus, a person's self-fulfillment may or may not be expressed within the forms of a historical religious institution. (For a discussion of psychological interests that have shifted from a scientific analysis of religion to the clinical use of psychotherapy as a "means of ultimate transformation," see Chapter 10.)

Religion as Social and Cultural Processes

Two famous scholars who interpreted religious life in relation to social forces were Emile Durkheim (see above) and Max Weber. Each sought the key to religious expression in a person's self-awareness within the social fabric. For Durkheim—who made his major contributions early in the twentieth century—religion was real insofar as it expressed the vital energy of social interaction. Religious life had its roots in a cause more basic than individual thought or feeling, namely social forces. What human beings designated as God was basically a symbolic expression of society's corporate definition of itself. Thus, Durkheim stressed that religious self-fulfillment was determined by a person's participation in the group norms, ideals, and expectations through which he or she gained a self-image. Personhood, for him, depended heavily on internalizing objective (intersubjective) social reality.

A few years later, Weber, while not basing his interpretation of religious expression on a universal condition of humanity, as did Durkheim, examined the social conditions in which individuals achieved a specific self-awareness as expressed in particular historical situations. Weber did not reduce religious feeling to social forces; rather, he understood the significance of inner religious meaning in the context of a general theory of social action. Basic answers to such universal human problems as suffering, evil, and death had profound consequences on social development. Similarly, Weber related charisma, the unexplainable spiritual power that some people have for others, to social processes. Charismatic individuals have power due to deep psychic links with their followers. Such individuals, then, could embody the reorganization of social patterns and develop new religious movements. In this way, Weber focused on the interaction of social forces within the individual and the group in order to account for the changes found in a religious tradition or a cultural way of life.

Durkheim and Weber influenced many later scholars who applied social science concepts to the interpretation of religion. A number of them relegated religion to the role of a "social mobilizer and integrator of a social group." They regarded social forces as the basic reality and saw society as the "fact" that is necessary for the development of an individual self.

With such an emphasis of the reality of society, sociologists have tended to interpret religious phenomena either in terms of religion's functions within the society, or in terms of the relations between religious structures and other social structures. Two of the functions most commonly discussed are (1) unification or integration of individuals into a social group, and (2) justification of rewards and punishments for obeying or disobeying the norms that restrain and channel individual behavior.

In the first case, social ordering provides a value scheme shared by most persons in the society. Sociologists believe that people gain a sense of identity through their affiliations with various groups, from small and temporary units (for example, a committee in an organization) to a whole culture that depends on a common language and other shared characteristics. As they see it, society, which of course is made of individuals, is a complex *system* of relationships between people. It requires an integrating force through which people can identify themselves in relation to a *pattern* of experience and action. In this view, religion provides the integrating force for a society and expresses social structures, which also apply outside the particular traditional religious forms. For example, American churches and synagogues are influenced to a considerable degree by "democratic" processes; at the same time, most have a distinct hierarchy, ranging from members to individuals with limited ceremonial or other functions, to rabbi, priest, or minister, who in turn fit into regional, national, and international religious structures. Individuals commonly become integrated into these religious structures through their adjustment to the hierarchial roles provided by social forces.

The second social function of religious life reinforces the first. As social conditioning integrates the individual into society, so it constrains or controls the individual so that the great majority of people in a society accept the control voluntarily as a condition of their existence. There are two factors at work. First, religious symbols (socially integrating images) define what is true and good; they provide an image of what is the best in human life. This image contains an implicit obligation, namely that one should live in terms of that definition of the true and good for one's own benefit as well as that of nature and society. To do otherwise is to move toward ultimate self-destruction. Thus, in most societies, indiscriminate killing or murder for private gain is considered bad; however, killing an "enemy" under socially approved circumstances (for example, war) can be a "good" act. Secondly, religious institutions provide or support the norms of other social institutions by placing not only ritual activities but all life under the judgment of an ultimate purpose (e.g., God's will or Buddha Amida's vow to bring all beings to the Pure Land). For all actions, a person can expect rewards for conforming to, and punishments for deviating from, the highest norms. Ideally, the motivating force taught in a Sunday-school lesson should carry over into a Christian's work and family life.

At present, it is commonly recognized that universal generalizations about the integrating function of religion hold true primarily in nonliterate societies, from which most of the data for such a theory have been obtained. The analysis of initiation rites or ritual sacrifices in nonliterate societies has emphasized the educative and integrative functions of religion in relatively small communities. It has become evident that the question of the function of religion is very complex. Studies of a variety of cultures over a period of time indicate that religion can be expressed differently at different times in the same culture and can be defined in different ways. Religion, thus, has various functions—some complementary and some antagonistic to each other.

Sociologists interested in religion were therefore compelled to focus on different kinds of social organization and their relationships to religious beliefs and practices. They examined various cultural conditions that determined specific types of beliefs or religious activities and analyzed differences within religious systems to see how the various parts of a system were interdependent. This kind of problem confronted Joachim Wach, whose *Sociology of Religion* defined religion in relation to natural groups (family, kinship, racial cults), different forms of religious organization, religion in relation to different social strata, the relation of a religious tradition to political systems, and the types of religious authority.

A close examination of the empirically definable social institutions reveals a variety of roles within religious communities as well as multiple relationships between the religious community and the rest of social life. Many recent sociological studies have been devoted to analyses of particular religious institutions and their relationships to social patterns. The social structures or institutions are taken as the concrete data through which values in personal belief are examined. In the context of these studies, variations in religious practice are often explained as a consequence of different social factors (national groupings, sex, age, and class).

The past twenty years have seen a particular interest in the institutional form of Christianity in America and Europe. For some scholars, this has resulted in an implicit identification between "church" and "religion," following the often unexamined linkage commonly made in Western speech between religion and Christian doctrine and rituals. Recently, however, some sociologists have criticized the identification of church with religion on the grounds that it provides too narrow a definition of religion and religious institutions. Besides omitting much relevant data, they say, such an approach fails to recognize that in a twentieth-century industrial society the "established institutions of religion" constitute neither the source nor the expression of pervading values.

In this vein, Robert Bellah and W. Lloyd Warner[7] have pointed out the impact of "civil religion" in America. They regard as religious activities such cultural expressions as annual Memorial Day ceremonies, the funeral rites for President John F. Kennedy, or honor paid to the ideals of heroes of American history—especially those who were killed, such as Kennedy or Abraham Lincoln. Similarly, American editorials and speeches favoring democracy, "righteousness," the virtues of the early (European) settlers, or values like strength, endurance and energetic effort are imbued with a sacredness that places the American people and the "American way of life" in the dimension of ultimate values.

In an analysis not restricted to the American scene, Thomas Luckmann, in *The Invisible Religion*[8] says that every society has "a configuration of meaning," which is internalized by the individuals of that society. This configuration has various levels of significance, and the highest level in the hierarchy of meanings expressed in special symbols is the "religious" expression of a society. Luckmann suggests that sociologists look for religious forces in modern industrial society under such themes as "self-realization," "mobility," "sexuality," and "familism."

The relevance of such thinking to the discussion of religious change and the dynamics of social change is especially apparent in the contemporary phenomenon of secularization. The notion of "secularization" as the loss of power by the traditional institutions of religious activity is inadequate as a complete sociological theory of religion. It fails to recognize all the ways in which the "transcendent" fits within the social fabric. According to the critics, the sociological understanding of religion cannot be limited to the analysis of certain institutions that have been labeled "religious," but must encompass all structures of society whereby man seeks and expresses his most profound self-awareness. Thus, technology, politics, psychiatry, or art may be regarded as "secular" by traditional theological norms, but for a scientific study, they may represent the most powerful social expressions of value-change.

Students of cultural anthropology have taken religion seriously as *one aspect* of cultural patterning. They are intellectual heirs of Durkheim, Weber, and Freud. Like these predecessors, anthropologists view religion as a product of human imagination that functions to establish patterns of cultural self-awareness and communication, and as a means to establish equilibrium within society after a crisis such as war or death of a leader. Or, characteristically, the central importance of initiation rites, such as circumcision or clitorectomy, is explained as a socially instituted mechanism whereby members of a group establish and stabilize sexual and social identity. Thus, religion is derived from cultural and social needs. As a product of the human mind and social interaction, however, it plays a decisive role in the patterns and forms that constitute any culture. Religion is peculiarly important because it not only provides general conceptions about the order of existence, but also imbues these interpretations of life with personal and cultural convictions. They become the unconscious assumptions on which conscious patterns of culture are built. Very often these hidden configurations lying beneath the outward cultural manifestations provide the moving dynamics for society.

One of the basic ways in which cultural anthropologists interpret religion is as a cultural habit. Religion is seen as a system of ideas and emotional responses whereby a culture creates, defines, and establishes habitual ways of action through which the society interprets and validates itself. In such a configuration of personal hopes, definitions of life, and techniques for solving problems reside cultural values, norms, and standards of living. This view of religion is found in the works of Alfred L. Kroeber,[9] who emphasizes that the essential elements of a culture are its patterns, which integrate people into an organization and provide the channels whereby segments of society can function as a culture. The particular relationships among individuals, between individuals and small groups, among small groups, and between the individual and the whole culture are preconditioned by antecedent organizations that play a powerful, conservative role in society. However, Kroeber warns, it is easy to assume that impersonal powers alone form society; on the contrary, individual human agents both create and embody cultural events. From a long-range view, it is clear that individuals predominantly express cultural traits rather than individual forms unique to that culture. At the same time, individuals act *as if* their individual personalities do change cultural events. And some studies indicate how individuals stretch and sometimes tear the fabric of society, which must then be rewoven. History is full of such examples, such as Napoleon Bonaparte, Joseph Stalin, or Mao Tse-tung.

The basis for interpreting religious forms as "cultural habits" is the assumption that a generalized framework of human activity underlies any particular formal expression of culture. All people face the same inevitable problems such as obtaining food and shelter and such social events as birth, illness, war, and death. While different value systems, rites, and beliefs provide various answers to human problems, the problems are defined by human biology and social interaction. As a matter of fact, cross-cultural comparison must start with the assumption of common human capacities and needs behind the different religious expressions.

While some anthropologists have interpreted religion within the total complex of the cultural fabric, others have concentrated on its function for establishing equilibrium in a society after some crisis. At the turn of the century, cultural anthropology emphasized studies of tribal societies, and the function of religion was understood to be the preservation of the integrity of the society through rites and rituals—with a considerable concentration on the initiation ceremony of the adolescent. Anthropologists who interpreted religion from a strictly naturalistic point of view saw this concern with the "transcendent in life" as the human effort to manipulate the mysterious in human life. From this perspective, the social phenomena of magic, religion, and science were viewed as different attempts to attain different and progressively higher levels of social awareness in order to fill gaps in knowledge and deal pragmatically with uncontrolled natural forces. While this interpretation has been questioned and criticized in detail by scholars who have made highly detailed studies of magic, religion, and science as social expressions, it is still influential in generalized anthropological interpretations of religion.

In recent years, an increasing number of studies have concentrated on the mechanism of change, which operates continually within a culture. Many reflect the assumption that religion is identified with conservative and unchanging value systems, but others question this assumption about the nature of religion. For example, the late Clyde Kluckhohn[10] called attention to the fact that a "functional interpretation" often begins with a static image of society—as if one social mechanism had remained unchanged through different historical periods. Such an interpretation tends to forget historical changes, as well as the personal motivations and rewards that help to determine structure and change in culture.

Without limiting the role of religion to a level of knowledge about the natural world, other anthropologists interpret religious myths and rituals within the more general context of social tensions and crises common to all cultures. Religion becomes the symbolic dramatization of ''a common system of sentiments,'' which is repeated not only periodically to condition the culture but especially at points of danger or threat to the personal or cultural life. Such crucial personal experiences as birth, puberty, marriage, and death, as well as experiences that hold a society of individuals together as a culture (for example, recounting the origin of the culture or community, reaffirming the necessity to keep a specific community in hostile or friendly relations, or celebrating the relation of mankind to the cosmos), all these require symbols and symbolic activities whereby the community identifies itself and preserves the value-patterns that are at the root of self-identification.

A recent scholarly attempt to discover meaning in myth uses an approach called ''structuralism.'' Structuralists include such diverse scholars as the Mexican poet-philosopher Octavio Paz, the Swiss cognitive-psychologist Jean Piaget, the British classicist G. S. Kirk, and the French cultural anthropologist and philosopher Claude Levi-Strauss. Instead of examining origins of religions or myths, the historical social-political-economic causes of religion or myth, the psychological needs that motivate a formulation of myths, the social-functional effects of myths, or the truth-value of myths, these scholars focus their attention on how myth operates below the level of consciousness in people's minds. This effort searches for the significant meanings and the structural laws beneath the consciously discernible patterns of meaning and intention. Such meaning is to be found in sets of symbols in cultural communication systems including mathematics, music, literature, ritual, language, art, and myth.

Instead of dismissing myths, stories and sayings from ancient and contemporary peoples as meaningless superstition, structuralists have found that these operate with rigorous logic to communicate meaning. For example, Levi-Strauss, in his four volume *Introduction to a Science of Mythology,* analyzes the myths of the Indians of North and South America in terms of the organization of abstract ideas within concrete images. He points out that these people recognize that certain objects, animals, plants, people, places, and events (whether actual or imagined) have sacred status in a community not because they are sublimations of repressed emotions (as Freud believed), not because they are a social force for preserving group identity (as Durkheim claimed), not because they have other practical uses in the society (as seen by anthropologist A. R. Radcliffe-Brown), and not because they represent the epitome of a progressive, evolutionary schema. They are important to the community because they communicate meaning. The stories embody general ideas; they make comprehension of the world possible in terms of dramatic images. The distinctions between the visual images of tribal totems provide a conceptual framework for comprehending the experienced social distinctions between clans. In a like manner, the distinctions between national symbols such as flags serve as a conceptual framework for comprehending the experienced emotional and intellectual distinctions between nations. Structuralists see this ''structural'' distinction as much deeper than social conventions in that it operates in the minds of a social group at an unconscious level. The function of social (tribal, national) symbols is to resolve the basic contradictions that everyone experiences and thereby communicate the meaningfulness of life.

From his studies of nonliterate peoples and myths, Levi-Strauss formulates general hypotheses about symbol-making that he claims are valid historically and cross-culturally. In *The Savage Mind* (1966), he argues that human beings have always thought equally well; the differences among groups lie in the concrete experiences they have to think about. The "mind" (thought) of the modern, technological scientist is in no sense superior to the "mind" (thought) of the "savage." Levi-Strauss rejects the often assumed contrast between "primitive" and "advanced" societies, the notions of "historical progress," and the "evolutionary superiority" of any race or people, or of any human symbol system. Thus, all religions and myths are understood as valuable and meaningful for the people participating in them. Finally, no one can prove that any particular symbol system within a society (such as mathematics or science) is more meaningful than any other particular symbol system (such as music or myth). All operate with the same organ of the body—the brain—for the same purpose: to communicate meaning to other human beings.

The structural concern with symbol systems and patterns of meaning is not confined to social scientists. It is also found among scholars of the "phenomenology of religion" who study both the meaning of religious symbols and actions and the force of ultimate reality that is asserted by religious people. One of the major goals of structural phenomenologists is to participate in an experience of meaning rather than decipher mental or neurological laws that govern changes in value orientations.

Many anthropologists, sociologists, and psychologists see religion as part of the total dynamic of human creativity and change. In each discipline "religion" is studied as a human creation (or negation), which is to be examined insofar as empirical data can be found and then understood in the context of a comprehensive system of personal and social development. In the effort to interpret human life within a more comprehensive model, some behavioral scientists have developed a general systems theory, or cybernetic model. Cybernetics is a science that focuses on mechanisms of self-regulation and the processes by which organisms adapt to their environment. Scientists using a cybernetic model view human beings as organisms that are capable of learning, self-regulation, and adaptation and respond to physical and social environments according to precisely specified systems of feedback and behavior. At present, there is no major systematic formulation of religious life in terms of a cybernetic model, but a number of behavioral scientists hold out the possibility of understanding religion in this way. Thus, personal and social expressions of religion would be interpreted in terms of energy exchange and organic adaptive mechanisms. Aligning themselves with functional and structural studies of religion, these scholars hold that religious activity can be interpreted as a mechanism for constructing personal and social identity whereby the organism develops capacities to respond quickly to its environment without disintegration or total destruction. These capacities would be particularly useful in situations of stress (death, radical social change, or inconsistencies experienced in truth-systems).

Such a systems model must account for unconscious motivational forces as well as for conscious learning devices. Religious experiences like hope, awe, peace, or integrity—as well as social organization, or doctrinal formulations—are then seen as different processes whereby emotional conflicts and the innovative forces necessary for self-maintenance can be reconciled. In this model, many interacting systems (language, society, feelings, visual symbols, physical perception mechanisms, genetic determination, biological needs) of energy-exchange are seen to interact, and the forces that provide the values of a society cannot be limited to traditional religious institutions. In this effort, as in those of the past century, social scientists limit themselves to interpreting those aspects of religious life that can be defined and observed empirically and that can be understood in terms of human creative processes and patterns of experience. This position, for other scholars of religion, seems oversimplified because it tends to reduce "religion" to something else, rather than considering religious phenomena in their own right.

SELECTED READINGS

Several volumes of selected readings in the different approaches of social science to religion are quite useful for understanding religion in terms of its function in life:

W. A. Lessa and E. Z. Vogt, eds., *Reader in Comparative Religion: An Anthropological Approach,* 2d ed. Section II, "The Function of Religion in Human Society," Section III, "Myth and Ritual," Section XI, "Dynamics in Religion," and Section XII, "New Methods of Analysis," provide good examples of the concerns with religion in anthropological studies.

L. Schneider, ed., *Religion, Culture and Society.* (New York: Wiley, 1964). A useful book of readings in the sociology of religion. The editor is sensitive to methodological problems arising from different kinds of religious experience. Some of these problems are exposed in Part II, "Problems in Definition."

O. Strunk, Jr., ed., *Readings in the Psychology of Religion.* (Nashville, Tenn.: Abingdon, 1959). Selections from both historical and contemporary psychological analyses of religion. See especially the selections in Chapter 2, "Religious Experience and Conversion," Chapter 3, "Religious Development," and Chapter 4, "Aspects of the Religious Life."

An excellent statement briefly explaining the scientific study of religion is "Religion," *International Encyclopedia of the Social Sciences,* edited by D. L. Sills (New York: Macmillan, 1968). Three prominent scholars, an anthropologist, sociologist, and psychologist, discuss past and present studies of religion in their respective fields. Each essayist places the study of religion in the context of Western intellectual history.

Psychological studies of religion include:

*G. W., Allport *The Individual and His Religion* (New York: Macmillan, 1950). This classic in the psychology of religion examines the nature, development, and influence of subjective religious life in the mature personality. See especially Chapter 2 for an example of methods used to collect data on religious beliefs, using a traditional approach to psychological inquiry.

*Ram Das, *The Only Dance There Is* (Garden City, N.Y.: Anchor Press/Doubleday, 1974). Talks to health science professionals at the Menninger Foundation, Topeka, Kansas and Spring Grove Hospital, Baltimore by a former Harvard professor-turned-yogin on the psychology of spiritual and religious life.

*W. James, *The Varieties of Religious Experience* (New York: Modern Library, 1902). A classic exposition of a scientific study of religion, available in an unexpensive edition.

*R. May, ed., *Existential Psychology* (New York: Random, 1960). A collection of essays by R. May, A. Maslow, H. Feifel, C. Rogers, and G. Allport reflecting the need to deepen concepts that define the human condition.

*J. White, ed., *Frontiers of Consciousness: The Meeting Ground Between Inner and Outer Reality* (New York: Julien Press, 1974). A book of readings on contemporary topics in transpersonal psychology, which focuses on the relevancy of consciousness as an object of study and as experience of transcendent awareness.

Studies of religion from sociological and anthropological perspectives include:

*P. Berger and T. Luckmann, *The Social Construction of Reality* (Garden City, N.Y.: Doubleday, 1966). This study in the sociology of knowledge is an introductory analysis of the objectivation, institutionalization and legitimation of "reality," which is seen as the product of social construction.

*C. Levi-Strauss. *Structural Anthropology,* trans. by C. Jacobson and B. G. Schoepf (Garden City, N.Y.: Anchor Books, 1967; first published in 1963). See especially Part III, "Magic and Religion," for an introduction to this contemporary anthropologist's "structural" approach to mythology. See also his *The Savage Mind,* translated by G. Weidenfeld (Chicago: University of Chicago Press, 1966).

*J. W. Sutherland, *A General Systems Philosophy for the Social and Behavioral Sciences* (New York: Braziller, 1973). A discussion of some of the implications of general systems theory for study in the social and behavioral sciences; it is meant for advanced students of social sciences.

*A. F. C. Wallace, *Religion: An Anthropological View* (New York: Random, 1966). A contemporary representative analysis of religion from a naturalist perspective, which typically focuses on the social-cultural functions of the religious forms in nonliterate and Western societies.

*M. Weber, *The Sociology of Religion.* (Boston: Beacon, 1963, first published 1922). One of the most famous social scientists of this century exposes his approach to religious phenomena in an analysis of the relationships between religious convictions and human conduct, especially in terms of economic patterns and social grouping. The book also contains a very helpful analysis by T. Parsons of Weber's contribution to the study of religious life.

*J. M. Yinger, *The Scientific Study of Religion* (New York: Macmillan, 1970). A substantial, but introductory, account of methods and problems in the study of religion by social scientists. Besides introducing the reader to the field of sociology of religion, Yinger discusses several prominent areas of current investigation in light of a field theory of religion.

4.

The Comparative Study of Religion

In the "objective" approach to the study of religion during the past century, a great effort was made to describe accurately a variety of religious expressions. This led to the collection, classification, and comparison of data from all cultures and from various historical periods. Scholars eagerly sought to discover similarities and differences among the data they examined. As researchers using scientific methods, they looked for principles of development or patterns of expression whereby the concrete data they had observed could be understood. It is not surprising that the first of these studies concentrated on comparative mythology, with its emphasis on language study, names of gods, and mythical interpretations of the origin and preservation of the world by divine beings. This kind of study, which looked for "parallels" by examining especially words and ideas, is typified by F. Max Mueller in his *Comparative Mythology* (1856).

During the last half of the nineteenth century, various academic chairs of comparative religion were established in European and American universities. The scholars filling these positions often focused on a comparison of doctrines found in the major world religions. They regarded their study however as an activity in the area of humanities rather than theology. They warned against confusing the *normative* interpretation of religion given in Christian theology with the *descriptive* discipline of "comparative religions" or "history of religions." Nevertheless, their interpretations were sometimes weighted in favor of attitudes and concepts found in the Jewish and Christian traditions, or in favor of the rationalistic, deistic position that there was a "natural" religiousness in all men.

Problems in Using a Comparative Method

The basic methodological problem was whether or not there could be an objective study of religion, which, on the one hand, interpreted a religious phenomenon in relation to its historical and cultural context and, on the other hand, retained some element of unique "religiousness" that could not be reduced to some other factor of existence for example, social or psychological forces. One answer grew out of the philosophical notion of a religious essence that is manifested through various forces in different historical periods of human life. Despite a concern to avoid philosophical presuppositions, the scholars of comparative religion used the insights of such systematic thinkers as G. W. F. Hegel and F. D. Schleiermacher, who helped establish a discipline of the philosophy of religion.

In the philosophy of religion, religion was seen as a "universal" with definable characteristics; a central problem was the relationship between the universal essence, and the particular manifestations or realizations of religion in existence. The universal idea assumed a "true character" of religion, which was in all men—it was a reality apart from, but was also manifested in, particular historical phenomena. The term "religion" was regarded not as a general concept only but as a reality whose relationship to the particular *expressions* of religion was to be studied and evaluated. This notion is still prominent in studies of the philosophy of religion. It is also found in general historical studies, which assume a developmental or evolutionary process, and in studies of the forms (morphology) of religion. In this context, to understand religious life means to be able to relate a particular historical expression of religion to some universal principles of religious meaning.

Certainly not all students of comparative religion regard religiousness in terms of a metaphysical essence, but they would insist that religious studies require a sensitivity to that dimension of life named "religion," which requires a discipline of study distinct from that of sociology, psychology, philosophy, theology, or linguistics. The term "comparative religion" is sometimes used to designate such a study, though this term means different things to different people. Used in a general sense, it designates the tasks of discovering data and comparing them. It seeks an unbiased comparison of data that have some common elements; for example, sacrificial forms, theistic notions, or feelings of awe or peace. It is based on the assumption that there are definable elements within human life that can be classified in terms of fundamental emphases, e.g., notions of divine beings, initiation ceremonies, or exercises in spiritual contemplation. Each classification is characterized by basic features that determine the meaning of phenomena collected within it.

The comparative method relies at its basis on empirical data. While the forms of data will vary, conclusions are supported or refuted by the strength of the data. Thus, scholars might appeal to data from classical religious texts and to commentaries explaining their meaning. They also record and analyze myths, rituals, and systematized practices in spiritual discipline and preserve and interpret existential statements of belief and the descriptions of inner religious experiences. This body of scholarship, like material found in other academic areas, also shows acquaintance with earlier scholarship.

Such a wide variety of sources presents a number of problems with regard to the meaning of symbols for those using a comparative approach. To meet some of these problems, a working knowledge of foreign languages and a willingness to struggle with the difficulties of translation are prerequisites for an accurate rendering of data as they appear within a foreign tradition. A scholar will need a working knowledge of Hebrew, Aramaic, Greek, or Latin to study the Jewish and Christian traditions, Sanskrit to deal directly with Hindu or Indian Buddhist materials, or classical Chinese to read Taoist and Confucian texts. Students of contemporary religion should know the native tongue of the people whom they are studying, as well as the classical textual language of the tradition to which the material belongs.

Besides studying parallel expressions of different religious traditions, some scholars using the comparative method examine how a religious form or tradition has changed over several centuries. They find "survivals" from an earlier stage in the development of a religious expression, which then continues to be reinterpreted and reformed in another stage. They try to locate basic patterns or fundamental structures exposed in the similarity of forms. The principal element of survival, or the structure seen in a comparison of phenomena, is regarded as the central feature whereby the religious expression is understood. This use of the term "comparative religion" is found in widely different kinds of contemporary studies, such as M. Eliade's *Patterns in Comparative Religion,* E. O. James's *Comparative Religion,* and J. Wach's *The Comparative Study of Religion.*

The term "comparative religion" has also been used more narrowly to refer to specific kinds of studies made from about 1875 to 1915. One specialized study, concentrating on philosophical and theological concerns, involved the comparison of religious doctrines, especially the beliefs of contemporary "great religions." A second specialized use of the term occurred in comparative mythology and the comparative study of nonliterate peoples. It designated the effort to collect whatever material was available and derive typologies or evolutionary sequences by comparing form and structures of religion. Thirdly, the term was used to indicate a special area of study within the general "science of religion." It represented the theoretical or systematic method of placing empirical and historical data side by side in order to show how a specific religious form compares with the general understanding of religious experience. Some scholars even hoped to use this method to judge the comparative value of religions, using only objective data and principles of comparison.[11] Using the term "comparative religion" in its broadest sense, we will note two dominant methods for interpreting religions: (1) historical studies and (2) the analysis of forms and patterns (phenomenology).

The History of Religions

The historical interpretation was justified by an appeal to documentation and by the claim that historical events are to be interpreted as a result of other historical events or as a result of human forces. This method of interpreting human life constituted a reaction against a doctrinal interpretation based on revelation, as well as against a philosophical interpretation based on assumptions about the nature of man or the essence of reality.

Students of history saw a great danger in a comparative study of religion that relied primarily on a comparison of similar forms. The historians maintained that the meaning of the forms or patterns of life is related most directly to a historical and cultural framework. Human events should not be abstracted from this framework and then compared with other forms taken from an entirely different historical framework. For example, the historians maintained that a close study of the Vedic sacrifice in India, as expressed in the *Brahmanas,* reveals a content and meaning quite different from the "sacrifice of God's son" as described by Paul in the Christian New Testament. While sacrifice can be regarded as a common form or pattern of religious expression, the *meaning* of Vedic sacrifice, claims the historians, is more closely related to its cultural context than to a comparable form of human expression from another cultural context.

In historical studies, the assumption is that the particularities of human life are more important than the overarching universal patterns of human life. Although the writing of history requires the assumption that men of the past and of different cultures are sufficiently similar to us so that we can interpret and understand them, the historian emphasizes that it makes a real difference as to whether a person is born in first-century Rome, in ninth-century China, or in twentieth-century America. The historian is concerned with the meaning of these differences; to know these distinctions is to get an understanding of oneself that can be had in no other way. Birth in a particular time and place conditions the forms and meaning available to a person. Time limits a person's possibilities, but any particular moment in time also has great potential meaning. Thus, the historian values the uniqueness and the significance of historical data.

The history of religions has had two major concerns: (1) to describe as objectively as possible the conditions and elements of a historical situation and (2) to recognize that the changes in religious life result from interactions with many cultural conditions surrounding a religious event. An emphasis on concrete historical data tends to crumble the abstractions and generalizations used in common speech. For instance, such terms as "Islam," "Hinduism," or "Buddhism" are convenient but very rough abstractions for a group of beliefs and practices that are quite divergent in different cultural and historical settings. Historians, therefore, are not content to understand the meaning of religious life by describing only the dominant or orthodox doctrinal position of a religion; they tend to emphasize the changes brought about by particular people or events, the differences between subgroups or movements within a tradition, and the particularities of the organizations, practices, and symbols used by different people. When they study the religions of the world, historians most often focus on cultural areas as the greatest determinants of human meaning. Their widest categories of interpretation, then, are not so much doctrinal systems or patterns of life as the religious life of South Asia, East Asia, the Near East, sub-Saharan Africa, or Western Europe.

The problem of the nature of causal relations between one historical event and another is solved by historians in a variety of ways, extending from a simple positivistic natural determinism to the affirmation that the individual possesses some unique quality or faculty called "self-will," which gives a person freedom of choice within a conditioned existence. The problem of historical causality is illustrated by the position of one student of religion who emphasized the historical condition of man, Ernst Troeltsch.

Troeltsch clearly distinguished between the notions of causality found in natural science and historical science. Causality in natural science, he said, takes the form of an all-pervading law of reciprocity. If the basic material of the world is "energy," "cause" may be seen as the transformation of energy from one form to another, which follows an observable pattern of change. While natural phenomena can be explained in terms of changes in the composition of energy, historical causation is regarded as something entirely different—a matter predominantly of psychological motivation.

Because historical reality has to do with human consciousness, historians see changes in cultural expression in relation to the conscious efforts of human beings—as well as unconscious elements. What is unique about the causal force in human consciousness is that the initiative for change is found *not only* in a person's past but also very forcefully in an expected result, or goal, or purpose. This complexity of motives gives a peculiar character to human events. The psychical condition of the individual or group introduces an incalculable element. Thus, human life includes the possibility of something new, something more than just a transformation of physical forces.

It is, in fact, this incalculable individuality, this ability to form a new reality, which is at the center of historical studies. Historical study does not attempt to learn the universal laws by which all particular phenomena are understood, but rather tries to understand the uniqueness of the historical phenomena it investigates. It attempts to reconstruct as closely as possible the phenomena under investigation as it occurred within its own specific and unique historical setting. Historical reality then, is quite different from natural or physical reality. Historians will focus not on a universal law but on that aspect of existence which is uniquely individual within the flux of phenomena available. They do not attempt a reconstruction of general physical laws, but seek to provide a sympathetic reconstruction of the historical causal connections in the context of which historical events have taken shape. The notion of progressive change in human society need not necessarily indicate an inevitable progress in values, such that there is an automatic change for the better. Religious history does not move necessarily from a "faulty" to a "perfect" religiousness. The special task of the historian of religion is to explain the historical conditions in which a religious person or community lives.

The Phenomenology of Religion

The concern to let the data "speak for themselves" led the students of morphology to use comparison as a basic interpretive tool. In the last quarter of the nineteenth century, they began by comparing such religious expressions as "sacrifice," "ritual," and "gods," especially as found in the religions of the ancient Near East and among nonliterate cultures. They sought to discover the predominant characteristics of religion within either historically or culturally determined environments. Wanting to be genuinely objective, they sought the meaning of religious acts in the available data and attempted to fill gaps in information about one religion through a careful comparison of structurally similar religious acts, like initiation rituals, found in other religions. This comparative study led to the classification of religious experiences by types, and of religious phenomena by internal structures. This method of comparison disclosed exciting possibilities for interpreting a wide range of religious phenomena and was related to the philosophical approach to understanding human experience known as "phenomenology."

As it relates to the study of religion, descriptive phenomenology can be defined as the art of interpreting the intent of religion. This intent is exposed in the particular patterns of religiousness found in different forms of religious life, for example, sacrifice, prayer, or sacraments. Since "pure religiousness" is not to be found anywhere in human experience, the phenomenologist attempts to precipitate the intent by exposing dominant patterns from a comparative study of concrete, historical religious expressions. This approach assumes that the outward forms of human expression have an inner organizing pattern or "structure," with power to order the meaning for the person participating in this expression. Such an organizing pattern can be discovered by comparing the outward expressions, by imaginatively entering into the activities performed, and by considering the explanations given by the participants, wherever this is possible. To understand the religious reality perceived and expressed by the participant is the ideal of the phenomenologist.

What has been said above should not imply that there is only one meaning for a religious phenomenon; indeed, religious meaning for the participant is many-faceted. Also, by correlating what different participants perceive, the phenomenologist gains an understanding beyond that of many individual participants. The fire of the Vedic sacrifice, for example, can mean "the messenger of the gods," the god, or the light, consuming power and the warmth of the flame. While a particular devotee may not know all the meanings of a particular religious symbol, the phenomenologist is concerned with exposing the richness and intensity or vitality of religious symbolism expressed by many adherents. Thus, students of the phenomenology of religion regard this study as a corrective to methods that do not concentrate on the peculiarly religious character of the phenomena for the society under study. While religious life participates fully in the conditions of human existence, says the phenomenologist, the religious meaning for the participant is never exhausted by investigating the historical context or social processes of formation. An ultimacy, a mystery, an open-endedness, a sacredness are integral parts of the religious meaning.

In the phenomenological study of religion, there are two foci of concern. One is the specifically religious power, or intent, of religious phenomena; the second is the attempt to locate structures, or patterns, of religious life in symbols, rites, and doctrines that men have used at different times. One of the classic books highlighting the unique quality of religious phenomena is Rudolf Otto's *The Idea of the Holy,* first published in 1917. While Otto was not concerned to compare systematically different structures of religious phenomena, as did W. B. Kristensen and G. van der Leeuw (see below), he asserted in this book the unique dimension of religiousness.

Otto began with a philosophical presupposition that "the holy" is an *a priori* category of value and maintained that religious feeling or awareness is a special and unique province in human consciousness. For him, the essential character of all religious awareness was feeling awe toward, yet fascination with, this "wholly other" reality (God). God was not simply a human idea of a feeling. God was a mysterious reality confronting the individual person with an incomparable, overwhelming power, a power that struck awe, even horror, into people's hearts, but also had paradoxically, a captivating charm for people. Generally phenomenologists of religion have tried to avoid a clearly defined philosophical orientation; they have asserted that any method of interpreting religion must include the recognition that *religious experience cannot be reduced to other elements of human life*. The lack of such awareness limits the study of religion to nonreligious factors. It is like reducing the aesthetic value of a great painting to the value of the canvas and pigments and the number of brush strokes made by the painter. On the contrary, investigators should make a detailed study of the peculiarities that make religious life significant for the religious adherent if they seek to expose religious meaning. They should try to learn the religious assumptions that give order and meaning to the adherent. This, for example, is the method of W. Brede Kristensen in *The Meaning of Religion*. Here he seeks to expose the meaning of "man," "the world," and "divine reality" as found in the ancient Near East by analyzing the patterning force of such notions as "sacrifice" and "kingship."

Another phenomenologist, Gerardus van der Leeuw, explained in *Religion in Essence and Manifestation* why the nature of religious phenomena requires an approach different from that of either the physical or the social sciences. Religious life, he said, is neither simply a subjective feeling nor an objective expression that can be isolated and studied as an independent entity. Every religious phenomenon (symbols, rites, feelings, awareness) encompasses both the apprehended object and the apprehending subject. A phenomenon is "what appears." While many people talk about "what appears" as brute fact, van der Leeuw (like many phenomenologists) held that all "facts" include a person's interpretations of sensory input. Whatever is recognized as "given" in human experience is at the same time "reconstructed" by visual perspective, by the conceptual framework that "receives" the information, by emotional patterns, and by evaluative ordering processes. "What appears," then, is a result of a significant organization of the awareness of reality according to a structure of apprehension. Such a structure is never simply a subjective interpretation of chaotic sense impressions nor merely a discovery of purely objective structures "in the world"; rather the meaning is a combination of the individual's interpretation and the objective patterns or forms apprehended.

It is important to locate "what appears" in the interaction between subject and object so as to avoid making religion either so exclusively subjective that it is inaccessible to any one other than the devotee or so exclusively objective that it has no relation to subjective apprehension. In practice, the religious meaning of any given datum or all religious data is so profound that it is inexhaustible. For van der Leeuw, a member of a Protestant theological faculty in Holland, the significance of the inexhaustible meaning of religion was that God, in the last analysis, revealed Himself and that human beings—including phenomenologists—could not understand Divine utterance in its fullness. Human beings stood always at the frontier of mystery; only when God came to people (in a "vertical" direction that cut into their "horizontal" human striving) could they break out of their limited perceptions. Not all descriptive phenomenologists follow van der Leeuw's theological understanding of the relation between the unfathomable Reality and the conditioned expression known in a particular moment of life; nevertheless, they do recognize that the issue of whether to use historical or symbolic forms to express the unfathomable source of all meaning is an important problem in interpreting religious significance.

As mentioned before, a central feature in the descriptive phenomenology of religion is the apprehension of the religious meaning of an action or belief through the study of its structure. According to van der Leeuw's summary, some of the basic steps of this apprehension[12] include the assignment of names to data (such as prayer, conversion, or festivals), the systematic interpolation of religious forms into the observer's life, the careful observation, but suspended evaluation, of what appears, the attempt to comprehend through structural comparison and contrast, and finally a statement of what is understood from the chaotic and ambiguous "reality" of immediate experience. The structure of a religious phenomenon is known when an investigator spontaneously perceives himself participating in it; the goal in observing a phenomenon is to know its meaning. The notion of "structure" here overlaps, but also differs from, that found in the structuralists' movement. Both the phenomenologists of religion and the social scientists such as C. Levi-Strauss seek patterns or underlying regularities in human behavior. The phenomenological approach, however, focuses on an investigator's empathic or intuitive experience of the ultimate meaning expressed by a religious devotee. Such an intuitive grasp, however, is not recorded as sufficient for the structural analyst in the social sciences who seeks to discover laws that govern the formulation of meaning and that ideally could be couched in formal mathematical terms.

On the basis of a phenomenological study, van der Leeuw held that there were three fundamental structures of religious life: dynamism, animism, and deism. "Dynamism" referred to an ultimate impersonal power, like the Sioux Indians' *wakan* or the Melanesian notion of *mana*. "Animism" was power of life experienced as an encounter between spirits, souls, or other beings who have will power. "Deism" was a general term for the worship of a supreme being. These were the three basic patterns, he suggested, for apprehending the source of all religious life.

From the standpoint of Hindu, Buddhist, or Confucian understanding of human experience, this conclusion is quite narrow and reflects a Western—perhaps more spefically a Protestant Christian—bias. Very few Western scholars at present organize their general understanding of religion under these three headings; nevertheless, the phenomenological method, with its focus on clarifying religious meaning by locating the basic structures of meaning, has been influential in academic circles, paralleling and sometimes overlapping with the "structuralism" of the social science.

While van der Leeuw sought to identify overarching patterns in religious phenomena, he rejected any attempt to analyze the historical development of religious expression. He did not try to describe patterns of religious meaning through comparisons of specific myths and symbols, as did another scholar, Mircea Eliade, in *Patterns in Comparative Religion*. In this book, Eliade interprets religious data according to various kinds (modalities) of symbolic awareness, in light of his definition of religion as "the appearance of the sacred." Humanity has perceived the sacred dimension of life through different modalities, he says. Some of these modalities are symbolized by the sky, water, the waxing and waning of the moon, seasons and cycles of vegetation, and the earth. In each modality, which is defined by a different symbolic structure, is an expression of the nature of life. For example, the transcendence of God is revealed in the infinity, inaccessibility, and creative power (rain) of the sky. There are, however, many forms of religion, each of which is an appearance—often an eruption—of the sacred in common, profane existence. Awareness of the sacred is the exact opposite of profane awareness in life; what is sacred is what is real. People apprehend the sacred through symbols and myths, and, according to Eliade, the task of the interpreter of religion is to expose the religious value found within the different modalities in which sacredness appears. The patterns of religious forms expose the organization of human experiences; when these experiences have *religious* value, they are imitations of the creative acts and models found in the sacred or divine realm.

For Eliade, symbols, myths, and rites—especially those found in nonliterate societies—represent a reevaluation of human self-awareness in terms of a transcendent, ultimate reality—a kind of evaluation that is radically different from that expressed in terms of historic, everyday situations. These mythical patterns of awareness (which Eliade also calls "modalities of the sacred") can be localized and studied. They have a power that is not derived from a particular historical or social set of circumstances; rather, they represent a unique dimension of human awareness that takes different forms according to different historical periods and cultural uses. The structures last and extend beyond a particular cultural form and reveal the religious meaning of the particular expressions as they are compared. By comparing the historical expressions of a religious phenomenon, says Eliade, the interpreter of religions can write a history of a symbol and present the religious meaning of religious symbols.

Religious Meaning and Cultural Expression

Eliade's effort to understand religious meaning according to different modalities of sacredness in particular cultural-historical situations shows a deep sensitivity to the fact that religious experience is always formed within a particular cultural context. This fact has become a central concern for several scholars who recognize the inexplicable quality of religion while emphasizing that religious meaning is heavily dependent on cultural forces and human capacities. One difficulty many interpreters of religion have is that people (whether scholars or devotees) use the same modes of apprehension (for example, language, emotion, social relations, visual experience, attitudes) in both religious and nonreligious experience. How can a scholar distinguish between religious and nonreligious elements if every religious form is conditioned by cultural conventions? How can a person apprehend the religion experienced by someone from a different cultural background or religious tradition?

While all the scholars we have mentioned in this chapter were sensitive to these questions, the studies of three others have dealt specifically with cultural forces in the formation of religious expression without reducing the religious content to social, historical, or semantic elements. The first is J. Wach, who, while recognizing the special religious quality of the data he studied, was particularly conscious of social-cultural modes of expression. The second, W. C. Smith, emphasized the uniquely personal quality of religious faith as it is manifested in historical traditions. The third, N. Smart, is particularly interested in the relation between religious experience and conceptual symbols, including philosophical formulations. These scholars, of course, recognized other cultural forces, too, and were aware of other dimensions of religious expression. They have been, however, notable spokesmen for the emphases mentioned within the general problem of the relationship between religion and culture.

In his posthumous book, *The Comparative Study of Religion,* Wach attempted to combine the comparative study of religious phenomena with a concern to relate the dynamics of religious awareness to social life, cultic acts, and conceptual formulations. While he asserted that religious expression always reveals ultimate reality to the adherent (and thus religious life cannot be reduced to other cultural forms), he was very conscious that in religious life people use modes of expression that are also used in the secular world, for example, concepts and social patterns. Wach, who was also a noted sociologist of religion, sought to expose the meaning of *religious* experience found in different human modes of apprehension: thought, ritual action, and fellowship.

For Wach, the core of religious life was a special kind of experience, which, however, could not be isolated from general human experience. He gave four criteria for a genuine religious experience: (1) it must be a response to what is experienced as ultimate reality; (2) it must represent a total response of the whole being; (3) its intensity must be such that it is the most powerful, comprehensive, shattering, and profound experience of which man is capable; and (4) "it involves an imperative; it is the most powerful source of motivation and action."[13] A genuine religious experience must be expressed socially, ritually, and conceptually if it is to be identified and preserved in history as a religion. Every religious tradition, therefore, has developed social, cultic, and conceptual forces to express this experience. While the study of concepts dominated in the German academic circles in which Wach worked until World War II, he felt that the researcher in religion should be sensitive to social and cultic forms of expression as well. The religious community in its particular expressions was of special interest to him, because it "cultivates, shapes, and develops in thought and action the expression of its religious experience."[14] However, those who want to comprehend a religious life that is not their own must be sensitive to all three forms of expression. To understand another person, Wach claimed, means to comprehend the dominant traits in another person's self-expression by grasping intuitively another person's orientation and identifying and piecing together clues to his or her intellectual meaning. As with the phenomenologists, such understanding requires that the investigator be sensitive to the significance of others' concepts and presuppositions.

W. C. Smith, in his *The Meaning and End of Religion,* criticizes some scholarly attempts to describe a person's religious experience in terms of an impersonal entity called religion. He maintains that because religious phenomena are human expressions one must be sensitive to the particular character of the individual's involvement as he expresses himself in prayer, ritual, or social responsibility. The investigator, maintains Smith, must distinguish between a religious man's personal faith and the cumulative tradition that is the object of study of the historian and morphologist.

Is there a method that can expose "the unfathomability of that personal faith"? A first step, replies Smith, is to understand the role that personal faith has played in the religious history of man. This entails not only observing cultural phenomena, but also recognizing that the interaction between a human being and the transcendent takes place through cultural forms.[15] The transcendent, of course, cannot be directly observed; its apprehension in the believer's heart can be inferred, however, by an imaginative sympathy disciplined by intellectual rigor and cross-checked by vigorous criticism. The faith of men can be studied, then, by being sensitive to the living quality of religious people who have exposed this faith in cultural forms. Smith advocates a personalist approach as a corrective to the objective studies that have emphasized an empirical methodology.

Ninian Smart, a British philosopher of religion, recognizes that what Western scholars term "philosophy of religion" is really a series of reflections on Christian theology in the light of Western philosophical problems. Unhappy with this parochial perspective, he has studied the religious thought of India and has wrestled with the problem of adequate religious terminology for comparing the claims of the major religious traditions. In his recent books, *The Science of Religion and the Sociology of Knowledge* and *The Phenomenon of Religion,* Smart criticizes a common assumption of such scholars as R. Otto and J. Wach that some kind of universal "core experience" is common to every religious phenomenon. Such an assumption, he suggests, is belied by the deep differences between various religious activities and between truth claims described in empirical studies. The major religious traditions have different "foci"[16] for a descriptive phenomenological analysis.

The "focus" of a religion is both the object of cultic activity and the public norm for group behavior. In a theistic tradition, the focus is the god worshipped; in Theravada Buddhism, however, it is nirvana. Faith in the focus of any religious group is expressed in practices, as well as reverence before images, and heroes, but the most sophisticated expression, according to Smart, is in systematic thinking. Thus, in Christianity, the focus is most clearly articulated in theology. The focus transcends the practice, doctrines, and experiences of the faithful, but any apprehension of it includes an account (and in any tradition there are several accounts) of the way the focus manifests itself.

Different kinds of understanding of the same religious data are quite possible,

Smart claims. For example, a scholar's interpretation of the focus will differ from that of a devotee. Likewise, a sophisticated group of monks or scholars within a tradition will not interpret the focus in the same way as outside social scientists and historians. Similarities in the data (such as similar forms of ritual) do not mean there are no important differences among subgroups within a tradition. In practice, cross-cultural comparisons of the religious foci need not be based on a belief in a single transcendent reality (such as God) or a single cultural process (such as rational interpretation). Likewise, while the "principles of numinous power"[17]—the essential qualities of divine influence—in theistic worship and sacraments provide a special content for believers, they cannot be understood independently from the linguistic, psychological, economic, and political structures of society in which myth-making occurs. The myth-making forces depend on specific cultural conditions, and thus myths function in different ways for different social groups.

The various approaches to the comparative study of religions mentioned in this chapter reflect different answers to questions each scholar asked: "How are we to understand the religious expression of another person in a different culture and a different time?" "How are we to perceive whatever is religious in others and in ourselves?" Such questions assume that we can talk meaningfully about "religion" or "religious life," but in human experience religion is related to other forms of human awareness. The last three chapters have surveyed various attempts to locate and interpret the meaning of what is religious in human existence. Some of the approaches can be integrated, and others are diametrically opposed, depending on assumptions about the nature of religious life and the appropriate means for investigating it.

There are, nevertheless, several common concerns in the objective study of religion. (1) There is stress on historical religious expressions and empirical documentation for any interpretation. A student of religion must have specific knowledge of the cultural background, historical situation, and concepts and acts of the people he or she is studying. (2) The principle of comparison emphasizes the fact that no *single* religious expression provides the only valid norm for understanding all other religious forms. The social scientist, historian, or phenomenologist of religion cannot be bound to only one cultural tradition and its expression of religiousness if he or she intends to say anything about religious behavior, institutions, and the symbols found in history. (3) Finally, there is the concern with the *meaning* of religious life. The purpose of the study of religion is not simply to collect, preserve, and exhibit unrelated facts about religion. It is, rather, to explore the forms and processes of religious life in order to understand the conditions for particular expressions and the significance of the forms for human life.

Every interpretation, however, involves the investigator's sensitivities, concerns, and presuppositions. If the investigator is not self-conscious about his or her pattern of thinking as a religious or nonreligious person, he or she will predominantly seek and find those elements in an unfamiliar religious expression which are familiar. The resultant understanding will simply represent an incorporation of all religious data that fit into the investigator's bias. Students of religious life need not accept as valid the ultimate norm of the devotee. They should, however, be aware of their primary presuppositions, be able to expose the assumptions and structures of another's religiousness, and even see relationships the adherent may overlook, for the scholar relates one religious experience to other kinds of human awareness and to religious patterns in various historical situations.

SELECTED READINGS

The historical approach to understanding man's spiritual life is discussed by *W. Dilthey, *Pattern and Meaning in History* (New York: Harper, 1961) and E. Troeltsch, "Historiography," *Encyclopaedia of Religion and Ethics,* edited by J. Hastings (New York: Scribner's, 1951); 6:716–23; and is exemplified by C. P. Tiele, *Outlines of the History of Religions* (Kegan Paul, Trench, Truebner & Co., 1896) and G. F. Moore, *History of Religions,* 2 vols (New York: Scribner's, 1949, first published 1913, 1920).

The phenomenological approach is found in *G. van der Leeuw, *Religion in Essence and Manifestation.* See also W. B. Kristensen, *The Meaning of Religion* (The Hague: Nijhoff, 1960); *M. Eliade, *Patterns in Comparative Religion,* edited by R. Sheed, (New York: Sheed & Ward, 1958, first published 1949); and the popular textbook, W. L. King, *Introduction to Religion: A Phenomenological Approach* rev. ed. (New York: Harper, 1968).

M. Eliade and J. Kitagawa, eds. *History of Religions: Essays in Methodology* (Chicago: University of Chicago Press, 1959). This series of eight essays by world-renowned American and European scholars includes discussions of both descriptive and evaluational problems.

N. Smart, *The Phenomenon of Religion.* This short but substantial book presents a critical assessment of some recent attempts to study religious expressions cross-culturally and analyzes the nature of ritual with special attention to the Christian Eucharist.

W. C. Smith, *The Meaning and End of Religion* (New York: Macmillan, 1962). See Selected Readings in Chapter 1 above for the basis of Smith's provocative reassessment of common assumptions in Western studies about the religious traditions of mankind.

J. de Vries, *The Study of Religion: A Historical Approach,* translated by K. W. Bolle (New York: Harcourt, 1967). The best and most readily available summary of the variety of methods used by Western scholars in studying religion. Emphasis is on the nineteenth and twentieth centuries, during which religion was viewed predominantly in terms of myth.

J. Wach, *The Comparative Study of Religions.* See especially Chapter 1, "Development, Meaning and Method in the Comparative Study of Religions." An introductory summary of the discipline of comparative religion and the mature conclusions of a notable scholar about the elements inherent in interpretations of religious phenomena. Wach deals specifically with the methodological problems of comparative religion in *Types of Religious Experience: Christian and Non-Christian* (Chicago: University of Chicago Press, 1951), Chapters 2 and 3.

J. Woordenburg, ed., *Classical Approaches to the Study of Religion* (The Hague: Mouton, 1973), vol. I, introduction and anthology. An 80-page historical survey of the last hundred years of the European scholarly study of religion, followed by 600 pages of brief excerpts from deceased major European contributors to research in religion. Volume II contains a bibliography and evaluations of the scholars mentioned in Volume I.

See also the readings listed at the end of Chapter 1, which represent contemporary views on the issues discussed in this chapter.

Part II

FOUR TRADITIONAL WAYS OF BEING RELIGIOUS

When adherents of different religions discuss a religious question, why do they so often speak past each other and then end in violent emotional disagreement? What is happening when an unconscious personal bias influences the observations of an "objective" observer? Why do a researcher's findings so often interest only like-minded people? One reason for these problems is that everyone tends unconsciously to understand and evaluate religious acts and claims according to pre-conceived notions. Thus, researchers must become aware of their emotional responses and conceptual patterns if they wish to investigate different kinds of religious life.

For many people, "religion" is a set concept, rigidly and narrowly defined. They have lost touch with the ultimate dimension in their experience and have allowed an unconscious program to direct their lives. In so doing, they have lost the ability significantly to transform their lives.

When many Westerners think of religion, they think of an institution, a faith, a set of doctrines. They often look down on the religious life of people in nonliterate cultures. Sometimes they criticize the overlapping of religious and secular aspects of life in some of these cultures or their lack of documents and commentaries. Ignorance may also encourage Western feelings of superiority toward other traditions or even rejection of them as insignificant and meaningless. Moreover, members of a traditional religious community—for example, Christians, Buddhists, or Jews—may assume that people who are not members of such a community have no inner spiritual life. This assumption raises the question of the meaning of religion.

As noted in Chapter 1, religion is the "means of ultimate transformation" in two senses. First, it embodies the power for transforming human awareness; it is not merely wishful thinking, nor is it just desire. Religious truth and action are intrinsically connected with the very source of existence, however that may be defined. Second, religion represents a practical technique for achieving the transformation of life, or ultimate transformation.

What is ultimate transformation? Is it a shift in a person's most comprehensive attitude, value system, or frame of reference? Is it a psychological shift from a sense of meaninglessness to a feeling of wholeness and integration? Is it a shift in social action, interpersonal relationships, or perhaps institutional and community relationships? It may be any or all of these changes—and more. The term "ultimate" in the definition of religion as a means of ultimate transformation expresses the phenomenologist's concern for distinctive *religious* significance. The expression of ultimate reality assumed in religious transformation requires a special use of language which may seem odd by conventional standards. For example, the images conveyed by such terms as "God," "*Tao*," "Brahman" or "nirvana" can obscure the reality of religious experience if the terms are used to indicate either conventional objects of thought or imaginative fantasies. In the religious context, they indicate the limit of human thought and at the same time the limitless possibilities of life. Such terms indicate that the transformation occurs at the profoundest level of the personality and involves the nature of reality. Religious transformation is the transformation of existence; it is identification with reality.

Various kinds of transformation are possible within each of the world's great religious traditions, and any given kind can be found in several traditions. Transformation may also occur outside of the major traditions. Part II discusses four different means of ultimate transformation, highlighting the dynamism of traditional forms, while Part III describes mental and political-social processes that function as a means of ultimate transformation. The discussion in Part II and Part III is based on a concept of religious data as symbolic expressions of changes going on in people's lives.

Part II's approach will be both phenomenological and structural. Phenomenologists focus on the subjective description of an individual's religious experience; they are also concerned with the meaning of religious structures symbolically expressed through thoughts, actions, institutions, and interpersonal relationships. They regard such expressions as acceptable data from which justifiable conclusions can be drawn, although new data will require new interpretations. The structuralist approach focuses on different structures as one way of identifying various dynamic religious processes of ultimate transformation. The term structure is used here to refer to a pattern of basic constituents or elements of a religious form and to the inner logic, the self-regulating organization, of a process of ultimate transformation.

The four chapters of Part II describe and make some generalizations about the basic elements of four traditional kinds of religious processes (structures) and the particular configuration that these elements present. Some examples of elements are awe, suffering, divine images, ritual prayer or meditation practice. The relationship between the elements is as important as the definition of them. Many religious expressions, for example, contain feelings of awe, institutional elements, ethical concerns, and visual symbols of the ultimate reality; the problem is to perceive the role of each in relation to other aspects of religious expression. Thus, bowing before an image in a specifically designated place occurs in the structure that exposes the Sacred through myth and sacrament and in the structure where mystical insight is attained through spiritual discipline, but bowing does not have the same *religious* significance in both types because it is part of a different structure of religious meaning.

The process described is, of course, an abstraction, a construct; its purpose is to help interpret a wide variety of data instead of describing a specific thought or action. There are as many specific religious processes as there are individuals—or moments in a person's life—but this fact is not very helpful for understanding the major similarities and differences of religious meaning found in human existence.

The four traditional processes, which do not necessarily exhaust the possibilities, are: (1) personal apprehension of a holy presence, (2) establishing the existence of sacred reality through myth and sacrament, (3) living in harmony with the eternal law proclaimed by seers and preserved by learned tradition, and (4) attaining mystical insight through traditional instruction in spiritual discipline.

While these religious processes are found in the major world religions, no one "way of being religious" characterizes any particular religious tradition. Within any given tradition, different processes dominate different parts of the tradition, and intermingling occurs with many structural variations. References to particular traditions are merely illustrative; no attempt is made to explore the full range of any historical tradition. No historical progression is implied in the order of the four chapters, nor is there any suggestion of development from cruder to more sophisticated religious forms. The general historical development of religion and the evaluation of different religious processes do not concern us here. In fact, an effort is made to describe each way from the standpoint of its adherents and to expose the inner religious dynamic of their process of ultimate transformation.

Each process of ultimate transformation is a structure that organizes some different and some similar elements in different ways. The differences of religious commitment, thought, and action within the various processes are not just differences in languages, cultural habits, temperaments, private inclinations, or social preferences. Nor are the differences basically due to a choice between a personal, inner insight and an outward cultural expression. Indeed, chapters 5 and 8 will describe two different processes emphasizing individualistic or subjective elements, while chapters 6 and 7 will discuss two more social or community-oriented processes. Each of the processes expresses both personal, inner elements and externally expressed social ones. Structural differences have much more to do with variations in the basic elements and in the particular functions of those elements.

Structural analysis of the different processes of transformation reveals important differences among them. Sacramental acts, spiritual discipline, and the personal religious experience of God as wholly other are dissimilar. Although each process seeks to resolve the most profound human problems, adherents of the various processes will define both problems and goals in different ways. Goals are based on value judgments that presuppose certain notions of ultimate reality, the nature of existence, and humanity; they require a certain technique or process to achieve fulfillment. At the same time, the religious expression of the nature of ultimacy is related intrinsically to the means (faith, ritual, or intuitive insight) of realizing this ultimacy. For example, orthodox Christians regard humanity and God as two radically different kinds of reality; they would not use yoga or zen techniques of self-realization to achieve union with ultimate truth. Thus, the different general processes (as identified by structures of religious meaning) are different *ways* of religiousness.

5.

Personal Apprehension of a Holy Presence

St. Teresa, a Spanish Roman Catholic nun of the sixteenth century, described thus the rapture that she experienced in prayer:

> When I tried to resist these raptures, it seemed that I was being lifted up by a force beneath my feet so powerful that I know nothing to which I can compare it, for it came with a much greater vehemence than any other spiritual experience and I felt as if I were being ground to powder. It is a terrible struggle, and to continue it against the Lord's will avails very little, for no power can do anything against His.[18]

Three centuries later, Joseph Smith, the founder of the Mormon church, after trying to find the truth among the contesting Christian denominations in America, got his answer in a vision:

> I had actually seen a light, and in the midst of that light I saw two Personages, and they did in reality speak to me, and though I was hated and persecuted for saying that I had seen a vision, yet it was true; and while they were persecuting me, reviling me, and speaking all manner of evil against me falsely for so saying, I was let to say in my heart: Why persecute me for telling the truth? I had actually seen a vision, and who am I that I can understand God, or why does the world think to make me deny what I have actually seen?[19]

In both cases, the people who experienced divine power felt compelled to express their religious experiences despite the fact that these did not conform to the expectations of Christian church authorities; a reality confronted them that could not be contained in accepted practices or doctrines.

During the last century in India, the Hindu teacher Sri Ramakrishna had extraordinary visions. He recalled one of his early experiences when he was a temple priest:

> No sooner had I sat down to meditate . . . than I heard clattering sounds in the joints of my body and limbs. They began in my legs. It was as if someone inside me had keys and was locking me up, joint by joint, turning the keys. I had no power to move my body or change my posture, even slightly. . . . When I sat and meditated, I had at first the vision of particles of light like swarms of fireflies. Sometimes I saw masses of light covering everything on all sides like a mist; at other times I saw how everything was pervaded by bright waves of light like molten silver. I didn't understand what I saw, nor did I know if it was good or bad to be having such visions. So I prayed anxiously to [the Divine] Mother: "I don't understand what's happening to me. Please, teach me yourself how to know you. Mother, if *you* won't teach me, who will?"[20]

In Japan, in 1837, a housewife by the name of Miki was acting as a medium during a healing ritual for her eldest son when she was possessed by a powerful deity, called the "Heavenly General," who is reported to have said: "I am the True and Original God. I have a predestination to the Residence. Now I have descended from Heaven to save all human beings. I want to take Miki as *Tsuki-Hi's yashiro* Shrine of God and mediatrix between God the Parent and men."[21] After several occasions in which Miki and her family resisted this power, she became the mouthpiece of this "Heavenly Ruler" and the foundress of Tenrikyo, the Religion of Divine Wisdom. How are we to understand the religious significance of these experiences from the four corners of the earth? Let us first look at the element of the "wholly otherness" of the reality that confronted these people.

The Unique Reality of a Holy Presence

When individuals are confronted by a holy presence, they become aware that existence is dependent on a radically different reality. At the same time, the "apprehension of a holy presence" should not be misinterpreted as the apprehension of some objective thing. The holy presence not only confronts a person in an overpowering way, but is the condition for any apprehension. In the struggle to truly see, the beholder senses that he or she has been seen. It is like being unaware that there is something like a bell until one is lifted up and struck. The divine reality is the ground of existence, the context in which a person is able to be aware of fully "being." Psychologically, this is a nonordinary state of consciousness where the presence of a usually unseen power sometimes becomes manifest for the believer, transforming that person because an extraordinary amount and intensity of psychic energy has been released during the experience. To put it theologically, God is the presupposition for any thoughts or feelings about the nature of life. The holy presence is the ultimate reality, the source of experience, and yet radically different from any normal physical experience.

When the holy presence is experienced as the "wholly other" or the incomprehensible, people react in awe and wonder. The incomprehensibility of holiness is not just a result of a lack of information or a misunderstanding, either of which can be clarified with further investigation. In apprehending the holy presence a person senses that *here* is reality that is not knowable in any other way. Beyond the immediate feeling and conceptual understanding is something that by its very nature cannot be reduced to an identifiable object but is regarded by a religious person as the source of existence.

This radically different reality represents a power that cannot be ignored; on the contrary, ultimate power requires the commitment of the total person. This involvement with the holy presence does not mean that a person is never aware of finitude or everyday experiences. It means, rather, that there is no dimension or aspect of life and experience that does not participate in the reality experienced as holiness. Divine power is not just one of several influences on a person's life; instead, every positive influence is experienced as a gift from God. The continuing influence of the worship experience in the tough daily life of a North Carolina tenant farmer is expressed as follows:

> I come out of there and I'm taller. I'm feeling bigger. I feel God has taken me to Him. He put His hand on my shoulder, and said, "Brother John Wilson, the reason that I want you praying to Me is so you won't be looking at yourself and feeling so low."[22]

The personal apprehension of the Holy Presence requires a dialectic of knowing that holiness is radically different from everyday existence and yet that everyday existence is dependent on the "wholly other." This is true whether the manifestation is recognized conceptually as an impersonal power, as a transcendent personal God, or as many powers in polytheism. We should make clear, however, that apprehensions of the Holy Presence such as those found in the Melanesian awareness of *mana*, in the Jewish Lord God of hosts, or in the life-giving force of the dawn or fire as depicted in the Vedic hymns are not all identical. The particular religious meaning of any concrete expression requires an analysis of the cultural and historical situation in which that expression is found; however, the religious meaning also includes the awareness of the unique quality of holiness.

To cite an example, in the Melanesian nontechnological society the Holy Power is called *mana*. *Mana* defies simple classification as either a personal or impersonal power. It can be conveyed in almost anything that exhibits "force" or "excellence." It is manifested in natural objects such as stones, bones, plants, or animals, and it is possessed by spiritual forces or disembodied spirits. It is a "strange," "sacred," and "marvelous" force that exhibits what is most real in the spiritual horizons of these people. Anything filled with *mana* is fertile or extraordinarily successful. At the same time, the power of *mana* is not identified with the everyday human effort to exist; it is a power or a unique expression of life that causes amazement.

Another example is found in the hymns of the *Rig Veda* where the seers of ancient India expressed their awareness that a sacred power dwelled in, and was manifested by, such natural phenomena as the sun, wind, fire, and juice from the *soma* plant. Part of a hymn to Agni (fire), for example, expresses the awesome wonder of the worshipper:

> 1. Thy auspicious face, O mighty Agni, shines in the neighborhood of the sun. Brilliant to see, it is seen even by night. Soft to behold is the food in thy (beautiful) body.

> 2. O Agni, disclose (wise) thoughts for him who praises thee; (disclose) the opening, when thou, O strong-born, hast been praised with trembling. Grant unto us, O very great one, such a rich prayer as thou with all the gods wilt hold dear, O brilliant one.[23]

Here fire, seen in the sacrificial flame, the sun, and the moon, is not just an everyday natural phenomenon; it is regarded as an effective force for physical and spiritual benefits. Similarly, the sun's energy, the fertilizing rains, the psychedelic experience derived from drinking *soma* juice—all these expose the presence of Holiness for the Vedic hymn-writers.

Within the Mahayana Buddhist tradition, particularly in the Yogacara school, the religious structure of the awareness of the "holy presence" is recognized in one part of the doctrine of the *tri-kaya,* or triple body of the Buddha. The Buddhists teach that individuals' visions of the Buddha are dependent on their capabilities and immediate states of consciousness. The quality of a vision of the holy depends on the aspirant's level of spiritual attainment. If the aspirant is at the level of ordinary people and animals, the Buddha is said to appear in the form of the *nirmana-kaya,* or apparition body, creating the illusion of concrete, enduring human features. When teaching the Mahayana insights to a select audience of spiritually advanced beings, called bodhisattvas, or when appearing in a vision to the particularly devout, the Buddha is manifested as the *sambhoga-kaya,* or bliss body, which is the transfigured body seen only through the eyes of faith. Finally, there is the *dharma-kaya,* the absolute body of Buddhahood, which is free of all definite qualities and constitutes what the advanced aspirant realizes he has always been by means of his spiritual practices.[24] The second form, the bliss body, is known through the process of ultimate transformation discussed in this chapter. In terms of the highest insight in Buddhism—that all forms are conditioned—this vision is recognized as a secondary awareness; it is nevertheless an important means by which people can move beyond the illusions in their understanding of themselves.

The holy presence people apprehend may also include powers that do not claim universal sovereignty but are essential to the happiness of their devotees. These include dead ancestors revered in ancient China and transhuman spirits in some nonliterate societies for whom people feel awe and reverence. In ancient Chinese religious life, not all the dead are regarded as powerful, nor are all living beings affected by all dead spirits. The power of departed spirits depends on factors such as their rank while living, their specific relationships to living beings, and special circumstances attending death (for example, in childbirth or by murder). A person's reaction to awareness of the dead or transhuman powers can be terror and dread on the one hand, or happiness and satisfaction on the other. While such unseen spirits do not have the total power of reality at their disposal, they are regarded as having special kinds of powers that must be taken seriously by the living. The reality of these powers is established in another "world," and, thus, if a person is to be happy, the spirits' wants and desires must be satisfied. Thus, one tries to avoid contact with them or to make them happy with gifts such as food and incense.

Relations with a holy presence can also be almost familial. In premodern times, many Chinese believed that they lived out their lives under the auspices of a host of unseen beings who, as part of the blood lineage, acted as advisors during times of confusion and doubt and as moralists about or witnesses to every act.[25] Here, as in Buddhism, the religious structure described as an "awareness of the holy presence" can play an important but sometimes secondary role within another more dominent structure, as expressed in the Confucian moral teaching that people should live daily in conformity with the cosmic law *(Tao)* (see Chapter 7). People of various cultures have felt that the spirits of their dead ancestors exerted a powerful influence on the moral behavior of their living descendents, perhaps more influence than the ancestors had exerted during their lives.

Personal Extraordinary Experience

In his well-known book, *The Idea of the Holy,* Rudolf Otto describes the holy presence as the *mysterium tremendum et fascinans* (the awe-inspiring and fascinating mystery). He points out three elements in the *tremendum:* the power that instills awe, an awareness of being overpowered, and the pact of drive, energy, or will. Since the publication of Otto's book, students of the holy presence like van der Leeuw and Eliade, have made significant contributions to the interpretation of this kind of religious awareness. They point out, for instance, that the holy presence is often revealed in a totally unexpected way, that it becomes manifest at critical moments in a person's life, and that coming into contact with such a power is a dangerous affair, for it imposes itself with irresistible force. The extraordinary character of personal awareness is the second element of this process.

Since the holy presence is experienced as that which is ultimately real, people have the possibility to act and to be in ways not otherwise available to their limited existence. At the same time, a person's amazement at the full scope of possibilities is colored with awe. That awe is not simply the sense of alarm or concern brought about by some concrete danger; this would be called fear, which is commonplace. "Awe," rather, combines the exuberance of sensing infinite possibilities with the knowledge that human beings are limited most profoundly by things of which they are often unaware. Thus, a person stands in awe of the holy presence, for it is overpowering. The vastness of the holy presence reveals the smallness of the individual who nevertheless receives tremendous power through this experience.

Such an awareness is reflected in the New Testament story in which the fisherman Peter falls at Jesus's feet and says: "Go, Lord, leave me, sinner that I am!" Then the gospel writer continues, "For he and all his companions were amazed at the catch they had made" (*Luke* 5: 8, 9). Awareness also stirred the Jewish prophet Isaiah when he said:

> Woe is me! for I am undone; because I am a man of unclean lips and dwell among a people of unclean lips; for my eyes have seen the king, the Lord of hosts. (*Isaiah* 6:5).

Similarly, in the Hindu *Bhagavad-gita,* the hero Arjuna exclaims after having seen Lord Krishna in all his glory:

> Having seen what was never seen before, I am thrilled, And (at the same time) my heart is shaken with fear; Show me, Oh God, that same form of thine (as before)! Be merciful, Lord of Gods, Abode of the world! (XI.45)[26]

With awareness of the holy presence comes the recognition of possibilities far beyond the wildest imaginings; the religious person is thrilled at this realization.

Combined with the sense of awesome power is a recognition that people are by their very nature related to this reality. Although the holy presence emerges from unknown depths of existence and appears foreign, a human being cannot disregard it, for being human requires a relationship to this power. To avoid this devastating encounter is to forego the one possibility of becoming fully real, say devotees. Thus, while attempting to avoid the holy presence, humanity at the same time seeks an encounter.

When individuals experience the holy presence, say the prophets, they find out who and what they really are. Their discovery is not one of conventional, daily, limited selfhood separate from the holy presence; rather, after such an experience, they know that they are related to the source of life. Religious prophets thus proclaim that all people are driven toward the awareness of dependence on the infinite because existence intrinsically depends on this ultimate reality. The awareness of holiness, then, is the insight into the way things really are.

The fullest possible human experience is a revelation of the source and subject of life. It is expressed in conceptual terms, for example by calling God all-powerful or all-knowing. Not only in the major literate religious traditions, but also among nonliterate societies, the heavenly sacred powers are recognized as seeing everything and therefore knowing everything. Such knowledge is a force in personal self-awareness. For example, although divine omniscience is a terrible power for those who hide from and evade the will of the holy presence, it works for the benefit of those who "live in Him (Her)." A short passage from the Muslim sacred book, the *Qur'an,* gives witness to the practical result of holy omniscience:

> And whosoever submits his will to God,
> being a good-doer, has laid hold
> of the most firm handle; and unto God is the issue of all affairs.
> And whoso disbelieves, let not his disbelief
> grieve thee; unto Us they shall return,
> and We shall tell them what they did.
> Surely God knows all the thoughts within the breasts.
> To them We give enjoyment a little, then
> We compel them to a harsh chastisement.[27]

A positive relationship with the source of their being gives people creative energy; without it, they feel a sense of waste. Recognition of the holy presence as the originator and controller of life makes people feel "blessed," "loved," "protected," and "saved."

Characteristic Responses to the Holy Presence

The experience of a holy presence is often like the awareness of another person; when it occurs people use terms and symbols that reflect human relationships. A personal God is said to "respond," "love," "provide," and "care for" devotees. In this kind of apprehension of a holy presence the *personal aspects* of love, care, and deliverance have been especially important.

The most powerful concepts and symbols have been used to express the awareness of intimate relationship to, and, dependence on, God. This is the case when God is called "the beloved." God is to be loved passionately and with complete loss of attention to the individual self. To know God only through doctrines and rituals, say impassioned devotees, is like knowing a casual acquaintance. Impersonal knowledge is inadequate and should never be confused with the awareness gained in knowing another person intimately. One symbolic expression found in several world religions for this most intimate of all relationships is sexual union. The intensity of the desire to know God intimately is expressed, for instance, in the "Gita-Govinda," a twelfth-century Hindu devotional poem. The yearning of the cow-maid Radha for her Lord is expressed in the following lines:

> She secretly sees you everywhere, drinking the sweet honey of her lips.
> Lord Hari [Krishna], Radha pines in the lover's bower.
> As she hastens in her eagerness to go to meet you, she moves a few steps, and falls in
>   a swoon.
> Lord Hari, Radha pines in the lover's bower.[28]

More familiar to Westerners is the symbol of children's love for their father in Heaven. Here God is seen as the provider, protector, and source of life who cares for his children. A stanza of a Christian hymn conveys the intermingling of warmth, trust, and commitment found in this personal relationship:

> Dear Lord and Father of mankind, forgive our feverish ways;
> Reclothe us in a rightful mind, in purer life thy service find,
> In deeper reverence, praise.

Another symbol used to describe the personal relationship between humanity and the holy presence is friendship. This can be the friendship between the spiritual "Master" and his disciples as depicted in the Christian Gospels or in the Buddhist *suttas*, or it can be the kind of friendship recognized in the intimacy of Sufi mysticism in Islam.

Perhaps the most common description of God's personal relationship to human beings is the term savior or deliverer. The savior overcomes powers that are hostile to life; thus, God is a great and victorious warrior. The savior is victorious over pain, sin, and death, expecially spiritual death, i.e., damnation or continual rebirth in the cycle of death and rebirth. The awareness of a savior, like that of a person's father, lover, or friend, emphasizes the human need of self-fulfillment through the power and grace of the divine reality.

When a personal apprehension of the holy presence is regarded as the prime way to be religious, there is great emphasis on (1) the internal life of the individual and (2) the intensity of involvement in the transcendent reality. The unique quality of religious experience is emphasized, and such experience resists any attempt to communicate it in everyday language. Such total commitment sometimes involves the devotee in activities and interpretations of life, for example, worship services or prayer, that are unintelligible or irrelevant to those who are not compelled by a similar apprehension of the holy. In fact, worship is regarded by advocates of this process of ultimate transformation as a special and necessary activity for those who want to enjoy the presence of God. Rufus Jones, in *The World Within*, eloquently expresses the need for worship and describes the core of worship:

> By worship I mean the act of rising to a personal, experimental consciousness of the real presence of God which floods the soul with joy and bathes the whole inward spirit with refreshing streams of life. Never to have felt that, never to have opened life to these incoming divine tides, never to have experienced the joy of personal fellowship with God, is surely to have missed the richest privilege and the highest beatitude of religion.[29]

Such a worship experience expresses the special character of the holy presence as well as the deeply personal means of responding.

Prayer is one of the most important ways of establishing personal communion with God. For those devotees for whom the personal apprehension of the holy is the essence of religion, prayer may be the definitive expression of all religious life. The late Protestant theologian Nels Ferré adopted this position:

> Prayer is the main highway to making religion real. Unless we meet God in prayer we never meet Him, for prayer is meeting God. Unless we meet Him, He can never become real to us. A person can be fully real to us only as we get to know him personally. . . . To be sure, God is always and everywhere present as the one who creates, sustains, and controls the world. But as such He is not personally present. We can meet God personally only in communion with Him *and such communion is prayer.*[30]

The final norm for truth and ethics in this process of ultimate transformation is the personal apprehension of the divine presence. Even where divine demands seem to be outrageous and in conflict with socially responsible authorities, or where the demands seem unrealistic in light of human limitations, they are to be fulfilled. In fact, people often consider the degree to which they hold to religious beliefs and practices despite abuse and ridicule as a measure of the power by which a religious experience has transformed and regulated their lives. What seems strange to the secular mind is exactly the reflection of the "wholly other." Thus, various extraordinary activities such as "speaking in tongues" (glossolalia), trembling, uncontrollable shouting and singing, states of apparent unconsciousness, or extraordinary feelings of bliss are sometimes taken as indications of being in contact with God. The most common reaction to such contact, perhaps, is praise to God for the transforming power that has come into the individual's life. For a large number of songs, psalms, hymns, and poetry in every major theistic tradition, praise is the theme. Likewise, the deep inner movement of the spirit is part of the dynamic of the reformers, preachers, and evangelists who are "on fire for God."

The urgency and intensity of a personal apprehension of a holy presence is seen in the devotionalism or pietism of the major historical religious traditions. Despite other contrasting features, the intense personal awareness of a holy presence is characteristic of such Christian leaders as St. Francis of Assisi and John Wesley. It is seen in the Roman Catholic cult of the Sacred Heart of Jesus, Protestant revivalism, or the Four-Square Gospel Movement. In Hinduism, this orientation dominates the medieval devotional movements, as typified by the Baul sect of

Bengal. It is also a dominant characteristic of the founders of Japan's "new religions," such as Miki, the founder of Tenrikyo.

The leaders of such devotional movements often react against the orthodox learning of the priests and emphasize individual, direct experience of God's love, mercy, or wrath. They emphasize that God is to be experienced directly, pointing out as a prime example that God will enter the life of the uneducated, the poor, the social outcasts. The emphasis is on God's grace as the only sure means of salvation (humanity's ultimate self-completion.) Mankind's only religious task is to respond to divine power with joy, praise, and servitude. This is the simple, easy way to self-fulfillment, say the devotees, if only people could abandon their own perverted, egotistical attempts to attain salvation by themselves.

Life of Faith and Servitude

When the awareness of a holy presence becomes the center of personal life, then, ideally, all human functions, abilities, and decisions are informed by the special impact of this experience. Yet, except for a few short, ecstatic experiences of the sacred presence, a person's response to the presence is often unclear. People most often become aware of holiness in an ambiguous context of fear, skepticism, enthusiasm, and a feeling of powerfulness. Their reaction is often described by the term "faith," the religious significance of which needs to be examined.

As a religious term, faith does *not* mean what it has come to mean in common speech in the West: an intellectual and emotional acceptance of something a person does not know with precision and cannot prove. Not only does such a definition emphasize a secondary character of the life of faith, namely, the agreement or disagreement with a theological proposition; it also shifts the focus from the transcendent source of faith to a concern with rules of logic and methods of empirical verification—which are only secondary considerations, say the advocates of faith, when wrestling with the most profound elements of human experience. Faith, rather, is a way of living, not merely a way of thinking, that places everyday existence in the context of eternal reality.

Once this has been stated, however, the "people of faith" make clear that the awareness of divine mystery leads to an ambiguity in their reaction to it. The strangeness of the holy presence results both in certitude and incertitude. This ambiguity cannot be removed if the holy presence is really regarded as "the other." On the one hand, faith includes something of an immediate awareness, and, on the other, the object of awareness (God) becomes the subject who shows wrath and love. It is often difficult to reconcile a person's everyday orientation with this paradoxical experience in which the object of love and awe turns into the source of the person's being. Similarly, since the awareness of the holy presence involves all dimensions of human existence, a reaction in faith includes unconscious as well as conscious sources of awareness. People are never sure if their most profound insights are demonic compulsions or if their gravest doubts and anxieties are divine revelation. Thus, faith is not a cheap solution to ignorance; it is the self-conscious response to the holy—in all its mystery, revelation, terrible power, and creative possibilities.

By *living in relation* to the source of all reality, people can hope for blessing and can recognize their purpose in this world as serving the purpose of this divine reality. Their deepest desires are fulfilled in being "servants of God"—a self-image found in every major theistic tradition. When devotees refer to God as "king," "lord," and "ruler," they acknowledge submission to God. The religious attitude of submission to God is given classical expression in Islam. The term "Muslim" means one who submits (to God). God in his uniqueness can have no peers. His divine will is completely sovereign, which makes a person's only acceptable response one of submission.[31] In Islam, even human submission is not an independent human choice but results from God's determination. Human beings are often weak or forgetful of their position as God's servants, but God is merciful. Nevertheless, those who continue in their arrogance after learning God's will find only terror and wrath on the day of judgment. Those who submit participate in glories beyond description.

When the holy presence is personally experienced, people are filled with awe in response to the strange, nonhuman qualities; however, this experience can only be communicated by human symbols, gestures, actions, or ideas. Believers face an unresolvable tension in trying to express the inexpressible in a particular symbol. One way to show divine presence is through a symbol such as a human person, an animal, a combination of both, or a geometric diagram. The symbol is used as a tool by means of which people focus their attention on the holy. Nevertheless, we find in the history of piety that some leaders have strenuously opposed any use of symbols and cultic acts as extraneous to the heart or center of a fully transcendent religious awareness. True faith, they say, must avoid putting the holy presence into any objective form. Or, they continue, God in his inner character is radically different from any of his manifestations. Thus, within such religious traditions as Judaism and Islam the pious refrain from pictorial symbols. The uniqueness of the holy, paradoxically, has also been expressed through the claim that since no name or symbol can do justice to such otherness, a multitude of symbols is necessary to suggest by analogy the unique character of the holy. Such a multitude is found in the variety of images of Hinduism: gods or goddesses with many arms and eyes, animal-like beings, and powers of nature. In any case, however, the "child of God" is aware of dependence on, yet difference from, the divine reality.

This survey of the major characteristics of the personal apprehension of the holy presence has emphasized: (1) the recognition of a radical separation between holiness and conventional, secular life, (2) the affirmation that God is known most profoundly through an inner, personal, *extraordinary,* and intense experience of awe and fascination, (3) a resultant witness to divine power that may lead the individual into a prophetic role, (4) the inner transforming effects of feelings of security, joy, and personal closeness to God, and (5) a basic response to this experience in faith and service.

SELECTED READINGS

The best and most easily accessible descriptions of this aspect of religious awareness are found in *R. Otto, *The Idea of the Holy,* and *G. van der Leeuw, *Religion in Essence and Manifestation,* especially Part I and Part III, Section B, "Inward Action."

Short excerpts of spokesmen for the divine presence in their lives, plus sympathetic interpretations and critiques of these claims, are found in F. J. Streng, C. L. Lloyd, Jr., and J. T. Allen, eds., *Ways of Being Religious* (Englewood Cliffs, N.J.: Prentice-Hall, 1973), Chapter 1, "Rebirth through Personal Encounter with the Holy."

Devotional forms of religious life often emphasize the personal apprehension of the Holy. Descriptions of these forms are found in the following: *N. Soederblom, *The Living God* (Boston: Beacon Press, 1962, first published 1933), Chapters 4 and 5; *F. Heiler, *Prayer* (New York: Oxford University Press, 1958, first published 1932), Chapters 1, 5, and 13; S. G. F. Brandon, ed. *The Saviour God,* (Manchester, England, Manchester University Press, 1963), Chapters 1, 4, 5, and 12; *A. K. Datta, *Bhaktiyoga* (Bombay: Bharatiya Vidya Bhavan, 1959); A. Bloom, *Shinran's Gospel of Pure Grace* (Tucson: University of Arizona Press, 1965), Chapters 4 and 5. A very useful summary statement on the structure of devotion is found in W. King, *Introduction to Religion,* Chapter 14, "The Discipline of Devotion."

For some documents expressing the object of the personal apprehension of the Holy, see M. Eliade, ed., *From Primitives to Zen* (New York: Harper, 1967), Chapter 1, "Gods, Goddesses, and Supernatural Beings."

A brief introduction to *mana* is found in W. Lessa and E. Vogt, eds., *Reader in Comparative Religion,* pp. 253–62. See also *W. Howells, *The Heathens: Primitive Man and His Religion* (New York: Doubleday, 1948), Chapter 3, "Mana and Taboo: A Force and a Danger."

6.

Sacred Action: Myth and Sacrament

Although some people define "genuine" religion as a deeply felt experience of a holy presence, others hold that religion is most clearly found in sacraments, sacred stories, and holy places. For the latter group, the most dynamic religious forces are the models of divine life found in ancient stories and ritual activities that give people symbols of meaning and self-identification. This is not to say that there are no images or symbols in the process of transformation discussed in the last chapter, or that rituals and symbols provide no feelings of awe, mystery, or joy in the process described in this chapter. The basic difference is that personal apprehension of the holy sets a high priority on *feeling,* while a religious structure organized around sacred action and words finds transforming power in the *meaning of symbolic expressions*. In the second process, the central vehicle for divine power is symbolic language. For the devotee, the sacred language is not just a product of temporal cultural and psychological forces; it is the divine image.

The power of symbols is generally recognized today as a force generating cultural values. Social scientists recognize that religious symbols both reflect social values and reinforce them. It is important to observe how symbols function as forces for social self-identity and value-reinforcement. However, what is their significance as religious language? One way to become conscious of religious symbolic power is to see how religious people interpret their sacred stories and rituals as the expression of their very being, as the revelation of the ultimate source of their lives. For example, Jacob Neusner, in portraying the major Jewish festivals of Passover, points to the ultimate significance of the Exodus from Egypt:

> To be a Jew means to be a slave who has been liberated by God. To be Israel means to give eternal thanks for God's deliverance. And that deliverance is not at a single moment in historical time. It comes in every generation, is always celebrated. . . . Jews think of themselves as having gone forth from Egypt, and Scripture so instructs them. God did not redeem the dead generation of the Exodus alone, but the living too—especially the living.[32]

This Jewish springtime celebration, with its unleavened bread and sanctified wine, is not simply an education for the children in the family or a reinforcement of social solidarity; it is an expression of thanksgiving to God and a re-presentation of God's redeeming activity.

In a similar vein, the Christian Ecumenical Council in Rome, called Vatican II, recently reaffirmed the ultimate significance of the sacred ritual of the Eucharist (Holy Communion):

The renewal in the Eucharist of the covenant between the Lord and man draws the faithful into the compelling love of Christ and sets them afire. From the liturgy, therefore, and especially from the Eucharist, as from a fountain, grace is channeled into us, and the sanctification of men in Christ and the glorification of God, to which all the activities of the Church are directed as toward their goal, are most powerfully achieved.[33]

Such importance is also placed on symbolic acts in Hinduism. Since early times, special rituals from conception to funeral rites at cremation, have marked the life of all males above the lowest class. These are called *samskaras,* which R. B. Pandey translates as "sacraments." One of the most important *samskaras* is the initiation of a young boy when he first goes to a teacher for his education. It is called *upanayana.* A central act is that in which the lad receives a sacred unbroken thread which he loops over his body from his left shoulder to his right hip and wears for the rest of his life. Regarding the significance of this rite, Pandey says:

> The sacrament of *upanayana* performed at the beginning of study marks the dawn of a new life. The student is now an *upanita*—one who is introduced to a life of perfect discipline. The sacrament symbolizes the student's entering the boundless realm of knowledge, it marks for him his destination, it asks him to be vigilant and steadfast in his path, and it reminds him of the need of complete harmony between him and his teacher. In his venture, the student is assured of the help of society, of all living creatures, and of the invisible powers. Brhaspati (the lord of knowledge), Indra (the lord of power), and Agni (the source of brilliance and energy) are held before him as his ideals.[34]

An ultimate claim is implicit in the symbolic gestures in the three sacred acts from different religious traditions, but there are *differences* in the basic *signification* of the ultimate. The rites both point toward and express meaning in different ways. Each ritual differs from the others in its identifying, integrating, and centering force and in its conceptual formulation and therefore structures its participants differently. The Jew does not appeal to and is not transformed by the "compelling love of Christ"; the Christian does not seek help from Brihaspati or Indra in order to enter the boundless realm of knowledge; and the Hindu boy does not leave home after the *upanayana* thanking the Lord of hosts for deliverance from Egypt. One response to the diversity of rituals and names for God in various cultures is the conclusion that all experiential forms are conditioned and therefore not ultimate. Some cultural philosophers who affirm "historical relativism" and some mystics (see Chapter 8) who stress the illusory character of any mental or visual form have indeed drawn this conclusion. The cultural philosophers reject a traditional myth for modern ones (for example, they argue that the reality referred to in traditional myths is a combination of psychological and social forces) and therefore regard the variety of traditional myths and rites as human projections of more basic survival needs. Among the extreme mystics, every symbolic form is considered to be just a mental and emotion projection, not an indication of some more basic sacred order or power. The differences exposed through particular forms reveal—according to mystic awareness—only illusion.

In contrast to the mystics' rejection of form as an indicator of reality, the users of myths and sacraments find great significance in specific symbols. They assume that gestures and other symbols create a world of meaning. An outward act is, first of all, a shift from an equilibrium of rest or from a static state; it reorders existence in some way. In general, some movements are more important than others; some are even extraordinarily significant and become organizing centers for interpreting other movements. Some physical movements that seem to have special importance for people are opening the eyes, standing erect, responding to another human face, or touching sensitive parts of one's body. Some activities have "value" as well as physical results. Thus, the consciousness that something is significant depends in part on general experience. The symbols and gestures that are often ritualized by society are patterns of value-formation even before a person becomes aware of them.

The psychologist Eric Erikson has described, for instance, the ritualizing behavior between a mother and baby—a description that has relevance for this discussion of sacred action as a form of ultimate transformation. If the baby wakes up frightened, the mother cuddles and caresses him, becoming the child's protector. If the baby is hungry, she feeds him, thereby becoming the provider. For the baby, she both is, and is the model of, the Mother Goddess; her repeated gestures order the infant's identity. In analyzing the mother's response to the awakening infant, Erikson says:

> If observed several days (and especially in a milieu not one's own) it becomes clear that this daily event is highly formalized, and that the mother seems to feel obliged (and to be not a little pleased) to repeat a performance arousing in the infant predictable responses, which encourage her, in turn, to proceed. Such formalization, however, is hard to describe. It is at the same time *highly individual* ("typical for the mother") and also tuned to the particular infant; and yet it is also *stereotyped* along traditional lines—as we can see best in cultures, classes, or families other than our own. The whole procedure is of course, superimposed on the periodicity of vital physical needs; it is an *enhanced routine* which keeps close to the requirements of survival.[35]

This enhanced routine develops, first, a significance that in an ultimate context is known as a sacred presence and, second, a regularized pattern of action and reaction that gives a particular order to life.

The self-images children and adults develop find form in the symbols their culture provides and usually reinforces, but the patterned-responses of the infant, the adolescent, and the adult determine what is considered "real" or "natural." Cultural images are the determining forces of self-identity not simply because a culture or a religious community self-consciously lends authority to its symbols, but because these symbols express something about the people they also mold. The symbols by which people communicate have the power—to the degree that they communicate—to bring a symbolic world into existence. Where self-awareness is *communicated through* a particular symbolic form, like the Passover, the Eucharist, or the *upanayana,* the symbol becomes the ordering and creative force in daily life. Devotees recognize the effective power of a religious myth to the extent that they create their lives in terms of, or as an extension of, that myth. Therefore, language—or even particular sounds—has life-giving or enlightening power. Correct knowledge in any culture functions as myth for those who affirm it, for it distinguishes "real" from "apparent" and truth from illusion. In the West, this knowledge is called "science" (from the Latin *scientia*, "what is known").

What then is a myth, and why is it so powerful? It is more than a story about supernatural beings. It is a symbolic creative force that orders existence into a meaningful world; it is most effective when it operates at the level that Westerners label the "unconscious." It is a perspective that has ultimate value. This value determines how a person's experience is broken up conceptually and then organized into a meaningful whole. For example, the judgment that there is a difference between "natural" and "supernatural" in the scientific claim about the basic reality of existence is part of a myth. Just as important is the fact that a myth provides an implicit form for evaluating the relative importance of human experiences and their conceptual labels. A philosophical claim that the natural world or a universal principle expresses the "real forces" of existence has an implicit norm for judging truth claims. Thus, within particular groups some words and gestures carry extraordinary power to define what is "real" and what is "true" in the nature of things.

Traditional religious communities use myths and sacraments to express the nature of things as *sacred* reality. This kind of reality is also the source of all knowledge and all life for those having a "personal awareness of a holy presence," the process of ultimate transformation discussed in Chapter 5. Just as the awareness of a holy presence is not understood by its adherents simply as the product of psychological needs, so the members of a religious community do not regard the expression of the sacred in sacred writings, stories, and acts as simply a product of social needs. The second process of ultimate transformation differs from the first, however, in that it emphasizes the transforming power of the symbols that give form to ultimate reality instead of stressing the personal inner awareness that gives peace and strength to the individual. The symbols declaring the sacred name of God, telling the story of the founders or divine heroes of the human race, or offering accounts of the creation of the universe crystallize the power of life in language and gesture; the resultant culture is both self-perpetuating and normative.

A myth, therefore, is more than one possible interpretation of life, and more than a literary technique to express personal hopes and fears. Similarly, religious ritual is more than a community's collective self-identification. Within a religious context, myth and ritual are more than expressions *of* something else; they are "the power unto salvation," the dynamic power embodied in language and gesture that manifests the eternal (divine) reality in everyday existence.

Certainly myth and ritual are not identical to the sacred reality they reveal; however, there is an intrinsic relationship between divine power and its symbolic image. According to a mythical means of self-realization, the essential character of life manifests itself in special (sacred) moments that are remembered and symbolically repeated from generation to generation by those living in the terms of the myth. Human existence is seen to be dependent on the eternal sacred power that is expressed through the symbols found in myth and ritual.

The Sacred and the Profane

The claim that a myth or ritual has power to transform life rests on the capacity of the myth or ritual to reveal the truth of life. They have the paradoxical capacity of using everyday (profane) language, activity, and material objects to expose the sacred, ultimate reality. For a religious devotee, sacred reality stands in contrast to the threats, frustrations, limitations, and ambiguities of everyday existence. Whereas everyday existence changes and is sometimes meaningless, the sacred is eternal. It is a different order of being in comparison with the world normally experienced by humanity. The sacred is truth, whereas people live in untruth (sin or ignorance); it is the unconditioned infinite reality, whereas the world is the conditioned, limited, derivative reality.

In this context, human life is transformed from chaos to order by imitating the reality of the sacred as it is most perfectly expressed in existence: for the Jew, through living in God's deliverance and promise; for the Christian, through living in Christ; and for a pious Hindu, through living in Shiva or according to the model given in an avatar of Vishnu. Actually, even profane existence does not exist independent of the sacred power. Profane life has its source in the sacred, but unless it conforms to the sacred reality, it is self-destructive. The basic religious question for people, then, is to ask where, when, and how this sacred reality manifests itself, so that profane existence can be molded to the sacred pattern.

Sacred Revelation Through Myth and Sacrament

Myth and ritual recreate in profane time what is eternally true in sacred reality. To live in the myth is to live out the creative power that is the basis of any existence whatever. The religious purpose of repeating myths and sacraments is not simply to establish a society, to explain the beginning of the world, or to ease man's frustration; rather, all these are secondary results of the basic purpose, which is to manifest "what truly is."

To know, and live in, the sacred reality is accomplished by repeating and reenacting the sacred symbolism. Because myth and ritual expose eternal reality, they can express what happened at the beginning of time. In the sacred stories of India and Japan, for instance, the activities of divine powers (*deva, kami*) become the foundation for some basic social institutions, morals, and sacred pacts.[36] These sacred beings (powers) not only bring the world into existence, but their activities, described in the myths, also provide the ideal pattern for human imitation. People reach their highest potential in imitating as closely as possible what took place "in the beginning." This orientation is in contrast to much modern thinking, in which human institutions and personal happiness are viewed almost purely as the product of human effort, and time represents a succession of efforts through which humanity perfects itself indefinitely. By contrast, myth and ritual inform people about themselves because these symbolic forms manifest or reveal the eternal—that which was, is, and ever shall be.

If we recognize that myth and ritual reveal divine activity, or sacred power, we must still be careful not to reduce the function of the myth to giving information about something, even if it is about the Sacred. The revelation of the sacred always includes the manifestation of power. Thus, among those Christians for whom the Eucharist is more than a remembrance of Christ's sacrifice, the act of "breaking the bread" by a priest is a unique release of sacred power. In Holy Communion, the participants not only learn that it is possible to be "born anew," but also regard themselves as new creatures. When the Roman Catholic priest breaks the wafer and places a small piece in the wine, praying, "May this mingling of the body and blood of our Lord Jesus Christ bring eternal life to us who receive it,"[37] he is not simply remembering the Last Supper of Jesus or expressing his personal good wishes; rather, he is offering a sacrament by which people will be transformed. In the Mass, the participant becomes part of Christ's sacrifice. While the priest is saying the above prayer, the participants chant three times, "Lamb of God, you take away the sins of the world; have mercy on us." Roman Catholics understand that the self-sacrifice of the individual is the transformation of a human act into participation in God's act; it is an ontological transformation—a person's very being is changed.[38] Catholics regard the change as more than an improvement of existing nature; it is a shift from the profane to the sacred. When the sacred power manifests itself, people learn something, but they also become something. Thus, the myth is more than an ideal; it is more than an explanation of life. Likewise, from the standpoint of the adherent, myths and sacred rituals are understood as manifestations of a power that transcends psychological needs or causes.

It is often possible to see the profound psychological significance myths or ritual actions have on people even when they are unaware of the cultural and historical meaning of these myths or actions. Myths can function as highly projective stimuli, sometimes pulling content from the unconscious. They constitute a medium for unconscious exploration, as in a Rorschach ink-blot test. However, for the believer in sacred writings, tradition, and sacraments, sacred reality is more than, and differs from, conventional human experience. It is even a different order of reality from those unusual experiences of the personal apprehension of a holy presence that are recorded in many cultures. In fact, those who maintain that the sacred stories and sacraments are *necessary* processes of transformation often regard conflicting unusual or extraordinary personal experiences of God as, at best, secondary or confused expressions of sacred power and, at worst, demonic events. For them, the appeal to individual, private, personal experience is a dangerous activity. Personal feelings—even very deep feeling—cannot be the criteria for the authenticity of an experience of ultimate reality. Only the sacred knowledge preserved by religious specialists, such as priests, can provide a norm for distinguishing truth from self-deception.

For those who use mythical-ritual techniques, sacred reality is decisively exposed through *reciting the myth*. A myth, in being told, manifests sacred power. When people know the truth of existence—how they came into being, the processes whereby they can get things that they need, a criterion for making a good rather than bad choice—they have power to live fully and happily. Life is at their disposal. Very often a myth describes a community's life as the central event of all time. It is a narrative that celebrates the value of a particular community in contrast to other communities whose members are regarded as strangers, barbarians, or enemies. Historical events are interpreted from the perspective of the prosperity and importance of the community. The repetition of a myth reinforces its values and conceptual labels; if people question the claims made in a mythical narrative they destroy the power that the value-laden symbols have in establishing personal identity within that social reality. Such critics of a specific myth live "in" another myth, another system of values and expectations that orders their self-awareness unconsciously.

Most Americans come closest to explicit mythical thinking when they learn and repeat the unexamined history of America and their home state in elementary school. They identify themselves within an accepted historical narrative, periodically reinforced by civic holidays. Many Americans, for example, have accepted the views of public schol history books as "objective" statements of fact without realizing that objectivity in history is a myth. Nor do they realize that the common notion of precolonial America as "a wilderness" with "free and unsettled land" waiting to be "tamed" by "God's people" is also a myth. Similarly, national holidays like Memorial Day, Independence Day, and Thanksgiving Day have provided symbols identifying Americans with an ideal past and future. For those for whom a community's history plays a normative role, understanding the past is not just gaining information about it; it is judging the present by the values implied by a narration of the past. On the other hand, the lack of personal identification with a myth makes it, at best, interesting but not revelatory.

All accounts of divine activity do not have identical assumptions about the nature of community, of the sacred, or the world. Myths must be interpreted within their cultural and temporal context. Thus, an understanding of the myths of Zeus requires some knowledge about the culture and times of the Greeks who recited them. Similarly, Norse legends, the Buddhist *Jataka* tales, the Japanese myths of divine creation, or even the contemporary myths of our time can only be understood within their proper context.

In general, however, it may be helpful to indicate two types of myth. The first expresses the devotees' awareness of the sacred in the natural cosmos. Those who are aware of divine power in nature establish rituals to reveal sacred productive and reproductive power and the joy of abundance. Their myths celebrate the intrinsic relationship between humanity and the sacred power in seasonal rites that follow a natural pattern. This focus is found predominantly in the myths of South Asia, East Asia, the islands of the South Pacific, and among nonliterate societies in the Americas. An example is the full-moon sacrifices performed in Vedic times in India, which permitted human beings to imitate divine activity.

Sacred Action: Myth and Sacrament

The second type focuses on serial time as the realm of divine activity. It is found in the Jewish, Christian, and Islamic traditions. There, myth and ritual do not emphasize a repetition of cosmic pattern in cyclical rhythms of nature but celebrate particular events within history as expressing the power of God. Here, people seek to know "that moment" when the sacred is clearly manifested; this moment presents the ultimate condition of salvation against, or for, which people must decide. By living according to the law given to Moses, by celebrating the divine incarnation in Jesus Christ, by establishing the "house of submitters to God" according to the *Qur'an,* Jews, Christians, and Muslims, respectively, participate in the saving acts of God who alone has both the power and mercy to redeem people from their folly. Despite these distinctions, there are nevertheless common elements in many myths and symbols whereby believers assert that the sacred is made manifest.

The Creative Power of Words

It is common today to think of words as conventional signs for something more real, such as an object or a subjective feeling. However, people in traditional societies and in certain traditional religions today regard particular words as having intrinsic power. For example, a benediction, a curse, the words used in a sacrament, and to some extent the proclamation of the Christian gospel or the Jewish sacred history of God's salvation, have ontological power; they manifest the divine. In contrast, the words of a common greeting like "Good morning" or the imperative "Shut up" generally have only psychological power; they establish a personal relationship between the speaker and hearer.

Words are powerful because they can put an experience into a form that can be used in relation to other forms (or concepts) to enhance self-awareness. The use of words to construct ideas brings a form into existence whereby we "know" reality. Such religious acts as calling on the name of God, pronouncing a blessing, or retelling a myth are uncommon uses of words. The religious use of words is nevertheless an extension of the common use of words; such use seeks to express the ultimate inexpressible reality.

When words are perceived to have creative power, they must be used carefully. To use God's name "in vain" is to act as if speech, or words, were mere human conventions; it is to forget that in using the name of God, or in speaking of powerful things themselves, power is generated. A priest, for example, can heal or destroy life since he knows the divine name(s). The names and myths of supreme beings—within the context of mythical thought—are gates of power that open conventional experience to the awesome sacred realm.

The power of the word can be enhanced in various ways. The potency of an oath can be intensified by repetition. Or the manner of taking an oath can heighten its power. In America, an oath is taken with the right hand up, palm forward, and the left hand on another sacred word, the Bible. Likewise, raising the voice or using rhythm and rhyme can heighten the power of utterances. Closely connected to this are the techniques of chanting, loud rejoicing, and mourning, which generate greater potency than mere speaking. Unusual words possess intensified power:

"Hallelujah" and "Amen" in the Christian West, *"Om"* in Hinduism, and *"Nembutsu"* in the Pure Land Buddhism of Japan. When a chant, blessing, curse, or myth is used, power—according to its devotees—does not come from personal desire or hope, but rather from sacredness. The sacred is being manifested; it has effective power to structure existence, organize human life, and create everyday events in terms of the eternal, divine model. When speech is used as a ritual act and is regarded as a transcendent force, the words used become extremely important. A devotee must use a specific invocation, benediction, or name for God, because only through this vocal pattern can the divine power be exposed or released. For example, the orthodox Hindu Brahmin priest holds that the Sanskrit verses of the ancient *Veda* are themselves powerful; the verse (*mantra*) is a succession of sounds arranged in a certain order that must be repeated exactly if the chant is to produce a blessing.[39] To translate the verse into another language would make it useless in the religious ritual. *Mantras* are also part of traditional Buddhism, reaching their most elaborate form in Tibetan Buddhism. While meditation was the central religious means of transformation among adepts in Buddhist history, ritual practice was advised for the laity, and was often the first step to control the mind and emotions. In an Indian Mahayana Buddhist manual called *The Lamp for Beginners,* for example, is the following instruction for a disciple who worships the Buddha image and thereby invokes the power of Buddhahood, i.e. "the deity,":

> He calls down the deity, saying: OM delight in the Law SVAHA!
> He establishes him therein, saying: OM well-founded diamond SVAHA!
> He consecrates it, saying: OM womb of the realm of reality, filled with a hundred blazing and shining gems of all Those Who Have Come SVAHA
> He dismisses the diety, saying: OM womb of the realm of reality, come, take away! SVAHA!
> And he asks for forbearance toward errors in the ritual he has performed, saying: OM womb of the realm of space SVAHA![40]

In Judaism, Christianity, and Islam, the power of the word is recognized in God's creative acts, which are preserved in written accounts of God's law as well as the history of God's self-revelation. Central to each of these religions is the belief that human beings have access to divine power uniquely through God's disclosure of himself at particular times in history, as recorded in the sacred writings of these religions. Thus, the reading of scriptures and the performance of religious rites or sacraments that have their bases in God's self-disclosure are regarded as sacred acts that emit power to transform lives. In Islam, the "word of God," the *Qur'an,* is the "recitation" of God's words as spoken to Muhammed through the angel Gabriel. For centuries in orthodox Islam, this unique character of the sacred word was recognized in the refusal to translate it from the original Arabic.[41] While the truths contained in the *Qur'an* were translated into many languages and interpreted according to the necessities of different historical situations, the *Qur'an* has been regarded by Muslims as the source for knowing God's will. Not to act in accordance with it is to oppose the very power of existence. To live fully, then, means to follow the prescriptions of sacred revelation.

Release of Sacred Power Through Ritual

The notion that power is released through a special use of words is part of a wider frame of reference in which action is seen as a power of change. In the context of the mythical-ritual way of being religious, the most fulfilling act is that which brings forth the power of the sacred. Those acts which bring forth the sacredness of life are called "sacraments." Such acts are very often an expression of the simplest and most basic life functions; eating and drinking, washing, sexual intercourse, or building a house; but also may include such activities as the making of fetishes, chanting, prayer, dancing, communion, confession, baptism, witnessing, ordination, initiation into discipleship, and the burning of candles, incense, animals, and sometimes people. The difference between the *sacred* use of these actions and their *everyday* use is that the sacred act discloses the "nature of things" and thus is never conceived simply as a biological, social, or political necessity. From the perspective of religious meaning, the power of the ritual does not come from any aesthetic appeal, nor from psychological comfort in the familiarity of a repeated act, nor from social authority; rather, the power initiates in the realm of the sacred, and the cultic act is an image or demonstration of the nature of ultimate reality. Just as in the awareness of the holy presence (see Chapter 5), the unconditioned total power of life is revealed. However, in the sacrament this sacred power is bound up intrinsically with specific forms carefully preserved by a religious tradition—either verbal or bodily gestures, or material symbols.

When ritual action is emphasized as central to being religious, the divine form must be repeated so that the divine power can be released. Also, cultic activity implies that sacredness is manifested in doing, in acting. The everyday events of existence become sacred through specific acts that transform the variety of phenomenal forms we experience according to the eternal pattern of the sacred. Such a view is clearly expressed in the priestly manuals, the *Brahmanas,* of Vedic India. They even claim that sacrificial action is more potent than the deities addressed in the sacrifice. The gods themselves used the sacrifice to gain divine power! Thus, people can become "real" (like the gods) through the sacrifice.

Certainly different religious rites have different purposes. However, their practical meaning is expressed in two terms for sacramental functions: "purification" and "rebirth." Through the religious ritual of purification, the finite and impure activities of people are placed back in the sacred sphere from which they ultimately derive. In everyday, profane existence, life-powers become choked with tensions and dissipate themselves. Life loses its freshness, its vitality; it becomes chaotic. To correct this, the religious ritual revives a dissipated life energy according to the eternal form or pattern of reality. Various elements are used to indicate the purifying action of the sacred, such as water, blood, incense, or fire. To purify, then, means to return a powerless form to the original power, which in itself is pure.

A particular example of purification occurs in the religious practices of some American Indians. Religious visions induced from ingesting peyote very often produce nausea and vomiting, a sign that purification is taking place because toxins are being released from the body. Likewise, certain tribes, the Oklahoma Creeks, for example, go to sacred places called "stomp grounds," where they swallow plant extracts, perhaps jimson weed and redroot, and alternate days of fasting with all night dances around the sacred fire. There the oldest men sing traditional songs and the women and girls keep time with tortoise shell rattles attached to their legs. Ingestion of the plants is supposed to purge the Indians of impurities due to wrong deeds. Pure Indians do not get sick. The fasting and dancing continue the process of cleansing and renewal, until finally, at dawn, all the people wash their bodies, particularly hands, face, and feet, in the juice of the plant extracts. Thereafter, the Creeks must come to the stomp grounds and take "the medicine" four times a year for four years. In this way, they regain their original state of purity.

The second sacramental function, rebirth, is closely related to purification. To return finite, conditioned existence to its infinite source means dissolution, or death, of the apparent reality—the worn-out, polluted existence. The ritual is the great reverser of apparent conditions. When the sacrificial animal is killed, for example, its natural existence ends, but in the sacred context, the end of the animal means the rebirth of the sacrificer's life. In the initiation rites of nonliterate societies in Australia, the male novice goes through an ordeal in which he loses his former, lesser self and gains a new self. The new reality he experiences and manifests has been made possible by his passage through religious rituals in which he learns the secrets of his spiritual and cultural existence. He can now become fully human because he participates in the hopes, expectations, and values of those who know the sacred lore; through this participation he has access to the hidden power of life. His "second birth," his spiritual rebirth, is the means by which he perpetuates and renews his life. Similarly, the imagery that St. Paul uses in his letter to the Christians in Rome suggests that Christian baptism is a kind of death and rebirth; he explains:

> We were dead and buried with him in baptism, so that just as he was raised from the dead by that splendid revelation of the Father's power so we too might rise to life on a new plane altogether. (*Romans* 6:4)[42]

Sacred Officiants, Places, Times, and Images

When religious people assume (1) that ultimate reality is wholly different from their everyday experiences *and* (2) that their knowledge of ultimate reality depends on specific divine images or traces left by the activity of the sacred, then the specific point of sacred disclosure has special significance. The sacred disclosure takes place where the "sacred" meets the "profane." Some concrete points at which the sacred meets the profane are the priest, the temple, celebrations at particular times, and the images of gods and goddesses. Because the sacred power is manifested in myth and sacraments, there is a special religious importance placed on the people, times, and places that serve as the point of contact between the sacred and profane.

The priest, for example, is religiously significant as the representation of the sacred. During the religious ritual, the priest loses his individual identity as a person and speaks "in the name of God." The masks used by the officiants in some African religious ceremonies, the ceremonial robes used by Christian priests, the purification rites performed by priests of Hinduism or Shinto are all necessary to separate the person of the priest in his everyday existence from his personification of sacred power during the ritual activity. Similarly, the painted bodies of the American Indian in ceremonial dances symbolize the nature of things. For example, Black Elk, a holy man of the Oglala Sioux, recounts the vision of an old man who explained the sacred meaning of body markings in the Sun Dance:

> The bodies were to be painted red from the waist up; the face too, must be painted red, for red represents all that is sacred, especially the earth, for we should remember that it is from the earth that our bodies come, and it is to her that they return. A black circle should be painted around the face, for the circle helps us to remember WAKAN-TANKA [the Great Spirit], who like the circle, has no end. There is much power in the circle, as I have often said; the birds know this for they fly in a circle, and build their homes in the form of a circle; this the coyotes know also, for they live in round holes in the ground. Then a black line should be drawn from the forehead to a point between the eyes; and a line should be drawn on each cheek and on the chin, for these four lines represent the Powers of the four directions.[43]

Such devices convert the frail human person into the manifiestation of divine power in concrete form.

Whenever a priest performs his sacred role, he re-presents the Sacred; he manifests anew the divine pattern or acts of God. In theistic religion, the priest becomes the representative and servant of God, mediating divine power to the world. In the ancient Vedic religion of India, however, where the impersonal divine power (Brahman) is regarded as the source of existence, the sacred ritual gains even more significance. The ritual becomes the machinery for transforming the unmanifest divine power into the everyday biological and social processes. Through his ritual activity, the Brahmin priest, in fact, has the responsibility to maintain the cosmic order. Nevertheless, in both the theistic and nontheistic interpretations of the sacred, the priest, under the special circumstances of officiating at the sacrifice or sacrament, becomes the vehicle or channel for exposing the ultimate creative force of the universe.

A sacred place is a gateway between the two worlds of the sacred and profane. A pious person visiting a place that is sacred in his or her religious tradition, such as a grotto, a shrine, or a sacred city (Mecca, Jerusalem, or Benares), is touching the cosmic boundary shared by both worlds. To be at a sacred place means to participate in life eternal; there an imperishable life force has been, and is, available. Even though most existence is seen as chaotic, dead, or meaningless, at a sacred place new life can come forth. Because the place serves as the point of contact with God or with infinite power, it takes on the quality of holiness or sacredness. While a sacred place may be beautiful, or fascinating because of its size, peculiar shape, or difficulty of access, the sacredness found in mythical-sacramental religious awareness is not a result of these factors; rather, it is the specific actions of the cult that make the place sacred. The sacred reality gives its quality to a place, thereby rendering that particular place religiously important.

A temple, especially, is a specific place where divine power reveals itself. Since the temple is the point of contact between earth and heaven, it is only natural that the temple reveal symbolically the character of the divine realm. For example, the ancient Babylonian, Egyptian, preclassical Greek temples, and the Hopi Indian *kivas* of the American Southwest were built and furnished in the image of the cosmic dwelling place of the gods. Similarly, the effort to build according to the divine plan rather than according to human ingenuity is seen in the detailed instructions for temple building in the writings of the ancient Hebrews, of classical India, and of China. Indeed, the architect's lack of personal freedom to design a temple was an indication of the sacredness or divine power in his work.

Just as mythical-sacramental thinking refuses to view the world as a continuum, or an even extension of space, so also it views time not as a continuous flow of human experience but in terms of critical points when the sacred defines, or outlines, the meaning of life. Thus, time is not broken up into identical segments; rather, some moments have a distinctive value. Some moments that are peculiarly relevant to human happiness and prosperity burst with meaning. Each season of the year has its special value: spring brings the power of life or salvation, and winter reflects the loss of life or the departure of God. Certain days and hours have their individual significance; some days, some hours, are more potent than others (for example, new-moon and full-moon days). "Sacred time" is celebrated with festivals that mark the intervals, the sections, through which time unfolds.

At the festivals, cult activity manifests divine power. The festivals mark the periods by which life's meaning is determined. Such a period is not the unending, identical segments of a minute, an hour, or a twenty-four-hour day. Rather, a period is marked out by critical points at which sacred power becomes manifest, as at Christmas and Easter in the Christian calendar, or Rosh Hashanah and Yom Kippur in the Jewish calendar.[44] A religious calendar—as distinct from a civil calendar—is a repetition of divine life. It is the means whereby those people who participate in it renew their lives. Thus, New Year festivals are preceded by chaos or destruction of order. They do not simply mark the beginning of a new year in an infinite continuum of time but provide a power through which the participants are again renewed and brought into an ordered existence.

The sacred image is also a point of contact between the sacred and profane worlds. The hero, god, or goddess of the myth often is represented in the material image of a person, and the power of the ritual is symbolized in such natural forms as water, blood, wine, grain, light, or sound. For the believer, there is a unique relationship between the image of the sacred and the sacred itself. The image reveals, exposes, and re-presents the sacred. When the sacredness of the image is emphasized, it is handled with care, excluded from profane view, or regarded as so sacred that only the priest may touch it.

The spiritual reality of the sacred, as distinct from the observable, phenomenal image, makes the use of this symbol important to the believer. The purpose of the material symbol is to reflect the quality of the sacred. Since the sacred is regarded as radically different from "normal" human life, it is not surprising that various forms are used to express it artistically—such as a halo, many arms, or a combination of animal and human characteristics. The power that is simultaneously behind, and expressed through, the symbol is the object of worship and the instrument of salvation.

In sum, the key elements in the process of ultimate transformation by means of sacred action are: (1) the assumption that there is a radical difference between the sacred-symbolic realm and the world of everyday life (chaos); (2) the belief that symbols, which are considered to be specific forms in the everyday, temporal world, have revelatory power to structure a cosmos; (3) the capacity of myth-ritual orientations to provide an identity for a person in a community of like-minded persons, and for that community, among other communities; (4) the power a participant perceives in *sacred* words and acts in distinction to everyday words and actions, and (5) the importance of special officiants, places, times, and images as points of contact between the secular and profane spheres.

SELECTED READINGS

M. Eliade, primarily using data from nonliterate cultures, elaborates the significance of this religious form in *Cosmos and History* (New York: Harper, 1954), especially Chapters 1 and 2; *Myth and Reality* (New York: Harper, 1963), Chapters 1, 3, and 6; *The Sacred and the Profane*, Chapters 1–3; and *Rites and Symbols of Initiation* (New York: Harper, 1965).

Two other important explanations of establishing the sacred through myth and sacrament are found in *G. van der Leeuw, *Religion in Essence and Manifestation* Part I, "The Object of Religion," and Part III, Section A, "Outward Action"; and in W. B. Kristensen, *The Meaning of Religion*, Part III, "Cultus."

*J. Campbell, *The Hero with a Thousand Faces* (Cleveland, Ohio: World, 1956, first published 1949). A psychoanalytic examination of myths and symbols from all over the world. Campbell shows that there are basic human experiences expressed in a mythic grammar.

*A. van Gennep, *The Rites of Passage* (Chicago: University of Chicago Press, 1960, first published 1908). While much anthropological information has been collected since this book was first published, it still makes an important contribution to the interpretation of sacred action in describing the magico-religious aspect of crossing personal, social, and geographic boundaries.

E. O. James, *Sacrifice and Sacrament* (London: Thames & Hudson, 1962). A study of sacramental forms in the religions of the Near East and Vedic India. Chapters 1 and 9 present James's understanding of the principles of religious meaning in sacraments.

*S. K. Langer, *Philosophy in a New Key* (Cambridge, Mass.: Harvard University Press, 1942). A study of the processes involved in forming symbols that are used in reason, sacrament, myth, and art.

F. J. Streng, C. L. Lloyd, Jr., J. T. Allen, eds., *Ways of Being Religious,* Chapter 2, "Creation of Community through Myth and Ritual," provides excerpts, sympathetic descriptions, and critiques of a mythic-ritual religious process.

Various recent anthropological studies of myth and ritual from different parts of the world are collected in two books of readings edited by J. Middleton: *Myth and Cosmos* (Garden City, N.Y.: Natural History Press, 1967) and *Gods and Rituals* (Garden City, N.Y.: Natural History Press, 1967).

Sacred Action: Myth and Sacrament

7.

Harmony with Cosmic Law

The traditional means of ultimate transformation discussed in the last two chapters are probably familiar to most readers. People in the West are accustomed to thinking about "religion" in terms of God, holiness, religious visions, personal faith, prayer, sacraments, religious symbols, and mythology. Religion is often defined as a belief system or an organized community, such as a church or synagogue. Nevertheless, for many people throughout the world, the means of ultimate transformation is not essentially a personal apprehension of a holy presence or a manifestation of the sacred through symbolic forms. For example, the late Indian philosopher Dr. S. Radhakrishnan writes:

> Hinduism is more a way of life than a form of thought. While it gives absolute liberty in the world of thought it enjoins a strict code of practice. The theist and the atheist, the sceptic and the agnostic may all be Hindus if they accept the Hindu system of culture and life. Hinduism insists not on religious conformity but on a spiritual and ethical outlook in life. "The performer of the good—and not the believer in this or that view— can never get into an evil state." In a very real sense practice precedes theory. Only by doing the will does one know the doctrine. Whatever our theological beliefs and metaphysical opinions may be, we are all agreed that we should be kind and honest, grateful to our benefactors and sympathetic to the unfortunate.[45]

In this excerpt, Radhakrishnan uses the term "religious" in a restricted sense of a belief system or doctrine and indicates that for him "a spiritual and ethical outlook" is even more basic in life.

In the religious processes discussed in chapters 5 and 6, the central dynamics of the transforming processes were inner personal experiences or verbal and ritual symbols; in this chapter, the focus is on harmonious social relationships that reflect a concept of a natural universal order of life. Of course, a deep awareness of the holy presence or participation in the symbolic power of sacredness is usually accompanied by ethical concerns. Moreover, individuals with a spiritual and ethical outlook, like Radhakrishnan, are also likely to perceive their self-hood in specific symbols or rituals and may even have a personal sense of a divine presence. Rather, the differences in the processes lie in the importance assigned to each focus in relation to the others. The process of the awareness of a holy presence includes an ethical concern, but it emerges from the overwhelming experience of personal confrontation with God. The process of symbolic transformation often includes a sense of awe before the sacred as well as a concern to live a rightous life in conformity with God's will, but these feelings develop from the ultimately transforming power in the symbols. Some forms of theistic religion do, however, emphasize social ethics more than others, as, for example, the Jewish effort to live the life of Torah (God's law) and the orthodox Muslim focus on submission to God's will as revealed in the *Qur'an* and in orthodox tradition.

In order to distinguish the third type of traditional religious process from the other two types discussed, we will use nontheistic expressions from China and India as the prime models. They will demonstrate that one religious option is a transcendent law of life that provides a universal moral order without a divine law giver. In this chapter, then, the central dynamics of ultimate transformation will be daily living in harmony with the cosmic (universal, ultimate) law.

In this religious process, the highest human attainment is the practice of moral conduct as expressed in the "natural distinctions" found in existence. Some of these "natural distinctions" are social, and others are physical; many are commonly accepted in different societies: the distinctions between men and women, plants and animals, infants and adults, heat and cold, wetness and dryness, and hardness and softness. Some of these distinctions reflect a social as well as a physical or biological difference. Similarly, the eternal social or moral order is seen by its advocates as an extension of a natural universal order in all existence. A prime example of this thinking occurs in one of the Confucian *Four Books,* which for centuries provided a standard of life in Chinese society. It reports that Confucius said:

> The life of the moral man is an exemplification of the universal moral order (*chung-yung,* usually translated as "the Mean"). The life of the vulgar person, on the other hand, is a contradiction of the universal moral order.
>
> The moral man's life is an exemplification of the universal order, because he is a moral person who unceasingly cultivates his true self or moral being. The vulgar person's life is a contradiction of the universal order, because he is a vulgar person who in his heart has no regard for, or fear of, the moral law.
>
> Confucius remarked: "To find the central clue to our moral being which unites us to the universal order, that indeed is the highest human attainment. For a long time, people have seldom been capable of it."[46]

Another of the *Four Books* records a statement by Mencius, one of Confucius's key spokesmen, that human beings have the innate ability to act properly because of natural (in contrast to learned) feelings:

> Man's innate ability is the ability possessed by him that is not acquired through learning. Man's innate knowledge is the knowledge possessed by him that is not the result of reflective thinking. Every child knows enough to love his parents, and when he is grown up he knows enough to respect his elder brothers. The love for one's parents is really humanity and the respect for one's elders is really righteousness—all that is necessary is to have these natural feelings applied to all men.[47]

Here, the means of ultimate transformation is not a personal experience, or an appeal to a uniquely powerful symbol, but a moral effort to participate in the universal natural order. It is a cultivation of one's true self. Prime examples of this religious process are found in the Confucian emphasis on the proper relationships between people, as suggested in the excerpts above, and in the concern found in Hinduism to live according to the eternal law, or universal order (the *dharma*). The concern to live life according to eternal moral principles is not limited to Eastern religious traditions, however. It found mythical expression in early Greek religion[48] and continued in the thought and life of various Greek and Roman philosophers. Emperor Mark Antony, for example, gives the following advice in one of his meditations:

> Let the performance and completion of the pleasure of the Universal Nature seem to you to be your pleasure, precisely as the conduct of your health is seen to be, and so welcome all that comes to pass, even though it appear rather cruel, because it leads to that end, to the health of the universe, that is to the welfare and well-being of Zeus. . . . Thus there are two reasons why you must be content with what happens to you: first because it was for you it came to pass, for you it was ordered and to you it was related, a thread of destiny stretching back to the most ancient causes; secondly because that which has come to each individually is a cause of the welfare and the completion and in truth of the actual continuance of that which governs the Whole. For the perfect Whole is mutilated if you sever the least part of the contact and continuity alike of its causes as of its members; and you do this so far as in you lies, whenever you are disaffected, and in a measure you are destroying it.[49]

Two interacting concerns will also play an important role in the Chinese and Hindu practice of morality as something of ultimate importance: (1) the placing of individuals in their present existence is not accidental, for individual circumstances result from a preexisting universal moral law; (2) a person is responsible to "the perfect whole", an organism affected by all individual decisions.

The focus on the moral order as the prime reality in life has continued in Western thought, but only rarely has it taken the form of an organized social expression. In the Near East and European West, moral concern has been derived predominantly from the processes of personal religious experiences or sacramental-symbolic formation (or both). However, in the twentieth century, the humanist Ethical Culture movement has clearly expressed the value affirming a universal moral law without appealing to any notion of God and God's revelation. In *Ethics as a Religion,* D. S. Muzzey describes the first two basic principles of Ethical Culture:

> First, Ethical Culture is a creedless religion. The bond of union among its members is a common devotion to the cultivation of moral excellence as the chief duty of man. Contrary to the widely accepted teaching that right conduct depends as a corollary on correct religious belief, we hold that it is the conscientious striving for righteousness in thought and action that has constantly refined and humanized the dogmas of the creeds. . . .
>
> Second, Ethical Culture insists that man has the capacity as well as the duty to lead a righteous life. Its postulate of the infinite and induplicable worth of every human being necessarily involves the belief that it is within the power of every human being to choose at every step between a right and a wrong course of action. . . .[50]

Later Muzzey explains that the cultivation of moral excellence is a universal moral law to be realized in every human action; there is no mysterious power demanding personal devotion or manifesting itself in uniquely significant symbols. The affirmation that human beings have both the capacity and the prime duty to attain moral excellence is also evident in Indian and Chinese materials.

Some key religious assumptions in the process of ultimate transformation through harmony with cosmic law are (1) the definition of a person as a participant in a natural, universal order; (2) the conviction that social ethics are the means of perfection, that human beings must participate in moral action, and that they have the capacity to cultivate moral excellence; (3) an emphasis on tradition and essential principles in differentiating right and wrong; and (4) the belief that a knowable moral order exists outside individuals and predates them, and that correct action will bring a person into harmony with forces at work throughout the universe.

Social Action as Religious Power

Where there is an emphasis on morality, any human activity is seen as religiously significant. The everyday, secular affairs of existence provide the medium for conveying concretely the eternal power and order of life. Cultural habits and customs can become profoundly religious when they expose the power and order of life. From this perspective, then, correct social behavior is a basic way to express the ultimate order of life. When rules of proper behavior are systematized into codes and laws, their authority does not ultimately derive from a group of people or from personal desire. It comes from the awareness that the written form, or "letter" of the law, is always a reflection of greater spiritual laws, which have the power either to create or destroy existence.

In all major religious traditions there is a concern to make spiritual life effective in everyday social existence. Nevertheless, in some religious orientations more than in others, man's common daily tasks are self-consciously used to expose a religious quality. In the Confucian focus on propriety (*li*), for example, the concern with human action dominates the character of religiousness. The Confucian Classic called the *Book of Propriety (Li chi)* expresses the importance of *li*:

> "Is *li* so very important as all that?" asked Tseyu again.
> "This *li*," replied Confucius, "is the principle by which the ancient kings embodied the laws of heaven and regulated the expressions of human nature. Therefore he who has attained *li* lives, and he who has lost it, dies."[51]

Confucius and his followers in classical China directed their attention to the *Tao* (way, process) of human relationships and provided little metaphysical speculation on the nature of existence. Their concern was with rules of morality as the means and power whereby the truly noble and wise person was perfected. The intellectual understanding of truth, or the subjective awareness of sacredness was secondary to the practical result of a person's life in relation to other people.[52]

Confucianism has been called the "religion of *li*" (ritual, propriety, good manners). Sometimes *li* is simply translated as "religion" to indicate both its practical and ultimate qualities. The character (禮) combines two elements: that of a sacrificial bowl (豐), and to manifest (示). The combination suggests a concern with an omen. For the Confucian scholars, social rituals such as public worship, funeral rites, and agricultural festivals not only provided the outward symbols for the order, but also served as an education for living in the natural order. The mourning rites at a funeral, for example, demonstrated the proper relationship between the mourners and the deceased. The closer the kinship with the dead, the greater the degree of grief that was required by the rules of propriety.[53] Children of the deceased were expected to mourn more loudly and for a longer period of time than nephews or grandchildren. Whatever the relationship of the mourner to the deceased, his action was expected to be appropriate to the nature of the personal relationships that structured society.

In Hinduism, as in Confucianism, there is a recognition that a deep relation exists between how one does something and who one is. Every group of people in society—in fact, every form of life—has its *dharma*, its way of being. Thus "religiousness" is seen as the attempt to express properly one's relationship to all other people and things, or to follow one's *dharma*. The root form of *dharma* is a verb that means to secure or uphold. *Dharma* is the law of life that holds the pulsating, flowing, dissolving impressions of our experiences in order long enough for us to distinguish one thing from another and thereby "define" what "is." It maintains or secures the characteristics of one thing over against another so that there can be order. It is that on which one can depend. Other translations are "law," "truth," "reality," or "religion."

The notion of *dharma* has had different and sometimes conflicting meanings among Hindus. In early India, it referred primarily to what one "ought to do" to perform the Vedic sacrifices correctly. Gradually, its meaning expanded to affirm the parallelism of the ritual order, the cosmic order, and the order of society. The term *dharma*, like the term "law" in the West, refers to (1) an eternal law, order, or "natural law" that is constant throughout existence; (2) its manifestation in particular virtuous or appropriate actions of social and biological organisms; and (3) its formulation in rules of behavior recorded in law books. This third concern requires a continuing effort to reformulate and interpret the meaning of the eternal law in light of immediate circumstances. However, every interpretation must conform to certain established principles recorded by early sages or forefathers in revered writings and/or oral traditions. In India, the earliest recorded religious material, the *Rig Veda,* is regarded by many Hindus as the earliest source of Indian law, but later law books and commentaries on them formulated explicit rules and regulations for various classes of people. One of the law books, *The Laws of Manu,* stresses the importance of *dharma* and suggests sources where people can learn what their duties are:

> The whole Veda is the (first) source of the sacred law, next the tradition and the virtuous conduct of those who know the (Veda further), also the customs of holy men, and (finally) self-satisfaction.
>
> Whatever law has been ordained for any (person) by Manu, that has been fully declared in the Veda: for that (sage was) omniscient.
>
> But a learned man after fully scrutinising all this with the eye of knowledge, should, in accordance with the authority of the revealed texts, be intent on (the performance of) his duties.
>
> For that man who obeys the law prescribed in the revealed tests and in the sacred tradition gains fame in this (world) and after death unsurpassable bliss.[54]

In the orthodox Brahmin tradition, the meaning of life depended on a person's birth into a certain class (*varna*) and on the stage (*asrama*) of maturity in life.[55] One's possibilities and limitations at any given time in life depended on one's *dharma*. To live contrary to that *dharma* would rupture the ordered flow of energy in the universe and cause chaos.

From the orthodox Brahmin point of view, four ideal classes comprised the inherently different groups of people in Hindu society. Besides these people, there were the others who were not ritually a part of the Hindu community—they were "out-castes." Living according to one's class-*dharma* enabled one to fulfill a natural destiny. Americans use such expressions as "he is a 'natural' comedian," or, "she has 'a gift' for playing the piano" to indicate an inherent capacity. On being born into a class, a Hindu received as a birthright certain assets and liabilities. In the total cosmic plan, the different classes complemented one another to provide a harmonious society. By following their *dharma*, people exercised their capabilities and thus manifested truth, or reality.

Fundamental to this understanding of Hindu religiousness is the notion of *karma* (action). According to the law of *karma,* there is an orderly expansion of energy that complies with universal law *(dharma)*. Every person continually molds his or her character simply because existence requires a person to *do* something or to *act* in one way rather than another. Every action has a consequence, the effect of which one must live out immediately, or at some future time, either in this life or in some other. No energy is lost. When people's actions comply with the eternal order of the universe, they grow and experience life according to their inherent character, which is determined by their place in the total cosmic plan. A person's existence is not wholly determined by a universal abstract pattern; to regard human destiny in this fashion would deny the dynamic power and causal force of individual actions. People develop their future capacities through present actions, and present actions either accord with or oppose the roles individuals have constructed through previous actions. Ideally, an individual should try to fulfill the potential of his or her present role. Thus, in the Brahmanical tradition in India, a person accepts birth into a caste and sex role without question, recognizing that actions performed in this life-span within a particular station will determine whether or not it will be possible to be born into a higher state in the next life. In this way, a person's *karma* can be an expression of the eternal *dharma*.

A different but related expression of infinite power expressed through social behavior is seen in the power of *tabu* among Polynesian peoples. A *tabu* is not simply a restriction placed on some thing or person because of a reasoned argument or as a social convenience. A plant, animal, food, or person can be declared *tabu* by a person who has power *(mana)*. Such an object is *tabu* because of its peculiar relationship with the transcendent power of *mana*. The term *tabu* suggests something that requires two terms in most European languages: (1) sacred, or holy, and (2) impure or polluted. Without going into the complexity of this notion, we want to indicate that people who live according to *tabus* are defined in relation to other people and the natural world. In a religious sense, *tabus* prevent the Polynesians from destroying themselves with extraordinary power and provide order and proper relationships among members of society who have different grades and kinds of power. To place a *tabu* on something means to fix it in place for a particular purpose—a purpose that cannot be defied without self-destruction.

Western religious life has also placed an emphasis on moral action, but it has most often been regarded as an expression of a person's commitment to God. In the Christian tradition, one of the most dramatic recent expressions of ethical concern is found in the "social gospel" of the late nineteenth century. This movement developed a program of social improvement by trying to imitate Christ's life of self-sacrifice. In Judaism, the effort to live in the covenant with God requires a definite course of conduct. God promises peace and blessing in return for obedience to his divine commands. This law of the Lord is a delight to the Jew—it is his means for salvation and joy. When people live in "the light of the face of God," they are open to God's love and power, which overcome all evil.[56]

Islam also places an emphasis on worshipping God through social actions. The Muslim professions of faith, pilgrimage, fasting, and giving alms are concrete forms of submission to God.[57] Historically, the social and political expression of living in submission to God's will took the form of the Caliphate. According to Muslim orthodoxy, the true community can exist only where God's law can be infused into the total way of life, and this has been most often interpreted in the past to mean the necessity of Islamic political sovereignty. Despite the variety of political forms the Muslim community has taken, especially in the twentieth century, its ultimate goal is to provide conditions under which the will of God can be done.

Cosmic Law as the Basis for Every Proper Action

From a religious point of view, the distinction between "good" and "bad" actions is not based on mere convention or personal convenience. When people act properly, they present what is real, what is true. Various religious traditions have confirmed this by saying that one does God's will, acts according to a cosmic order by following natural law, or expresses a rational universal principle. Ultimate reality is the basis for physical and moral existence, and it is revealed in harmonious social relationships. The justification for acting one way rather than another, then, is based on the claim that such an act expresses the law of life.

In those religious traditions in which a concern for acting in harmony with cosmic law prevails, people are thought to have an inherent capacity to act in a fully moral and proper way. Rather than assume a radical break between the realms of sacred and profane, adherents assume that ultimate reality is the potential source of all that happens and that everyday events are the actual, explicit expression of cosmic power. The potential, unmanifest power is the source of all existing reality. Everyday existence is not the opposite of this potential, but its actualization in ordinary events and experiences. In a sacred-profane dichotomy, the two elements are antagonistic and the profane threatens the sacred by exhausting it or wearing it down. The notion of a continuum, however, sees profane existence as an imperfect and incomplete projection of cosmic power and perceives a reciprocal relationship or movement between the manifest and the unmanifest.

Thus, the Confucians appealed to natural distinctions between things in the universe to substantiate the necessity for different social observances. Although Confucius sought justification for social ethics primarily in the actions of the ancient sages, his successors emphasized an intrinsic relationship between humanity and nature. People were counseled to participate in the natural rhythm of the *Tao* by revealing in their actions the natural distinctions between things as well as the appropriate relationships among them. As there are intrinsic qualities peculiar to each of the five elements (or ''agents'') in nature, or the four seasons, so there are natural distinctions between mother, father, ruler, son, daughter-in-law, farmer, and scholar.[58] Harmony in society and order in nature required that all parts of the social organism examine what relationships were appropriate with all other parts. For example, a man's relationship with his mother differs from his relationship with his son, and these ''natural'' differences were to be expressed through different social forms. Similarly, various styles of etiquette, language, and clothing marked the differences among farmers, scholars, and government officials. When these distinctions were not made, the natural harmony of life was thrown into chaos. To know the truth about oneself and others meant to live harmoniously with all things according to one's place in the ever-moving rhythm of the *Tao*.

In orthodox Hinduism, also, people who acted according to their *dharma* did not regard it as mere social convention. By living in the *dharma,* every person secured and upheld the order of life. The cosmic order *(dharma)* was revealed, or brought forth, when people lived out their social responsibility (also *dharma*). The rules and regulations by which a person lived, then, were a religious force. To live by the rules of one's class and stage in life caused the cosmic order to appear clearly in an undefiled way. To have distinctions and various grades of power was natural.

Living Authentically by Cultivating One's "Nature"

From this religious point of view, one does not choose to act correctly out of fear of punishment or in mere compliance with social authority. Right action (justice, righteousness, following the law) is, rather, the means for an authentic existence. A person ''is'' when his or her actions show the true nature of things. Spiritual death occurs when a person's actions are contrary to eternal law.

The effort to live according to one's true nature is seen in the Confucian ideal of humanity, *jen. Jen,* or true humanity, is self-fulfillment through proper relationships with others. The natural order of things requires people to perceive themselves in a context of relationships. A judge handing down a verdict, a father speaking to his son, a man and a woman making love, warriors in combat—each of these concrete situations could be an expression of either harmony or disharmony in the cosmic order. In each of these cases, harmony is expressed when the actions expose such virtues as honesty, kindness, courage, and wisdom. To be human, however, never means being egotistical or making an arbitrary decision; it means to practice the appropriate action in a given situation so as to bring out the central harmony of the universe. There is no question about the ability of human beings to perfect and cultivate their humanity. All people can develop themselves if they have guidance from those who know the nature of the world, and if they set about diligently to express the truth. From the Confucian perspective, spiritual perfection is meaningless unless it manifests itself in and grows out of actual human relations.

Living according to one's *dharma* in Hinduism was also the means for fulfilling one's potentiality. To the degree a person was identified with the tasks and possibilities of his or her social role in the hierarchy of things, he or she was "real"—manifested the *dharma*. Ideally, people sacrificed their individuality where it conflicted with the duties and requirements of social expression. The loss of egocentricity made it possible to present in a perfect and unclouded image a person's role or station within the cosmic order. The ideal was not to struggle for some abstract, "highest" goal for all people, but to discover an individual's inherent nature.

Accordingly, to do what someone else should do was a perversion of true spirituality. Just as there was assumed to be a natural biological distinction between men and women, between adults and children, and between rocks and trees, so there was a natural distinction between duties of different people. For a person to do the duty of someone of another class or stage of life was as incongruous as a rock growing like a tree or a fish chanting Vedic hymns. In this context, the passage in the *Bhagavad-gita,* "Better one's own duty, (though) imperfect, Than another's duty well performed" (III. 35), does not sound so strange.

Another example of religiousness that emphasizes the quality of human actions for establishing "what is real" is the power of *tabu* among Polynesian societies. Of course, there are major differences between the social expressions of the Indian *dharma,* the Confucian *jen,* and *tabu.* Among Polynesians, individuals had power *(mana)* to the extent they were able to effect *tabus.* A person's claim to power in Polynesian society had to be manifested in concrete demonstrations. The chief of a tribe, for example, was acknowledged as possessing *mana* when he extended his administration, when he was successful in battle, and when his people had all the physical necessities of life. Any conflict of authority was settled decisively by one person's *demonstration* of his physical or social power over another person. Whoever was successful had *mana.* Similarly, a person's political authority was measured by the *tabus* he could impose. One person's *tabus* were regarded invalid when they were overruled by the *tabu* of a more powerful person. Thus, the different kinds and quantities of *tabus* reflected the power in concrete situations.

Discovering Truth by Living in the "Tradition"

How can people be sure that their actions express the nature of things? One answer is, by tradition. Many modern readers are hostile to the term "tradition." It may even evoke the mental image of, and emotional response to, a carcass. Those who view tradition as what was done centuries ago often find it unsatisfactory today. On the contrary, a living tradition is something that is preserved, treasured, and well guarded because it is a practical solution to the problem of how people can live together in the most creative way. Its claim to truth is that it reveals the way things are. Often the beginning of a tradition is credited to ancient seers who were also sages—people who acted wisely because they knew the truth.

A living tradition is so precious that it is placed in the custody of priests or scholars whose formal learning is required to keep it pure. These specialists preserve the tradition, ideally, by passing it on exactly as they learned it. At the same time, they are called on to explain and interpret the eternal pattern of living in order to make it relevant to people of different circumstances. In this way, a body of assumptions about life is passed on from generation to generation. Later generations preserve the tradition by approaching life in terms of these assumptions, although these may be interpreted differently at different times. The body of often *unarticulated assumptions in a life-orientation* constitutes the most lasting and pervasive quality of a tradition.

In China, the Confucian tradition was preserved by Confucian scholars. They read and studied the ancient texts of history and rites to learn what ancient sages had said and done. They wrote commentary upon commentary explaining the meaning of ancient sayings and applied Confucian norms to political theories of government in their day. While it is clear that throughout Chinese history the Confucian political philosophy was only rarely applied as the sole governmental policy, the study of the Confucian classics by government officials had an important influence. Especially important was the recognition of a hierarchy of social responsibilities from the emperor down to the lowest peasant. The hierarchical system of authority, which began in family relationships, according to Confucian thought, was the basis for all social order in Chinese society.

In India, Brahmin priests preserved and articulated the orthodox tradition, for they were "lovers of *dharma*." Brahmins were jealous of their sacred heritage, and they directly exposed only the three upper classes to their sacrificial power and learning. Nevertheless, they regulated social relations between all members of society. The ancient law books, compiled by the Brahmins, reflect the concern to regulate every detail in the daily life of the individual. In cases in which the sacred scripture of the Hindus did not define specifically enough the appropriate rules of conduct, other sources of *dharma* were accepted, for example, the practice of those who knew the *Vedas,* and custom. The concern was to integrate the conduct of every individual with the basic stance, or assumptions, of the sacred tradition.

In Christianity, Judaism, and Islam, tradition has sometimes played a crucial role in shaping religious life but the foundation for any elaboration of tradition has been based on the revelation of God's will as recorded in sacred writings. At present, besides the assertions of the Ethical Cultural advocates, perhaps the clearest Western system of interpretation based on human conduct is found in the notion of law. Law courts daily make practical decisions about right and wrong. In arguing a case, a lawyer will appeal to precedent on the grounds that there are consistent patterns of life and continuities between situations; a judgment in favor of something in the past constitutes a positive moral basis for a similar judgment in the present situation. Exact adherence to legal procedure for clarifying and establishing the rights of an individual in relation to others in a society is important, and the interpretation of law as given in the courts is accepted as a power that determines the possibilities or limitation of social interaction. The fact that the American legal system provides a growing body of tradition does not, of course, make it identical to any of the traditions discussed. Nevertheless, in our modern society, which prides itself on having surpassed "traditional societies," there is a social force at work that emphasizes the role of specially trained people in deciding what is true and right.

Some of the most important elements in the process of ultimate transformation through harmony with the cosmic law are: (1) the assumption that morality and ethical conduct in daily social relations can transform earthly chaos into order; (2) the notion that "right" actions and behavior conform to the greater harmonious ordering of the universe; (3) the claim that universal laws are the source of laws men have codified; (4) the recognition that universal laws preceded human efforts to learn and comply with them, (5) the belief that individuals have the capacity to learn universal laws by cultivating their natural sensitivities within their social and physical environment, and (6) the recognition that cultivation occurs "naturally" when people understand tradition and their leaders are models of virtue.

SELECTED READINGS

Two useful general introductions to the expression of religion through right social action are *J. Wach, *The Comparative Study of Religions,* Chapters 4 and 5; and W. L. King, *Introduction to Religion,* Chapters 3 and 13. Both studies include some cultic expression as part of their explanation of religion in social activity.

*J. Wach, *Sociology of Religion* (Chicago: University of Chicago Press, 1944). Chapters 4 and 5 of this well-known study deal with the importance of social relationships in religious life.

Two introductory explanations of Hindu *dharma* are found in *S. Radhakrishnan, *The Hindu View of Life* (London: George Allen & Unwin, 1927), Chapters 3 and 4; and *T. J. Hopkins, *The Hindu Religious Tradition* (Encino, Calif.: Dickenson, 1971), pp. 73–86. More detailed studies can be found in *The Cultural Heritage of India* (Calcutta: Ramakrishna Mission, 1962, 2nd ed.), vol. 2, Part IV, "The Dharmasastras."

*L. G. Thompson, *Chinese Religion,* 2d ed. (Encino, Calif.: Dickenson, 1974), Chapter 3, "The Family," introduces the reader to the importance of communal relationships in the cosmic order. C. K. Yang elaborates on different aspects of the situation in his *Religion in Chinese Society* (Berkeley and Los Angeles: University of California Press, 1961). See especially Chapters 2, 4, 10, and 11.

*H. B. Earhart, *Japanese Religion: Unity and Diversity,* rev. ed. (Encino, Calif.: Dickenson, 1974), Chapter 4, "Formation of Shinto," shows how Shinto (way of the *kami*) provides the basis for harmonious living.

For introductions to the social expression of religious life in the Western religious tradition, see *K. Cragg, *The House of Islam,* 2d ed. (Encino: Dickenson, 1975), Chapter 4, "Law"; *J. Neusner, *The Way of Torah: An Introduction,* rev. ed. (Encino, Calif.: Dickenson, 1974) Part II, "Torah: A Way of Living"; and *J. Neusner, *The Life of Torah: Readings in the Jewish Religious Experience* (Encino, Calif.: Dickenson, 1974) and H. W. Schneider, *Religion in Twentieth Century America* (Cambridge, Mass.: Harvard University Press, 1952), Chapter 3, "Moral Reconstruction."

F. J. Streng, C. L. Lloyd, Jr., and J. T. Allen, eds., *Ways of Being Religious,* Chapter 3, "Living Harmoniously through Conformity to the Cosmic Law." A collection of readings expressing advocacy, sympathetic interpretation, and critiques of this way of being religious.

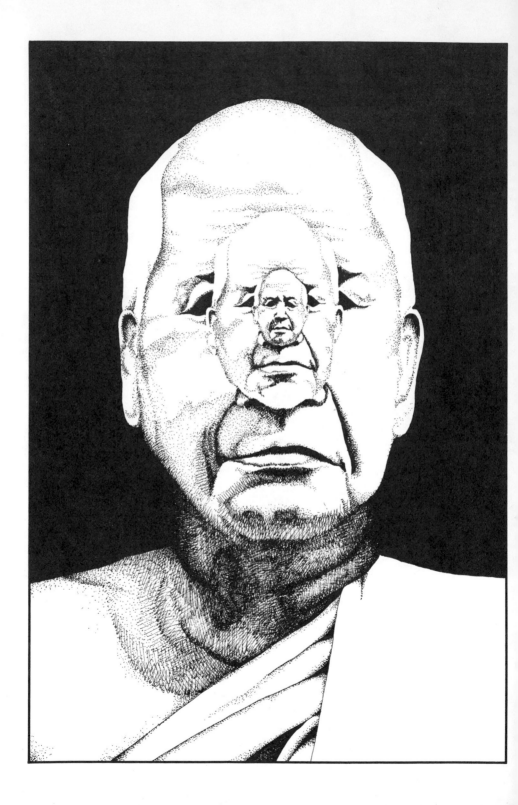

8.

Mystical Insight Through Spiritual Discipline

A fourth way of being religious is through what is often called "mysticism." In considering the topic, this chapter will focus on disciplined practice in religious traditions, a practice, usually guided by a spiritual teacher, that facilitates transcendent states of awareness. This awareness makes it possible to live in everyday experience with freedom and insight. Thus, the process that leads to illumination and the subsequent art of living fully is just as important as the mystical experience itself. When people gain spiritual insight, they descend into the depths of their being by following a path prescribed by religious seers who have already experienced the ground of their being. The searcher strives toward a consciousness in which depth experience, rather than rational coherence, empirical measurement, or the divine word, reveals the truth of life. The seeker thereby transforms a bondage to a limited image of himself or herself into a full comprehension of life and abandons objects of desire to win a freedom for true living.

Some of the key elements in this process of ultimate transformation are (1) the perception of ultimate reality as internal and subjective, though hidden by the psychological and physical factors that are mistaken for one's "self"; (2) the elimination of self-deception through a spiritual discipline, such as meditation, accompanied by moral, psychological, and physical control techniques; (3) the concept of the highest goal in life as freedom from compulsive habits and physical causes; (4) the belief that insight into (direct awareness of) one's true self transcends both conventional perception and supernormal psychic vision; and (5) the notion that insight is a transforming power that changes one's attitudes and daily life-style. This process of ultimate transformation shares elements with the other three processes discussed earlier, though the common elements function differently in different structures. For example, "mystical insight through spiritual discipline" shares the following elements with "personal awareness of a holy presence": a focus on individual, inner experience of transcendent truth; a perception that people are responsible for their own spiritual darkness; the belief that spiritual forces lie beyond normal rational understanding and conventional social expectation; and, often, a rejection of the clerical, ritual, and intellectual expectations of a culturally acceptable religious institution. The process of mystical insight also has some common elements with the process of "living in harmony with cosmic law": the recognition of continuity between the eternal and the temporal aspects of life; the belief that people have distorted the eternal ultimate reality, the most "natural" reality, by pursuing short-lived pleasures; and the view that faith, discipline, and determination can reveal the natural source of joy for all living beings. Although the structures of the various processes of ultimate transformation contain common elements, each structure also has some unique elements. The shared elements, however, function differently in different structures and in general play a secondary role in one structure and a primary one in another. This chapter will discuss the major elements in mystical insight under three general headings: the disciplinary process, the mystical experience, and the subsequent art of living fully. The models for this process are taken from yoga and Buddhist meditation, but there will also be references to materials from various religious traditions.

Release from Bondage Through Discipline

Spiritual discipline is a technique or process for overcoming human limitations. It is a method for releasing a person's spiritual potential. But what is this bondage, this limitation, from which people are to be released? It consists of the conventional thought processes and common emotional responses, such as sorrow or frustration, which most people take for granted as natural or inevitable. The limiting character of these natural thought processes and emotions is recognized in the great contradictions that run through human life—the frustrations, anxieties, and disappointments.

Anxiety and pain can awaken religious insight, however. The concern as to who one is and why one exists lie deeper than the concern for a logically perfect system of philosophy. The question of the meaning of life is experienced as a personal challenge. *Why* should I do what others expect of me? What *is* right? What is the connection, if any, between what I feel myself to be and what I want to be?

If people are to know their true nature, say the masters of spiritual discipline, they must avoid attachments to things that seem to be important, such as money, fame, status, or the physical body. In fact, any distinctions that form the basis of evaluations and emotional judgments are seen to enmesh a person in commitments to love or hate, enjoyment or disgust—in short, to bind that person to existing predispositions. To refrain from constructing self-perpetuating images and emotional attachments is not easy. As a matter of fact, social conventions, natural desires, and mental images derived from sensuous experiences are usually accepted as adequate sources for knowledge about life. However, say the spiritual masters, conventional resources for knowledge are limited and perverted in comparison with spiritual insight. The conventions seem so "natural" that ways must be found to break patterns and habits of daily life. One technique used by yoga, Buddhist, and Jain meditators is "restraint of the senses." It is described in the Buddhist Pali canonical literature as follows:

> When his eyes see a visible object, [the monk] does not label it, nor grasp at its details; but rather he sets himself to restrain what might be an occasion for evil & impure states, for desire & regret to attack his sight, were it not restrained; and thus he guards his sight & restrains his eyes.

And when his ear hears sounds, or his nose smells odors, or his tongue tastes flavors, or his body touches a tangible object, or his mind perceives a mental event, he does not label it, nor grasp at its details; but rather he sets himself to restrain what might be an occasion for evil & impure states, for desire & regret to attack his mind, were it not restrained; and thus he guards his perceptions & restrains his mind.

And as he practices this noble restraint of his senses, he experiences an untainted happiness within himself; and thus the monk guards the gates of his senses.[59]

Classical Hindu yoga offers one of the most explicit exercises for eliminating the illusions of everyday life. Yoga has two aspects: one is a practice of the techniques, and the other is a philosophy explaining the "way things are" and the results of practice. The specific exercises include external methods of eliminating agitation: restraint, cultivation of good habits, practice of yoga positions, controlled breathing, and detachment of the senses from external objects. There are also three internal aids for attaining complete peace: holding the mind steady, meditation, and concentration *(samadhi)*.[60]

The goal of yoga, as given in the first verses of the *Yoga Sutras* of Patanjali, is the elimination of the continual shifting of the mind. During the perfect practice of yoga, pure consciousness abides in itself, but at other times—as in everyday experience—it becomes identified with a shifting mental and emotional attachment to physical, mental, and emotional objects. Patanjali divides mental-emotional processes into five kinds; some cause more spiritual problems than others. The kinds are: (1) generally valid sources of knowledge, for example, perception, inference, and authoritative assertions; (2) misconceptions; (3) imagination; (4) sleep; and (5) memory.[61] Most people are caught in a self-deception whereby they identify one or more of the five kinds of mental-emotional processes with unchanging pure consciousness. These mental states may be useful for acquiring images of a changing personality in conventional experience, but when any one of them is regarded as expressing the pure state of self-awareness, it is a fundamental self-deception. This basic deception about a person's inherent nature causes frustration and anxiety in anyone's attempt to learn about the deepest truth of life. Frustration necessarily is produced because all mental-emotional states are impermanent. The state of change is one of activity, and activity exists only where there is tension between things. The ideal state, according to yoga, is one of unchanging equilibrium.

The view of life expressed philosophically in the classical system of yoga was identified with another philosophical system called *samkhya*. It held that there were two kinds of ultimate reality and that both were necessary to account for the variety of existing things and the fact of change itself. One kind of ultimate reality is the pure unlimited consciousness or "spirit" *(purusha),* which is experienced in the highest state of yogic meditation but exists continually in a perfect undisturbed state of equanimity in all people. The other kind of reality is called *prakriti*. It is the original source of all change and differentiation in common experience. It is made of three sorts of primordial nature: the capacity for clarity, bouyancy and joy *(sattva)*; an active force *(rajas)*; and a principle of resistance and inertness *(tamas)*. These three, in different proportions, constitute the "material nature" of every form in existence. Most people experience themselves only as a changing personality, their material nature. They do not "remember" the *purusha* within and thus wrongly identify it with that which is not consciousness *(prakriti)*. From the perspective of samkhya-yoga, most people accept as natural the delusion that characterizes every person's changing experiences and consequently fail to recognize their pure consciousness, which remains (in the final analysis) untainted by the tumult, tension, and pain that they think is real. When people identify themselves with the material-mental forms of daily life, and especially when they regard emotional responses and sensations as spiritual life, they become enslaved by their failure to distinguish between unlimited "cosmic consciousness" and physically and emotionally conditioned consciousness. The late Hindu mystic Sri Aurobindo Ghose (who did accept a nondualistic conceptual system) has stated the importance of releasing oneself from habits of thought:

> Man is shut up at present in his surface individual consciousness and knows the world only through his outward mind and senses, and by interpreting their contacts with the world. By Yoga there can open in him a consciousness which becomes one with that of the world; he becomes directly aware of a universal Being, universal states, universal Force and Power, universal Mind, Life, [and] Matter and lives in conscious relations with these things. He is then said to have cosmic consciousness.[62]

From a nonyoga point of view, it is normal for human beings to recognize as real only their physical, psychological, mental, and emotional life. The pure spiritual self is difficult to perceive, and most people affirm only the material-psychic-mental construction that we call "a person." They do not want to leave the warmth of the familiar image of themselves. This is true even when change may open up new possibilities for self-awareness, such as cosmic consciousness. It is usually easier, many people feel, to accept some pain than to revolutionize their understanding of what it means to *be*—to exist in the most profound way. People rationalize their lack of success; they escape through laughter and imagination—if not through drugs and alcohol; they learn to calculate any risk very carefully so as to avoid unnecessary pain.

From the perspective of spiritual insight, however, the acceptance of suffering and time-space limitations on human nature is an expression of the most profound ignorance. If people do not realize that they limit themselves by what they construct mentally and emotionally, they can never know the true (ultimate) self. In order to realize the true self, one should follow a spiritual discipline, such as yoga, which burns out the influence of one's past *karma* (forces of inertia resulting from past action) and produces liberation. Thus, one unbinds pure consciousness from its entanglements with conventional fears, frustrations, and ignorance.

Spiritual discipline is not merely theoretical. It is a practice, a technique, an exercise taught by those who have personally verified its usefulness. The seers of Hinduism and Buddhism have recognized that relatively few people are determined to plumb their depths and see directly the nature of existence. Nevertheless, all individuals have a potential for directly experiencing the truth—if not in this life, then in some subsequent life. If people would only direct their attention away from illusory satisfactions and concerns to their true nature, they would attain a growing detachment from pain, frustration, guilt, and meaninglessness—the fate most people assume to be natural. In the ancient Hindu spiritual texts called the *Upanishads,* the religious seer warns the seeker of truth to plumb a depth of the self that is beyond conventional pleasures and expectations:

> The Self is not to be sought through the senses. The Self-caused pierced the openings (of the senses) outward; therefore one looks outward and not within oneself. Some wise man, however, seeking life eternal, with his eyes turned inward, saw the self. . . .
>
> The small-minded go after outward pleasures. They walk into the snare of widespread death. The wise, however, recognizing life eternal do not seek the stable among things which are unstable here. . . .
>
> That by which one perceives both dream states and waking states, having known (that as) the great, omnipresent Self, the wise man does not grieve. . . .
>
> He who knows this Self, the experiencer, as the living spirit close at hand as the lord of the past and the future—one does not shrink away from Him. This, verily, is that.[63]

One difficulty, of course, is that the seeker after spiritual perfection must abandon the assumptions that most people feel are necessary for existence and meaning. To eliminate such assumptions is extremely difficult, but to use logic or everyday experience to see the dynamics, the brilliance, the perpetual explosion of life, say the accomplished meditators, is like trying to catch one's shadow. With each movement of the hand or any part of the body, the shadow changes shape, and when we put our fingers around the shadow, it enlarges in proportion to the width of our fingers. With the aid of regular spiritual practice under the guidance of a master who has perceived the truth, it is nevertheless possible to attain a superconscious awareness.

The discipline that leads to spiritual insight is a process that purifies a person's awareness in order to reveal ultimate reality. Progress toward perfection requires great moral effort, avoidance of false views, and regular meditation practice. As in the process of harmony with cosmic law, there is a recognition that every human action either benefits or harms a person. Thus, morality is of great importance, especially at the beginning stages of spiritual practice,[64] but lacks the ultimate transforming power it had in the process of harmony with cosmic law. Morality must be informed by the highest spiritual insight if it is to produce what adherents of this fourth process regard as ultimate transformation: the freedom from all form, all shifting of the mind.

Because morality is part of the discipline, it is not unusual to find extraordinary austerities, severe mental, psychological, and physical disciplines, and some cases of physical punishment or fasting until death. The effort toward purification through austere physical discipline is, for instance, a hallmark of Jainism. The following passage describes the austerities of Mahavira, who founded the historical tradition of Jainism, after he entered an order of ascetics:

[For] more than four months many sorts of living beings gathered on his body, crawled about it, and caused pain there.

For a year and a month he did not leave off his robe. Since that time the Venerable One, giving up his robe, was a naked, world-relinquishing, houseless (sage).

Then he meditated (walking) with his eye fixed on a square space before him of the length of a man. Many people assembled, shocked at the sight; they struck him and cried.

Knowing (and renouncing) the female sex in mixed gathering places, he meditated, finding his way himself: I do not lead a worldly life.

Giving up the company of all householders whomsoever, he meditated, Asked, he gave no answer; he went, and did not transgress the right path.[65]

While householders (laity) are to follow ethical rules and adepts are to practice austerities, these efforts are only adjuncts to the central dynamics of this process of ultimate transformation. In seeking mystical insight through spiritual discipline, the goal is not conformity to society's moral expectations or to natural biological and social patterns, as it is in the process of living in harmony with cosmic law. Instead, the goal is union with ultimate truth, which may be attained through knowledge of self and the practice of spiritual disciplines. Spiritual disciplines are techniques to free people from social habits and personal desires. Adherents of this process regard "cosmic law" as nothing more than a sometimes useful mental construct.

The process of mystical insight can also be compared to the process of sacred action. Those who seek mystical insight also use ideas, images, and feelings, but they use them to counter their conditioned habits, attitudes, and reflexes, not to enhance their experience of God. Indeed, the literature of Hinduism, Buddhism, and Jainism suggests a great concern to correct the false views that bind people to illusory images of themselves. The great spiritual merit Buddhists earn in chanting, hearing, and copying their sutras should not overshadow the fact that transcendental awareness is the goal of Buddhism. Visions may be part of the processes of sacred action and mystical insight, but there are differences in both vision and seer. A committed Buddhist meditator may experience visions of a celestial buddha or bodhisattva—a remarkable and rare experience. In the process of mystical insight through spiritual discipline, however, verbal or visual symbols are not of prime importance as they are in the process of sacred action. The adept in mystical insight relies on the symbols as pointers but realizes that they are mental and emotional fabrications that can also bind those who develop attachment to them. Symbols can be effective releasers of power in this process, as in the process of sacred action, but the power of mystical insight is not released in order to manifest a divine (sacred) reality as in a sacrament. Rather, spiritual power engendered in meditation releases the meditator from the forms that the devotee to myth and ritual assumes are eternal sacred revelations. Myth and ritual—from the standpoint of highest wisdom—is just another form of mental and emotional projection.

For those who adopt the process of mystical insight, it is the ultimate way by which people can realize their true potential. Religious rituals, myths, and emotions of love and faith can help direct people away from their self-imposed limitations but can also become limitations for those who regard them as ultimate rather than as catalysts for release from signs or symbols. The highest spiritual awareness can come only through direct, personal transcendence of the restricting and dead character of any philosophical idea or religious act. Knowledge of the deepest truth requires getting beneath the information about the world. To be free means to be free from one's information.

Within the process of attaining spiritual insight are different grades of advancement. In Muslim Sufism and Christian mysticism, as well as in the methods of Hindu yoga and Buddhist meditation, stages of advancement lead from the first steps of a new awareness through further steps of purification and rebirth in a new dimension of reality. While the disciplinary process is especially exacting and clearly defined in the beginning stages, the more accomplished a person becomes the more he or she must become disengaged from disciplinary techniques. This may sound strange at first, but no thought, perception, or activity can contain in itself the nature of truth; ultimate truth must be experienced by the individual as a release even from the techniques of knowing any "thing." Thus, the disciplinary process must be discarded as at best a vehicle that moves a person toward the ultimate. It, too, can become a chain of illusion that binds people rather than freeing them to fulfill the possibilities of their ultimate nature.

In the Hindu movement called Advaita Vedanta, for example, discipline helps a person dispel the illusion that the world consists of ultimately separate, and independent, physical or mental entities. However, to attain freedom *(moksha),* a person must see that even the act of dispelling illusion is a construction and an illusion. There can be no correction of that which really is. There is no illusory self separate from the absolute. The individual *in his illusion* thinks that he is not free; in reality, there is only freedom. The purpose of discipline, especially as a means of purification, is to bring the individual to this point of awareness. Thus, discipline is not an end in itself. The difficulty of prescribing a spiritual discipline that must be transcended led the Indian Mahayana Buddhists of some 2,000 years ago to say that the training for the highest wisdom, that is the path of the bodhisattva, was a teaching in which nothing was taught, a position that "stood" nowhere, and a training that made no distinction between nirvana and the shifting world of forms *(samsara).* Thus, the text called *The Perfection of Wisdom in Eight Thousand Lines* credits the following statement to the Buddha's accomplished disciple, Subhuti:

> Even so should a Bodhisattva stand and train himself. He should decide that "as the Tathagata [the Buddha] does not stand anywhere, nor not stand, nor stand apart, nor not stand apart, so will I stand." Just so should he train himself "as the Tathagata is stationed, so will I stand, and train myself." Just so should he train himself. "As the Tathagata is stationed so will I stand, well placed because *without* a place to stand on." Even so should a Bodhisattva stand and train himself. When he trains thus, he adjusts himself to perfect wisdom, and will never cease from taking it to heart.[66]

This way of striving to the point of "letting go," even of the path and the projected goal of spirituality, is emphasized in the Zen Buddhist use of *koans,* the riddles a Zen master gives to help a student break away from intellectual conventions and thus see directly or spontaneously. One of the most famous of these is: What is the sound of one hand clapping? In the Buddhist tradition, some of the most famous *koans* were recorded, commented on, and expressed in poetic verse, as in the following:

> Wu Tsu said: When you meet an enlightened man on the road, do not greet him with words & do not greet him with silence. Tell me: how do you greet him?
> *Comment:* If you can greet him deep & sharp, nothing can hinder your happiness. But if you can't, you had better start looking at everything.
> An enlightened man met on the road:
> do not greet him with words or silence
> punch his jaw & split his face
> he'll get the message.[67]

Among the Chinese Taoists there is also a clear expression of the need to "let go," to relax, in order to realize that ultimate reality is not attained by striving but is already implicit in the earliest effort. Some comments in the ancient Taoist text, the *Tao-te ching* (Revered book of the way and its character) suggest that the *Tao*, the ultimate reality that is also the "way," works quietly and effortlessly but effectively:

> Who can find repose in a muddy world?
> By lying still, it becomes clear.
> Who can maintain his calm for long?
> By activity, it comes back to life.
> He who embraces this Tao
> Guards against being over-full.
> Because he guards against being over-full,
> He is beyond wearing out and renewal.[68]

Thus, in the course of training in the Taoist brotherhood, "meditation" is a growing relaxation from artificial conventions of thought and action. Growth and understanding do not mean intellectual comprehension of the forces within a person, nor living according to prescribed rules, but opening oneself to spontaneous living. The goal is "actionless activity" (*wu wei*). A sage is one who does not interfere with the natural flow of the *Tao*.

Spiritual discipline requires compliance with strict moral rules; it often includes intellectual wrestling with doctrines and beliefs and some form of initiation rites. Nevertheless, these techniques are regarded only as means. Should they become identified with the truth, religious words and actions may become great chains that bind a person to that which is less than the ultimate. Thus, spiritual exercises must be done with care and alertness.

It is important to place oneself under a master who can give guidance and encouragement in times of difficulty and who can stimulate insight. At the same time, the master always points beyond his or her phenomenal intellect and abilities. While the student shows great honor and respect to the master and places complete trust in him or her, the student must ultimately cultivate the reality within, not merely take over the ideas and activities of the master. From the standpoint of spiritual discipline, ultimate reality is not something far off; it is already here. The importance of spiritual discipline is that it dispels people's blindness to this fact. It allows reality to become manifest; it releases people from their self-imposed smallness.

Transcendent Consciousness in the Moment of Mystical Experience

The purpose of spiritual discipline is to attain spiritual insight. This often involves forming a new image of life or destroying old images of life in an ecstatic moment of transcendent consciousness, variously referred to as *samadhi* in yoga; nirvana, *bodhi,* or *shunyata* in Indian Buddhism; *satori* in Zen, and *unio mystica* in Catholicism—to name a few.[69] This consciousness is regarded as the highest type of awareness and as the validation of the notions presupposed in the spiritual practice. Such moments often have a dramatic and colorful character, which piques the interest of curiosity seekers and is thus the best known aspect of all the religious phenomena collected under the concept of mysticism. Their religious significance however, lies not in the *form(s)* of experience but in the revelation of a universe of spiritual, psychic, intellectual, and physical power that preexists any form.

Such power is inexpressible in conventional language. Even talk about a consciousness of "something" obscures the revolutionizing experience of the spontaneous flow of ultimate reality. The effort to know ultimate truth may lead to an experience of spontaneous awareness or, in theistic terms, grace. Such an awareness has been put into several metaphors and symbols. Three of these are union, illumination, and freedom.

Union is an especially appropriate description of the revolutionizing experience that occurs when people overcome the spiritual poverty caused by their separation from the source of life. In this metaphor, the spiritual goal is to return to the original identity found in the single source of all beings. For example, the well-known Christian mystic Meister Eckhart spoke of God's being as inherent in all things; even more forcefully, he said that the Father begets his Son in the individual person's soul. Thus, the Father begets his own nature in the person. Similarly, the Advaita Vedanta seer Shankara claimed that all phenomenal "things" are, in essence, the eternal Brahman. For him, the most profound spiritual truth was that "I" *(atman)* and "divine being" are one.

Although both Meister Eckhart and Shankara insisted that all existing things are derived from one source and thus find their ultimate fulfillment in a reunification with this source, there are important differences in their views. One is that while Shankara claimed that unity can be realized in this life, Eckhart felt that man can never entirely escape his limitations as a creature. There was, said Eckhart, a "little point" in the process of the soul's reunion with God at which the creature recognized his creatureliness and therefore could not sink completely into the divine void.

There is a basic distinction between a theistic form of mysticism and an impersonal form of mysticism. The former emphasizes the absolute character of God before whom the devotee surrenders his or her ego and lives as completely as possible in response to the love and grace of God. In the latter, ultimate reality is seen to be beyond any image of divine personality. According to the advocates of Advaita Vedanta Hinduism or Zen Buddhism, those who cannot give up the image of a personal God are imposing on ultimate reality the distinctions between persons made in everyday experience. Only insight can dispel this ignorance by revealing the original undifferentiated whole.

The notions of enlightenment (illumination) represent another basic image in the attempt to articulate the nature of mystic consciousness. Enlightenment removes the blinders that have prevented people from seeing themselves and the world as they really are. It is meaningful especially where ignorance or spiritual blindness is the basic spiritual illness. The name "Buddha," for example, means "the enlightened one." In the moment of enlightenment, a person awakens as if out of unconsciousness.[70] The enlightened person, however, not only sees the light but becomes the light—and thereby gains the power to show the "suchness" of things. The illumination is like that of the sun, which brings forth new life and causes a new world to appear.[71]

The process of illumination can be described in several ways. One image is the uncovering of reality behind existence. This emphasizes the removal of some obstacle between the seer and what is seen. A second image is the improvement of sight so that the truth is experienced spontaneously and naturally. Related to the latter image is the notion of a "third eye of illumination." This eye is symbolically located at a point between the eyebrows and is regarded as a faculty that perceives without falsely discriminating—as is unfortunately the case with the two physical eyes. Whatever the description, illumination releases a power for ultimate transformation of the individual.

Freedom is a basic religious image used to express the new reality experienced through spiritual insight. It is especially meaningful where the basic image of the human spiritual problem is bondage; it is often used in Hindu yoga and in Buddhist meditation. Spiritual insight is the power to liberate the self. The phenomenal "I" or "me," as experienced in everyday life, is constructed with mental and emotional patterns that cause fear, greed, and anxiety. Spiritual insight informs people of the mental and emotional prisons they have constructed, but even more important, this knowledge has transforming power to free people from the bondage that they normally impose on themselves.

To be free means to have the capacity to use one's creative potential in love, judgment, understanding, and vitality. People usually cannot make use of their potential because they are attached to their anxieties. They are attached to their anxieties because they are bound by superficial goals, values, and self-images. Where there is freedom, there is the capacity for faith, for there is also the capacity for doubt. Human beings have the capacity to make mistakes freely, and thus a capacity to act "correctly" spontaneously. To live spontaneously in an open, noncompulsive relationship with all existing things is to be free.

The Art of Living

The moment of insight changes the mystic's perspective toward the meaning of existence. The subsequent way of life, however, depends on whether the mystic finds the "real" on a completely transcendent plane or in the everyday events of the world. There are some expressions, in Hindu and Christian devotional mysticism, for example, in which the ecstatic experience, the beatific vision, is regarded as the highest attainment. In this case, life in the world is considered a burden to be dropped as soon as possible. The act of contemplation or blissful experience is the highest good. Also, in such religious traditions as classical Hindu yoga or Jainism, the eternal self *(purusha* or *jiva)* within people is regarded as bound by worldly fabrication and the highest goal is to release the eternal self from this bondage. In such cases, any return to "normal" experience is regressive.

In contrast to this withdrawal orientation, some mystics recognize that avoidance of life can leave a person as much in bondage as participation in it. For example, in the meditative schools of Chinese Taoism and in some schools of Mahayana Buddhism, such as Zen, the goal is a new *way of life*. The *sheng jen* (holy sage, "man with a calling") or the *siddha* (spiritually perfected saint) holds that spiritual discipline is a guide to maturity. At the point of transcendent consciousness, such a spiritual master realizes the nature of truth and from that point on seeks to express spontaneously what he or she is. New sensitivities and new relationships with the environment well up when a person applies the new knowledge of self to everyday experience. Living becomes an art rather than a task. That is to say, life is self-consciously fabricated or composed into events or patterns that have ultimate significance. When the spiritual master manifests truth in daily living, he or she becomes the truth.

In such religious exemplars as the Zen master Hui-neng of the seventh to eighth century and the twentieth-century Hindu *yogin* Sri Aurobindo, mystical insight has led to a fuller, more spontaneous participation in life. According to them, a person's personality, everyday activities, and experiences are not regarded as bad in themselves. They, too, can be used as means for expressing the truth in particular and concrete situations. In fact, their view of reality requires living life out fully and completely, since it is as real as anything can be. When people lower their self-imposed psychological and intellectual barriers, the divine or potential activity takes form within their lives spontaneously. A person who lives free from bondage to the world is one who lives free to enjoy all facets of worldly experience. The spiritually perfected person is indeed aware of the deception in the conventions, fads, and styles of life to which the ignorant look for meaning. At the same time, such a person can use these conventions in order to communicate with other people, and yet remain free from their binding power because he or she knows their relative character. In being free, one is exposing the true nature of things.

To ask: "What is this true nature of things?" is to have missed the point of practicing a spiritual discipline and attaining insight. The instruction at the beginning of the meditation process includes metaphysical statements on which the practice of spiritual life is based, but at the end these must be recognized as only relatively true. The different conceptual formulations found, for example, in early Buddhism, Jainism, yoga, or Advaita Vedanta can be learned and analyzed as philosophical systems, but the accomplished saints know that these are only signals to be used and then discarded.

The spiritual master, then, uses everyday language and eats and sleeps as a normal person, but living is a self-conscious art. Perfected beings are not limited in the experience of joy or in depth, because they are no longer deceived by the limitations of the world, but accept it as a part of full existence. The conventional absolutes that govern preenlightenment human experience and divide the world into "things," such as "you" or "me," and "right" or "wrong," no longer pull them from side to side, press in, and close off possibilities for life and action. Faith and doubt are seen as parts of the same process and are necessarily reciprocal for those who are fully aware that their lives are part of the dynamic process of change. The world, then, is not a "thing" to be observed; it is a dynamic power to be participated in by creating every concrete moment spontaneously out of the depths of one's being.

In conclusion, some of the key points to remember about mystical insight through spiritual discipline are: (1) the importance of the notion that people have ultimate reality within themselves (such as the Buddha-nature of Brahman); (2) discipline, though difficult for most people, releases them from the conventions and compulsions that produce suffering and illusion; (3) the simplest and most profound problems are self-made and can be solved if one's spiritual blindness does not obscure one's ultimate reality; (4) while several religious traditions use various techniques for spiritual discipline and describe transcendent state of consciousness differently, the goal of all people using this process of transformation is release from the attachment to physical and social conditioning, and (5) these ultimate states of consciousness influence people's moment-by-moment experiences in everyday life.

SELECTED READINGS

*E. Underhill, *Mysticism* (New York: Dutton, 1961, first published in 1911). This is still regarded by many as the classic exposition of mysticism. It emphasizes the goal of union with absolute reality through personal, introspective awareness.

R. M. Jones, *New Studies in Mystical Religion* (New York: Macmillan, 1928). A series of lectures that analyze the relationship of mystical awareness to psychology, personal discipline, and institutional religious forms, showing what this awareness might mean in the context of twentieth century Western society.

General introductions to mysticism most often emphasize the disciplined effort of the individual mystic to be reunited with the one eternal reality. Representative of this interpretation are J. Politella, *Mysticism and the Mystical Consciousness Illustrated from the Great Religions* (Kent, Ohio: Kent State University Bulletin, 1964); W. T. Stace, *The Teachings of the Mystics* (New York: New American Library, 1960); and *S. Spencer, *Mysticism in World Religion* (Baltimore, Md.: Penguin, 1963).

Two important studies of comparisons in mystical awareness by noted scholars are *R. Otto, *Mysticism: East and West* (New York: Meridian, 1957, first published 1932), and *D. T. Suzuki, *Mysticism: Christian and Buddhist* (New York: Collier, 1962, first published 1957).

Students who want to interpret Eastern awareness in terms of the psychological framework of the Eastern theories of man can profitably read Swami Akhilananda, *Hindu Psychology* (London: Routledge & Kegan Paul, 1948); Lama Anagarika Govinda, *The Psychological Attitude of Early Buddhist Philosophy* (London: Rider, 1961); and R. E. A. Johansson, *The Psychology of Nirvana* (Garden City, N.Y.: Doubleday, 1970). Comparisons between Eastern spiritual therapies and Western psychological therapies are found in G. Coster, *Yoga and Western Psychology: A Comparison* (London: Oxford University Press, 1934); H. Jacobs, *Western Psychotherapy and Hindu Sadhana* (London: George Allen & Unwin, 1961); and *D. T. Suzuki, E. Fromm, and R. DeMartino, *Zen Buddhism and Psychoanalysis* (New York: Grove, 1960).

Three studies of Buddhist meditation processes and the theoretical framework used for getting beyond everyday thoughts and activities are *P. Kapleau, *The Three Pillars of Zen* (New York: Harper, 1966) (see especially Part I, Sections 1 and 3); *D. T. Suzuki, *Zen Buddhism,* edited by Wm. Barrett (New York: Doubleday, 1956), Chapters 1, 4, and 6; and *F. J. Streng, *Emptiness: A Study in Religious Meaning* (Nashville, Tenn.: Abingdon, 1967) (see especially Chapters 6, 9, 10, and 11).

F. J. Streng, C. L. Lloyd, Jr., and J. T. Allen, *Ways of Being Religious,* Chapter 4, "Spiritual Freedom through Discipline (Mysticism)," gives excerpts from advocates, sympathetic interpreters, and critics of this way of being religious.

Part III

MODES OF
HUMAN AWARENESS
USED TO EXPRESS
RELIGIOUS MEANING

Part II described four traditional models or ideal types of religious life. The emphasis in Part III will be on the transforming possibilities of experience in this world.

In both traditional societies and in the modern, technologically oriented West, some people have been sensitive to important dimensions of their lives—rational thought, social responsibility, human relationships, beauty, and an awareness of time and the physical world—as means for an authentic existence. Similarly, some social reformers, artists, and scientists have claimed that the ultimate power of life is to be found in resources other than those of the traditional religions.

Although these dimensions and claims have been found to be less than ultimate by many adherents of traditional religions, they have been used by these adherents to communicate traditional religious meanings. The observation that traditional religious feelings and sensitivities can be expressed in secular ways does not go far enough, however. In the modern world, some people assert that the skills and procedures developed in these human dimensions can become religious processes of self-discovery. The study of the dynamics of religion in various processes of ultimate transformation shows that traditional ways of being religious (Part II) are not just extensions of human capacities and that humanistic ways (Part III) are not just extensions of traditional religious assumptions and activities. Both the traditional and the humanistic ways are proper subjects of an objective and comparative study of religion.

Just as Part II focused on ways of being religious, rather than on different religious traditions, so Part III will be concerned with some key aspects of the internal dynamics of various ideologies, institutions, and experiences, rather than with such contemporary movements as communism, existentialism, or cubism per se. Part II, however, analyzed, explained, and interpreted various elements of the processes found within those institutions and traditions commonly regarded as religious. Part III examines various aspects and uses of the dimensions of human life to show their particular capacity for expressing human experience, to describe how they are sometimes useful vehicles for expressing religious concerns, and to indicate why some people regard them as means for ultimate transformation. Although some people may use human sensitivities in a religious way—either to express transcendent reality or achieve a humanistic ultimate transformation—others may find no religious meaning in them at all.

The problem, then, is to decide when one of these dimensions or modes of human awareness is religious for a person or group and when it is not. Not all forms of social life, thought, relationship, art, and science are religious even in a nontraditional setting. The modes are religious to the extent that the individuals involved connect them with some institution, experience, attitude, or thought that they regard as ultimate. To the extent these modes do not have ultimate value for an individual or group, they are nonreligious.

Modes of human awareness function religiously in at least two ways: within and outside traditional religions. First, within a religious tradition, they may express an ultimate reality that completely transcends them. In this way, music, visual arts, thought, and social institutions are *forms* through which the ultimate (regarded by adherents as a transcendent reality) becomes immanent or is revealed in everyday existence. The singing of a hymn, the study of a theological claim, or the effort to implement *dharma* in daily life can express the aesthetic, rational, and social dimensions of life within a religious tradition. These forms are also ways of apprehending and manifesting a traditional religion and expressing a transcendent reality—the mysterious, ineffable, cosmic, or divine reality, however it may be defined. From the perspective of those within a given religious tradition, ultimate reality is the source of the cultural or historical forms within which it is hidden, but the forms are also the product of conditioned, secular factors of life. Many people with traditional religious orientations are concerned that an emphasis on the modes of human awareness is a secularizing process. Thus, believers have from time to time called artists, philosophers, and social workers deviants from the true path.

Secondly, such modes of awareness as art, social reform, rational reflection, and the attempt to improve physical life can function religiously outside traditional religious institutions as means of ultimate transformation. They are processes whereby human beings order their lives, find enjoyment, and understand themselves. In each of the next five chapters, at least one section will show how social-political institutions, reason, interpersonal relations, art, and science serve as a means for the highest fulfillment in life.

The difference between those who adhere to traditional ways of being religious and those who use various modes of human awareness as means of ultimate transformation is basically one of attitude toward the criterion for authenticity. Adherents of traditional ways have a deep concern for applying the ultimate dimension of life to everyday existence, but their ultimate dimension originates and culminates in a nonworldly reality. They approach ultimate questions from the standpoint of a transcendent reality and find resources for solutions in transhuman power: a holy presence breaking into personal experience, sacred (or essential) archetypes, eternal order, and spiritual bliss. Those who use an aesthetic or rational mode of awareness as the prime means to learn the truth about themselves and the world do not appeal to a transcendent source. Nevertheless, a mode of awareness can function as an ultimate dimension if it is the basic determinant of meaning or behavior. Thus, the modes of human awareness can be either adjuncts to traditional religious processes or the means of ultimate transformation for those not recognizing a transcendent reality. In both cases, of course, people make choices according to their capacities to know and express the truth.

To understand that art, reason, or human relationships can lead to religious fulfillment, the researcher must be open to the claim that some dimensions of reality can be apprehended only through these or other modes of human awareness. That is, when people become aware of their aesthetic sensitivity, their ability to use reason, and so forth, they become conscious of their capacity for "becoming" as a human being. "Being human" is something different from just "being." The world is not made only of "things," but also of ideas, art, architecture, cities, and images of oneself and the cosmos. To exist as a human being means to interpret existence. Human existence is not just "there"; nor is it just the sum of all experience. To be human means to make judgments, to select, and then to construct meaning about one's personal experiences and those of other people and about the past and the future.

The strongest advocates of humanistic religion see humanity today as not fully mature but with considerable potential. They believe that people must put away such childish fantasies as a heaven after death or a nirvana, and the adolescent-like anxiety over the lack of human capacities to meet life's challenges. For example, the moral philosopher Kai Nielsen puts it this way:

> To be free of impossible expectations people must clearly recognize that there is no 'One big thing' or, for that matter, 'small thing' which would make them permanently happy; almost anything permanently and exclusively pursued will lead to that nausea that Sartre has so forcefully brought to our attention. But we can, if we are not too sick and if our situation is not too precarious, find lasting sources of human happiness in a purely secular world. [72]

The greatest human need, then, is to find meaning, joy, and fulfillment in the here and now—a life that is not informed by the hope of resurrection, caught fast in the rhythm of an eternal moral law, or emptied of meaning by the lack of durable mental and emotional relationships. The ultimate here is not what a few extraordinary teachers, guides, prophets, and authorities regard as eternal; it is the meaning the human being finds in life itself.

Instead of seeking final or absolute answers to life's problems, people should use their capacities as fully as possible in the present. This does not mean that the status quo is fully acceptable. It means that human beings must learn to eliminate pain, injustice, anxiety, boredom—even death—by making conscious decisions, learning from their mistakes, and transcending arbitrary or accidental failures. Human life is not something static, whose quality has been set for all time. "True spirituality" is the use of presently available techniques of human—which traditional religious advocates call "secular"—development. Julian Huxley, a renowned advocate of humanist religion, urges all people to participate in what he calls "transhumanism." He writes:

> The new understanding of the universe has come about through the new knowledge amassed in the last hundred years—by psychologists, biologists, and other scientists, by archaeologists, and historians. It has defined man's responsibility and destiny—to be an agent for the rest of the world in the job of realizing its inherent potentialities as fully as possible. . . . Whether he wants to or not, whether he is conscious of what he is doing or not, he *is* in point of fact determining the future direction of evolution on this earth. This is his inescapable destiny, and the sooner he realizes it and starts believing in it, the better for all concerned.[73]

Freedom from absolute ideals or eternal values does not necessarily result in the elimination of responsibility, hope, or the need to decide what is and is not meaningful.

The political, rational, interpersonal, aesthetic, and physical ways of ordering existence are discussed in separate chapters below because each has become a different means of exploring truth. Knowledge today has become fragmented and specialized. Although these modes of awareness have been integrated into the religious and cultural outlook of nonliterate and, to a considerable extent, traditional societies, in modern societies, they are specialized disciplines, with skills and techniques based on different values, emphases, and evidence. Art and science, for example, are often viewed as antagonistic ways of approaching truth. Those who accept historical and scientific inquiry as the basic means of structuring human awareness and revealing ultimate reality believe that it allows people to transform life from a meaningless, crude, frustrated, and unhappy experience to one of significance, creativity, excitement, and growth. On the other hand, those who seek ultimate reality through aesthetic experience might argue that scientific and historical values are not the only ones that can ultimately transform human life.

9.

The Religious Significance of Social Responsibility

People grow up with the recognition of *social*—as well as aesthetic, rational, and physical—limitations and possibilities. Part of the maturing process is acquiring the sense that individuals are partially regulated by their interactions with other people. As part of a community, a person can do some things, but not others, and learns that there is a difference between good and bad.

Social relationships provide channels for expressing human values, especially particular patterns of values that we call "morality" or "ethics." Moral actions expose a dimension of *human* existence that other types of mental or physical action do not. They deal with rights and obligations in relation to others—a situation in which the term "justice" has particular significance. While people have interpreted the nature of "the good," moral order, or human capacities differently, they have acquired a part of their self-awareness in relation to a particular society in which certain customs, obligations, restrictions, and ideals mold the meaning of life. Just as people are dependent on the concepts and language patterns in their intellectual environment for verbal communication, so they are dependent on the moral habits (such as honesty, justice, obligations to government) of their society in learning how to act.

The close relationship between religion and social interaction has long been recognized by students of religion. Indeed, Chapter 3 indicated the relevance of sociological studies of religion, and Chapter 7 described the central character of one traditional way of being religious as living out the prescriptions of an eternal order in everyday activity. This chapter will focus on the fact that moral relationship to other human beings can be a means of ultimate transformation within a variety of historical religious expressions, as well as outside religious communities. For the latter, there need be neither transcendent, absolute law nor God's law, but only a recognition of the value of human life in terms of man's rights to equal political and economic opportunities. In this context, the full development of social-ethical relationships provides a person with religious significance; these relationships are the vehicle for becoming an authentic human being.

Ethics as a Mode of Becoming Human

What dimension of human existence makes ethics possible? As a member of a community—whether a family, clan, city, religious society, or state—one asks the question: "What shall I do?" in relation to other people. However, not only is each person related to other individuals; he or she also reacts to a third reality made of the purpose or ideal of human life. The ideal may be embodied in forefathers, great seers, or a future universal ideal of humanity. This third reality often provides the norm for action and reflects the basis on which all actions are judged.

The patterns of proper action by which people identify themselves vary from culture to culture, and they undergo change in human history. Sometimes there is a tension between the different patterns of social-ethical response within a society. An individual who believes that the community's activities are causing spiritual death may seek to form a new community of like-minded people. The new community may become a religious community, such as a monastic group or a commune, and separate itself from the rest of society both physically and morally. Such communities in East and West have offered individuals opportunities to abandon what they regarded as a decaying society in order to cultivate a different life. This chapter will consider the character of religiousness in three approaches to ethical imperative: divine will, right knowledge, and political and economic means of ultimate transformation.

In a society that recognizes God's will as preserved in divine laws, morality is often combined with a cultic expression of corporate prayer, services of praise, and seasonal festivals. The value of a person's activity is often measured against the ideal expressed by the patriarch, seer, or founder of the community. Thus, the lives of Abraham, Jesus, and Muhammed are the true expression of God's will and purpose for "his people." Community members imitate the goodness of God (to the best of their ability) and live according to divine prescriptions that help define what is a good life. In this orientation, ethics has functioned within the traditional framework of organized religious structures.

The acceptance of a given society's ideals and rules constitutes another kind of ethical involvement, one that may not require an organized religious sturcture. This alternative can be expressed in various ways. It is seen in the pre-Socratic Greek philosophers who advocated that human beings accept their fate *(moira)* and endure with a stout heart the inequalities and injustices that are recognized by all—since this is the way things are. It is also seen—though in a radically more positive light—in the value found in living according to one's *dharma* in orthodox Hinduism, or in the Confucian ideal of living according to the natural distinctions found in the *Tao*. In this orientation, there is no suggestion that human beings are irreparably evil or cannot be morally perfect. As a fragment of an eternal orderly process, people have the full potential to live in social harmony. The morality of an action is judged in relation to an individual's role in a cosmic harmony; there is no question about *legislating* or creating goodness, but only about administering or exposing it.

A third orientation bases morality on the human capacity to have rights and responsibilities in relation to others. Proper relationships are not determined by a transcendent order or eternal paradigm; they are determined by recognition of the human capacity to seek rational goals, that is, to set goals, assess their values, and construct social mechanisms, such as legislatures and courts of justice, to implement the ideals. A basic notion in this orientation is that all people regardless of birth or religious views have legal *rights*. If people recognize that they have rights simply because they are human, they must recognize that this human quality extends to other people as well. Thus, rights automatically become *obligations*. A person's claim to rights implies that others are obliged to recognize those rights and that they, in turn, have rights that place obligations on anyone else. Of course, in a society built on an established social hierarchy, the rights and obligations operating *within* a stratum may not extend to members of other strata. On the other hand, the concept that every human being has certain natural rights that society is expected to guarantee establishes a new context in which to consider ethical relationships. This concept can exist without reference to an organized religion and may even constitute a "religious" expression in its own right.

Ethics as an Implementation of Divine Will

One way of identifying oneself as an ethical being is to recognize that the social-political order should embody a transcendent eternal law. Chapter 7 pointed out some of the characteristic religious elements that pertain to harmony with cosmic law. This eternal law should not be confused with governmental legislation nor even with a particular type of government. For example, in the Brahminical understanding of *dharma,* the purpose of social life and political government was to *administer* the eternal law, not to *legislate* social life according to the will of the people. Similarly in China, the Confucian cultivation of true humanity sought to bring forth such virtues as filial piety, wisdom, and honesty as reflections of the universal moral order. The emperor was supposed to be the chief example for all society as the connection between heaven and earth. His failure to adminster justice and provide peace and minimal prosperity constituted grounds for rejecting his rule. However, there was no question about which form of government best provided benefits for the governed; the only question was whether a given ruler adequately fulfilled his duty.

Where people respond to divine revelation, ethics takes the form of implementing God's will in everyday life. The revelation becomes the focus of creating a community of God's people and is celebrated in the rehearsal of his will and redeeming activity. People in such a community are related to each other through their being called by God. Social patterns are derived from an interpretation of the special revelatory experience.

Jews, Christians, and Muslims ideally acquire knowledge of good and evil while apprehending the awesome, but loving, character of the Lord. The divine law is an expression of God's care, just as his mercy manifests his patience and love. Human morality, then, is a response to God. A person who trusts in God's justice as the source of good and punishment of evil must reconcile this trust with the evident lack of righteousness in the world. One way to deal with the problem is to predict that even though sinners may escape immediate punishment, their descendants will suffer for the sins, or retribution will come in a future life—as portrayed in the

Hebrew book of *Job*—but in the last analysis the logic of morality is shattered in the apprehension of the Holy One, whose ways are inscrutable.

The attempt to live adequately in the light of God's law and love has resulted in varied ethical interpretations by the members of every religious community. One problem common to all theistic communities is whether divine power is best reflected in the given social patterns of a culture or in the personal faith and decisions of believers. The former pattern stresses cultural values and emphasizes the consequences of social behavior for the total communal life. In the latter, purity of heart, clarity of conscience, and right motives are the foci of attention.

The former ethical alternative is typified by the medieval Roman Catholic Church and by the Sunni Muslims, who saw the caliphate as the political form of God's will. The Roman Catholic Church found God's will both in natural law, which governs human relations, and in revealed truth, whereby humanity is related to God through grace. The medieval theologian Thomas Aquinas, for example, claimed that European society ideally should expose God's law; human institutions were to embody the eternal order. Both secular life and the church were realms of the Christian life, each having its proper role in establishing God's law.

In Sunni Islam, all social and political life derives, ideally, from divine revelation. Until the twentieth century, there was no separation of secular and religious law in the Muslim community. The law *(fiqh)* that prescribed social actions was based on the *Qur'an* and traditions of the Prophet *(sunnah)*. Among the Sunnites, four schools or systems of the *fiqh* were accepted for interpreting moral action. From the handbooks of these schools and from the expositions of the religious scholars *(mufti),* orthodox Muslims learned what they must do. It was the responsibility of the Muslim ruler *(khalifah* or *imam)* to administer this ethic.

The ethical perspective that stresses moral actions originating in purity of the heart is exemplified in the Jewish prophetic tradition and the Psalms. Here, human moral action is seen as justified by the holiness of God. God's communion with the Patriarchs should lead each generation to teach its descendants how to act. In relationships with others, a person should reflect God's care for the world; then blessings will abound. Ideally, moral duty is not obedience to an external law, but an obligation placed in the human heart. The psalmist's ideal of "a pure heart" *(Psalm* 24:4) is the point at which knowledge of God and decision meet in human life. A person's moral duty is to witness to the Lord's holiness and blessing. We see this concern, for example, in the daily life of the Jewish community in America, which abounds in welfare and social agencies to care for community problems. On a more personal level as well, the fellowship of the tradition means that Jews coming into a strange city for the first time need only make themselves known to members of the local Jewish community to find an immediate "family" relationship and a concern for their personal needs. This deep social identification also produces religious scholars, historians, and novelists who dedicate their entire lives to the preservation of the Jewish tradition.

With such an emphasis on outward action as the result of inner divine motivation, it is not surprising that the Jewish tradition stresses the importance of an ethical life. The ideal is for a person to express personal religious motives in practical moral activity. It was proclaimed by the prophet Micah (6:8):

> He has showed you, O man, what is good;
>   and what does the Lord require of you
> but to do justice, and to love kindness,
>   and to walk humbly with your God?

People, then, cannot be deceitful, unjust, or unkind without polluting the divine power at work in their hearts. Where the Holy One impinges on humanity, there one has a moral obligation that must be fulfilled, lest one break the covenant with God and become guilty.

The emphasis on personal obligation was also seen in the Reformation of Western Christianity. Appeals were made directly to man's conscience as moved by the Holy Spirit. While not all Reformation movements led to social and political change, the German reformer Martin Luther regarded every moral secular calling as a possible field for a full Christian life. This eliminated the special virtues of religious orders vis-à-vis a secular life. Protestant groups, emulating John Calvin's efforts to establish a Christian society through local political action, emphasized the individual's responsibility for positive involvement in social institutions. Likewise, John Wesley, reacting against formalism in the Anglican Church, worked for a revitalization of the Christian's inner life to bring about a self-conscious life of social responsibility. Perhaps the most dramatic expression of the Protestant Christian ethical imperative is seen in the ''social gospel'' movement in England and America, especially during the first three decades of the twentieth century. The social gospel was a program of secular social reform that sought to give practical expression in political and economic areas of life to the Christian experience of redemption. Not only did it lead to the development of social services within Christian churches, but it also led to cooperation between church bodies on moral issues and aided the growth of such religious social agencies as the Salvation Army, the Young Men's Christian Association, and the Young Women's Christian Association.

Ethics and Right Knowledge

While the masses of society have found security in following the customs and social standards dictated by the past, or those prescribed by living political-religious authorities, there have been skeptics in the East and West who have questioned the value of their contemporary social rules. For example, in Greece in the fifth century B.C., some philosophers claimed that the customs and social authority commonly accepted were only artificial restraints imposed on personal freedom. In the following century, this view was elaborated by Antisthenes, a student of Socrates, and was continued by the group of philosophers eventually known as the Cynics. They claimed that popular convention was no basis on which to judge right and wrong and that people should fix their attention on "the requirements of Nature." They did not regard even commonly accepted moral positions as an eternal good; nor would they recognize any validity in the self-serving distinction between Greeks and barbarians. Thus, the facts of noble birth and precedence were not sufficient justification for authority and value.

A pure skepticism was unacceptable to some Greek thinkers, notably Socrates, Plato, and Aristotle. These men, however, did share the skeptics' view that the existence of something did not justify its acceptance as an eternal value. Similarly, they shared the pre-Christian Greek recognition that moral action is intrinsically connected with correct knowledge. To act virtuously a person must *know* the truth—even if that truth is only a recognition of ignorance. Knowledge for Socrates meant practical wisdom—as distinct from a mystic intuition. He believed it was possible to know virtue by analyzing various spheres of action and to teach it. The object of moral concern is the good, but to know the good requires an analysis of the conditions in which it can be expressed. Thus, laws that help to effect the good do so because they are reasonable and they should be followed because they bring about useful effects rather than because they are divine commands.

Similarly, Plato held that virtue cannot be identified with custom or political authority; rather, virtue is dependent on knowledge. Knowledge is available through contact with the "supreme ideas" that transcend every particular expression of them. There was, therefore, a gap between the appearances of actual existence and transcendent reality. In the sphere of ethics, Plato distinguished between the everyday rules of civil and political life and the virtue of the philosopher. The former could be expressed in the conduct of a statesman by moral effort, while the latter could be attained only by inquiring into the nature of absolute virtue. In the last analysis, the survival of society depended on its ability to discover ultimate ends.

The concern to define virtue and law in terms of ultimate ends was continued by Aristotle. His *Politics,* however, reflects a deep concern for administration, which is supposed to provide opportunities, especially for property-owning males (the "aristocrats"), to live noble lives. Women and slaves, he thought, had shown an incapacity to use such opportunities profitably. Nevertheless, he believed that moral relationships promised a noble and full life for those who could perceive values above wealth and power. The state existed to prevent some members of this upper class from exploiting other members.

Like the Greek philosophers, the Buddha and his followers emphasized that moral action is not valuable unless it is related to a radical mental and spiritual reassessment of life. The Buddhists, however, went further in emphasizing that social morality is important as part of a program for emancipating human beings from worldly illusion and sorrow. While the Greek philosophers thought that their knowledge applied to conventional everyday affairs and depended on rational distinctions, the Buddha claimed that the goal of life was not to express a universal moral ideal, but to achieve freedom from all mental and emotional bondage. Also, the Greek philosophers, especially Plato and Aristotle, regarded state and society as the framework in which to realize the noble life; the Buddha and his followers in

South Asia believed that political and social life should support the ultimate effort to be free from worldly sorrow but could not express the highest state of freedom. Because of these latter two considerations, Theravada Buddhism has sometimes been regarded as a community that remains aloof from social ethics. Nevertheless, although social ethics are relative to the goal of freedom from sorrow, they are a vital part of what it means to follow the path of the Buddha.

Verse 183 of the *Dhammapada* (one of the most widely read Theravada Buddhist scriptures) reads: "Not to commit any sin, to do good, and to purify one's own mind: that is the teaching of (all) the Buddhas." This suggests that morality is not a trifling matter. At the same time, moral action is intrinsically bound up with mental-psychic training. Other teachings elaborate the view that "sin" arises from human greed ("craving"), which is produced by mental and moral actions *(karma)* as long as people delude themselves by accepting the conventions of life as eternal truths. The origin of "sin" does not lie in something external to human life, such as a devil, but is a product of human greed and ignorance. Similarly, virtue is not simply obeying certain social prescriptions; it is living in such a way as to free oneself from all the limitations of mind and emotion.

In this light, the highest virtue is to teach the *dhamma* (truth, law) of the Buddha. This was the "social responsibility" that the Buddha accepted after he attained enlightenment in Northeast India. This teaching includes following certain rules of morality, such as refraining from taking life, stealing, and lying, as well as perfecting such virtues as charity, wisdom, and forbearance. These ethical prescriptions emphasize personal and interpersonal ethics and stress that the individual should change within if outward actions are to have any spiritual meaning. While it is true that personal perfection does not require the development of a system of political ethics—as Aristotle advocated—the welfare of society requires that the Buddha's *dhamma* be taught and that the state protect and support "perfected beings" and those seeking perfection. Again, unlike Aristotle's view, any member of society can work toward perfection and should be accorded respect—not on the basis of birth, but because of spiritual and moral attainment.

Political and Economic Life as the Means for Ultimate Transformation

Where the everyday affairs of politics and economics are not central to the realization of the highest human potential, or where prevailing customs and governmental structures are viewed as unchangeable laws, people often do not feel responsible for improving the general welfare. However, when people see that living conditions contribute significantly to a profound self-awareness in their relations with others, "good government" and "economic productivity" become foci for the growth of the human spirit. Justice, equality before the law, and freedom are goals worth living and dying for.

Social reformers and some revolutionaries assume that all people have the capacity for moral integrity. For them, the basic problem of life is social injustice implicit or explicit in political and economic institutions. They feel that a transformation of inhumane social and political institutions is the most direct way to correct life's deepest problems. A solution to these problems requires, first, a perception of how economic and political structures create human suffering, then the courage to confront the social authority that perpetuates injustice, and, finally, the persistence and ingenuity to overcome it.

When social and economic values are regarded as intrinsic to a fulfilling human life, the failure to implement basic civil rights is sinful and leads to self-destruction. The passion for political freedom and economic justice is the very life breath of humanity. Nevertheless, it must be cultivated and perfected continually. Albert Camus, for example, urges people throughout society to continue to work for justice and freedom:

> There is no ideal freedom that will someday be given us all at once, as a pension comes at the end of one's life. There are liberties to be won painfully, one by one, and those we still have are stages—most certainly inadequate, but stages nevertheless—on the way to total liberation. [74]

These words provide a glimpse of a mode of human awareness that focuses on humanity as a group of political-economic beings. For Camus, social ethical patterns of life were neither mere conventions nor unchanging holy laws. For social and political reformers (and revolutionaries), social responsibility is a force whereby human beings can effect the salvation by creating more perfect social-political structures.

During the past two centuries, the concern to transform society has been found in two dramatic forms of "secular religion." One is the development of capitalistic institutions connected with democracy as in much of the West. As Max Weber has pointed out, the principle of voluntary association found in Protestant churches, the emphasis on individual responsibility to God's will, and the recognition that this world is "the theater of God's glory," all of which accompanied the Protestant Reformation, provided part of the ideology for this development. The other form is the Marxist doctrine of scientific socialism. It, too, has historical roots in Christianity as, for example, in the concern for one's neighbor and the hope for a future realm of glory (the classless society). Both movements (1) regard social (political, economic) improvement as an ultimate goal, and (2) emphasize the value of discipline and personal acceptance of responsibility by all individuals, and (3) affirm that human learning and productive capacities are means for realizing unlimited new benefits.

Two basic ideals express the concern for improving the everyday conditions of life. The first is human dignity—the recognition of a qualitative difference between man and lower animals, plants, and machines. No person should be exploited by another. Thus, the American social movements of Black Power and Women's Liberation are seeking to correct social and economic structures that deny the rights of blacks and women to live as full persons. One spokesman sees Black Power as a profound religious expression:

> Black Power . . . is a humanizing force because it is the black man's attempt to affirm

his being, his attempt to be recognized as "Thou," in spite of the "other," the white power which dehumanizes him. The structure of white society attempts to make "black being" into "nonbeing" or "nothingness." . . . The courage to be, then, is the courage to affirm one's being by striking out at the dehumanizing forces which threaten being.[75]

The rights gained by affirming oneself as a human being lead one to accept obligations toward another person as a human being. Each person's need for another *person* (with similar rights) is important not only for social and political justice but also for economic well-being. The laborer, the entrepreneur, and the consumer will recognize each other's rights and responsibilities to the extent they recognize each other as human beings and not merely as cogs in the economic machinery.

Similarly, individuals and governments cannot forget the fact of the dignity of human life lest they destroy each other. Perhaps the best known expression of this is found in the American Declaration of Independence:

We hold these truths to be self-evident, that all men are created equal, that they are endowed by their Creator with certain unalienable Rights, that among these are Life, Liberty and the pursuit of Happiness. That to secure these rights, Governments are instituted among Men, deriving their just powers from the consent of the governed. That whenever any Form of Government becomes destructive of these ends, it is the Right of the People to alter or abolish it, and to institute new Government . . .

People are not subjects governed by a lord; they are citizens with certain guaranteed rights. They accept responsibility for legislating, as well as administering, rules. Such rules permit all citizens to have freedom to pursue happiness if all citizens accept the responsibility to allow their neighbors the same freedom.

A second idea basic to religious realization through political and economic means is the acceptance of the capacity and moral duty continually to develop new legislation and technology for increased material welfare. This emphasizes the value of modification and change for developing new possibilities. Thus, the essential character of a system of government, scientific theory, or technology is the capacity for continuous change. What is not socially useful is crushed and buried. The very notions of rights, responsibilities, liberty, and welfare change; the acceptance of human responsibility sets in motion the social, scientific, and political energies that make the pursuit of happiness possible for all citizens.

Modern technology has involved more people with each other than ever before in human history. Such involvement begins with advanced possibilities for communication, including the international exchange of ideas. It results in the exchange of commercial products and services. The social and economic structures necessary to relate the lives of millions of people, however, also threaten those who established them. The impact of modern technology on social relationships can be seen in labor-saving machines, the development of centers of commerce through improved transportation, accessibility of information from geographically distant places, information storage and retrieval, and, of course, nuclear power. Along with increased productivity, however, advanced technology makes it possible for a few people to gain physical and intellectual control of the masses. It also can lead to the wholesale destruction of plants, animals, and environment in order to fill the material desires of a small segment of the population. Thus, those who see the political and economic realms as an opportunity for human happiness have a moral responsibility to provide a realistic, but flexible, concept of ultimate authority.

Because the masses in many countries today demand participation in determining their lives, and because advancing technology will give many nations the capacity to destroy other nations regardless of geographic location or population, multitudes of people who have never seen or known each other have become neighbors. Formerly, the ultimate unit of social consciousness was the family, clan, race, religious community, or nation. Now, while people have special groupings to which they still belong, some leaders recognize that moral obligations extend around the world. What political structure will allow every person and all people, to realize material benefits and political rights as human beings? Will people simply continue to exist as a variety of separate and sovereign nations? Can we look for a world government that will not dissolve the individuality of a people, or of a person, into the monotony of uniformity? One of the great challenges for those seeking ultimate transformation in economic and political life is to secure a situation of stable flexibility for improving human welfare.

SELECTED READINGS

*J. Wach, *The Comparative Study of Religions,* Chapter 4, "The Expression of Religious Experience in Fellowship." Wach's emphasis is on the expression of man's confrontation with ultimate reality in a cult-community and institutional structure.
E. Cell, ed., *Religion and Contemporary Western Culture* (Nashville, Tenn.: Abingdon, 1967), Section 8. A selection of eight readings from the writings of well-known contemporary Christian theologians on the relationship between religious life and social order.
H. R. Niebuhr, *Christ and Culture* (New York: Harper, 1951). A classic analysis of Christian social ethics. The author distinguishes between five types of patterns in which Christian faith has been related to cultural patterns in Western history.
C. A. Moore, ed., *Philosophy and Culture: East and West* (Honolulu: University of Hawaii Press, 1962), Part IV, "Ethics and Social Practice," and Part V, "Legal, Political, and Economic Philosophy." A collection of papers by well-known scholars from various continents.
The variety of ethical forms taken by religious commitments in different Asian contemporary societies can be seen in C. K. Yang, *Religion in Chinese Society,* Chapter 14, "Communism as a New Faith"; M. K. Gandhi, *The Gandhi Sutras,* edited by D. S. Sarma (New York: Devin-Adair Co., 1949), Chapter 2, on the spiritual importance of *satyagraha;* *W. L. King, *In the Hope of Nibbana* (La Salle, Ill.: Open Court, 1964), Part II, "Content and Application—Buddhist Ethics in Practice"; *G. E. von Grunebaum, *Modern Islam: The Search for Cultural Identity* (Berkeley and Los Angeles: University of California Press, 1962), especially Chapter 2, "The Problem of Cultural Influence," and Chapter 9, "Problems of Muslim Nationalism."
C. J. Friedrich, *Transcendent Justice: The Religious Dimension of Constitutionalism* (Durham, N.C.: Duke University Press, 1964). After analyzing different forms and devel-

opments of constitutionalism in Western culture, the author in the last chapter discusses the implications of a humanist constitutionalism in the present age, when the traditional religious foundations of constitutionalism have almost vanished.

F. J. Streng, C. L. Lloyd, Jr., and J. T. Allen, eds., *Ways of Being Religious,* Chapter 6 ''Achievement of Human Rights through Political and Economic Action.'' A collection of readings expressing advocacy, sympathetic interpretation, and critiques of religious life discussed in the final section of this chapter.

10.

The Power of Rationality

Reasoning power—like social responsibility—is one of the modes of human awareness through which people construct their *human* existence. Reasoning is the ability to see a similarity or a cause-effect relationship in two different experiences and to give that similarity or relationship a name. For example, people sense heat in both sun and fire, but they also distinguish between the empirical phenomena of sun and fire. They abstract an attribute such as heat from these two different things, but they also abstract other elements of sense experience and relate "sun" to "moon," "planets," and "stars," forming a classification of "heavenly bodies." In this way, most often without being conscious of it, people experience the world by selecting and relating identifiable elements in life.

Ideas are abstractions from sensations and patterns of meaning. The use of general or abstract concepts makes it possible to concentrate on certain character-istics of experience and exclude others. The purpose of this procedure is to locate and apprehend those aspects of experience that are of continuing importance in self-awareness.

The power of rationality is also apparent in "discursive thinking." Human experience can be broken up into discernible mental units (ideas, concepts), and strung out, one idea after another. People are aware of relationships between the named elements of their experience and can express these relationships in symbols—in European languages by verbs and prepositions. Thus, experiences are not only "defined" but also "arranged" or ordered in a way that conforms to struc-tures of meaning called "rules of grammar." Communication between two people—to say nothing of agreement—can only occur if they share a set of ac-cepted rules of meaning.

This chapter will discuss the human capacity for reasoning as it relates to a person's self-awareness. Reason enables people to learn who they are and to estab-lish norms for deciding what they will do as human beings. Can verbal abstractions (words) and their logical interrelationships constitute a valid means of apprehend-ing reality? The goal in this mode of awareness is to provide such a means. It is not possible in these few pages to discuss all the procedures and problems of logic, the formation of language, and the discipline of syllogistic logic. Suffice it to say that reasoning is a conditioning process that determines *how* reality is to be known—not only *that* reality is known. Reason and conceptual formulations are useful as an ad-junct to traditional human religiousness, as in theology, for example, but logic and philosophy become means of ultimate transformation themselves when no trans-rational norms are affirmed.

The Construction-Power of Definitions

Most people assume that distinctions between objects such as trees, buildings, and the sky, or between values such as "good" and "bad" are self-evident. At the same time, some experiences—mistaken notions, bad judgments, paradoxical occurrences—cause some people to question this common notion of reality. Similarly, sustained investigation and intellectual analysis often strain the capacities of common-sense concepts and judgments. On critical analysis, some facts, such as "the sun rises" or "a person's body lasts as long as his life," are recognized as *interpretations*. Where some people see the sun "rise," others conclude that the earth turns as it goes around the sun; where some think of the human body as lasting until death, for others it changes constantly as it incorporates nutrients and eliminates waste. While common-sense definitions form useful interpretations of some—indeed many—human experiences, they are often ambiguous and do not allow for the distinctions and refinement through which specific features of human experience can be further analyzed.

One element in the reasoning process in both theological and nontheological discourse is the formulation of definitions. Definitions establish the distinctive character of something in comparison with something else. Very often terms or concepts are themselves definitions. Concepts provide a mental "set" for experience. Thus, they are powerful forces in the process of self-awareness. Highly abstract definitions, which exclude all possibility of their opposites, provide not only the forms or images whereby people identify reality but, even more importantly, establish a process of inclusion and exclusion that enables people to identify their experiences and come to terms with life. For example, the distinction between "infinite" from "finite" reality not only "names" two aspects of human apprehension, but allows the prefix "in" to order a mutually exclusive relationship between them. The use of reason allows individuals to take responsibility for their existence by extending their experience in a general way; however, that process of self-extension is a focusing, and thus an organizing, power.

The more abstract reasoning becomes, the further removed it is from any particular person's experience. Although concepts abstract only some aspects of an experience, they provide a medium for human relationships between individuals with very different experiences. "Love," "truth," "reality," and "meaning" are such high levels of abstractions that they can negotiate certain levels of reflection and communication that might not otherwise be possible. Part of an individual's understanding of these concepts derives from personal experience, but much more results from the human capacity to construct a symbol that is larger than private experience. Symbols are necessarily inexact and general, for they abstract from multiple sense impressions and meanings and apply to many individual experiences. Indeed, partly because meanings are not dependent on private experience alone, symbols seem to take on a reality of their own. For example, the questions "what *is* love?" or "what is reality?" imply that "love" and "reality" are things like trees, tables, or books, which are external to the speaker.

In fact, the unique capacity of a concept to mean something quite arbitrary in relation to a specific event is what makes it so negotiable. For example, when people begin to talk they often have different content for the concepts they use. It is only through clarification in use that the differences become apparent. The conversation then either comes to a halt because the concepts mean different things for the different participants or a new meaning is agreed upon. In clarifying the meaning of terms, the participants in a conversation are constructing a realm of discourse in which they can participate. The degree to which this discourse expresses the participants' experience—even if it selects only very few aspects of their experience—is a measure of the power concepts have to construct a person's self-awareness.

Philosophers have different explanations of the way a definition functions. Each way interprets the relationship between conceptual knowledge and reality differently. We will discuss two prominent explanations given in Western philosophy. First, a definition can be understood to be, in Aristotle's imagery, "a phrase signifying a thing's essence." The essence is that unchanging character of something from which all the "peculiarities" of that thing must necessarily follow. For example, if a Christmas tree is defined as "an evergreen tree decorated with ornaments at Christmas," something would be classified as "a Christmas tree" when it manifested these essential characteristics. The attempt to know something by learning its essential character has played a large role in Western logic, as well as in Indian thought and in Chinese, especially Neo-Confucian, philosophical reflection. To suggest that there are such essences, and then to define and ever more perfectly redefine experienced phenomena to conform to an ideal image of a "pure nature," is one way to relate knowledge to reality.

Second, a definition may be considered valid if it is appropriate to a particular context of thought. For example, the definition of "tree," "star," or "person" does not depend on its perfect expression of all possible trees, stars, or persons. Rather, the validity of the definition depends on the purpose for which it is used. If the validity of what we know is more directly related to our use of terms than to some external essence beyond the language system, two consequences follow.

The first consequence is that, as the philosopher Ludwig Wittgenstein noted in his later writings, the definitions of everyday speech are pliable; the same word does not refer to exactly the same thing each time it is used. For example, the term "Christmas tree" can refer to various objects that have some things in common but no single element common to all. One tree may be an evergreen with a pointed top covered with candles; another may be an evergreen with a *round* form and Christmas lights on it; a third may be a metal tree with a pointed top and Christmas lights on it. The term "Christmas tree" may specify any one of these objects, although no single element is common to all.

A second consequence of understanding a definition in relation to its use is that changes in definition have more to do with the context in which the definition is used than with an exact or perfect description of some objective reality. Thus, the purpose of classifying "man" as one of the vertebrates in biology has a quite different function than that of the Hebrew paslm writer who claimed that "man" was "little lower than God." Similarly, the elaborate classification of animals among the American Indians had a quite different purpose from that of contemporary zoologists. The earlier classification was made on the basis of color and the functions assigned to various animal species in magic and ritual. Its purpose was to perceive personal life in relation to animal powers, and the similarities and differences represented personal needs of people in relation to their ancestors and their participation in the natural order of things. The scientific method, on the contrary, emphasized "objective," impersonal, and nonhuman sets of classification in the context of environmental conditioning and reproduction. Thus, scientific classification is not "self-evident" or more perfect than the classification of the American Indian medicine man; it is more relevant to the question of biological maintenance.

Rationality is a mode of human awareness that gains part of its validity from the fact that it is a constituent element of what we mean when we talk of human existence. Awareness of what it means to exist requires, among other things, that a person experience this capacity for abstraction and the structuring of meaning through projections, extensions, and inferences. Rationality provides the mechanism for disciplined analytical and synthetic thinking. In the case of either general common-sense thinking or a disciplined inquiry into problems of logic, people construct a conscious conceptual pattern that gives them meaning. These patterns also provide the means for articulating and clarifying traditional religious claims. However, rationality is seen by some philosophers to have life-transforming power when it is skillfully used, because it clarifies understanding and eliminates conceptual confusion. Where rational processes lead to a new understanding of life, they release humanity from its dependence on physical and emotional forces. Philosophers use this mode of awareness as a primary source of insight into human experience, and some affirm that it provides the fullest comprehension of life possible. In contrast, an advocate of one of the traditional religious processes, such as a devotee of a holy presence known in awesome wonder, would regard the capacity to think rationally as, at best, only a limited or supplemental means of ultimate transformation.

Use of Reason to Interpret Revelation or Spiritual Insight

All the religions that emphasize a direct revelation of God (for example, Judaism, Christianity, and Islam) as recorded by prophets, tribal leaders, or disciples, as well as religions that revere an honored tradition (for example, orthodox Hinduism and classical Confucianism) use human rationality to define and interpret the "given" truth. A great effort has been made in the major historical religious traditions to define, clarify, and preserve the original content of expressed truth. In the effort to interpret correctly the original revelation, insight, or wisdom, reason is used (1) to interpret a statement of eternal truth or revered tradition by a close analysis of the meaning of words and their use in sentences; and (2) to decide when to apply the assertions about life to a particular situation, whether the situation occurred a generation after the original articulation of truth or thousands of years later.

This concern to preserve meaning has led to the growth of libraries of commentaries that often enjoy at least a semicanonical authority and become institutionally important in providing the foci for "schools" or "denominations." This is seen for example, in the Jewish *Talmud,* in the Hindu *Smriti,* the Confucian commentaries, and the writings of Martin Luther, John Calvin, or John Wesley in Protestant Christianity. Similarly, in the Japanese Buddhist Pure Land schools, the writings of the founders of these schools, Honen and Shinran, are studied and elaborated upon by their followers as much as, and often more than, the ancient Sanskrit and Pali scriptures. Indeed, the history of the development and growth of the major world religions can be understood only by taking seriously the changing interpretations within a tradition, which often resulted from the reinterpretation of a particular portion of the sacred documents or a reevaluation of an earlier tradition.

The effort to get back to the true intention of the original sacred law, divine story, or metaphysics is complicated by the fact that religious symbolism often has many dimensions. This is clearly seen in the symbols of ultimate reality. Such notions as "the divine nature of Jesus Christ," "Brahman," "God's will," and "emptiness" give rise to a variety of interpretations, often paradoxical or logically contradictory. The attempt to define, systematize, and explain the meaning of the most profound religious symbols has led to tensions within a religious community when different aspects of the reality known in religious experience have been articulated; sometimes the differences have been used as a justification for religious wars.

It is because an interpretation is regarded as normative that followers of one interpretation or another so tenaciously hold to their positions. These interpretations of the true meaning of a religious vision often determine social relationships, the use of certain rites instead of others, and ethical decisions, as well as beliefs. The power of theological formulation to crystallize and perpetuate certain conceptual formulations from generation to generation has clearly been as important in religious life as the original expression. Every attempt to clarify and preserve the original intention of the revered writings requires the use of concepts and language by an interpreter.

Two specific examples show how reason was used in parts of major religious traditions to communicate a translogical vision of truth. In Islam, the primary norm for belief and practice is the *Qur'an.* Within several generations after Muhammed, several schools of interpretation had been established in the Islamic world, ranging from literal interpretations of a fundamentalist sort to a more liberal perspective in which some questions were left to God's decision. In the third century of the Islamic tradition, a dialectical theology *(kalam)* emerged that sought to articulate the truth of the *Qur'an* and refute the innovators by rational methods. Al-Ash'ari (died A.H. 324) is an example of a theologian who in his later life tried to reaffirm the traditional Islamic position with the help of logical demonstration and philosophical argument. While for him reason had no independent validity, and while his central concern was to reveal the meaning of the Prophet's words, his method was different from those Islamic scholars who appealed only to the literal meaning of the words of the text, as in the school of Hanbal.

In ancient Hinduism, as the Arian culture spread from North India toward the south and east, the Vedic religious leaders had to crystallize and systematize their understanding of the eternal truth that had been handed to them from the remote past. This took the form of aphorisms *(sutras)* into which the essentials of their religious insights were distilled. By about two thousand years ago, there were several orthodox perspectives *(darshanas)* claiming to provide the insight and proper techniques for knowing the highest truth. Each perspective had proponents as well as critics from outside the orthodox Hindu tradition. The teachers of the different perspectives were called on to justify by reason and clear articulation the basis for their views. Of course, philosophical concepts were meant primarily to point the person in the right direction. Realization of truth required some form of spiritual practice. Nevertheless, the power to cleanse the mind from error and ignorance depended, in part, on knowing the nature of things—which was partially stated in propositions. Throughout, the commentaries demonstrate an intellectual capacity for clarifying, classifying, and explaining by means of logical inference.

Reason as a Supplementary Source of Knowledge in Traditional Religions

The concern for exposing the true meaning of a divine revelation or revered tradition may lead to a reevaluation of the forms by which that truth is known. One of the most powerful ingredients in reinterpretation is man's rational capacity. This is especially true when a religious tradition assumes that divine or eternal power reveals itself in every moment of existence. Also, when a historical religious vision spreads into new cultures and new times, tensions may arise between those using the symbols that had persuasive power for the originators of the tradition and those using new symbols to redefine the meaning in their own terms.

When symbols once useful for interpreting life are no longer felt by later thinkers to have a power of revelation, an attempt is often made to find a deeper meaning hidden in the original form. The effort to go beyond the forms and reach for the essence or eternal truth has resulted in a heavy dependence on reason and a search for an expression that is universally applicable. Similarly, in the major cultural traditions are thinkers and scholars who recognize reason as an alternate and complementary means of knowing truth.

In Christianity, the degree to which reason is accepted as a positive force in learning the truth pivots on the question of how reason is related to revelation. The Roman Catholic scholastic theologian Thomas Aquinas (died A.D. 1274) argued that reason could and should be used in proving God's existence independent of any revealed knowledge. This was so, he asserted, even though philosophical reflection was not the only or highest form of religious knowledge—the highest truth could be known only through special revelation and had to be taken on faith.

Similarly, Anglican Bishop Joseph Butler (died A.D. 1752) claimed that God revealed himself through the natural and moral order as well as through the special revelation of Jesus Christ. He argued in *The Analogy of Religion* that we know the moral perfection of God by an examination of our own nature. He felt that just as there are natural physical laws, so there are general moral principles to be discovered by empirical investigation and comparison, and these moral principles are identical to those revealed in Scriptures.

An example of a more recent Christian theologian who took the use of reason seriously was Paul Tillich. The use of reason, he claimed, is important to spiritual reflection in that it is a tool for asking questions about man's being. Philosophical truth is concerned with ultimate reality, as is religious faith. Such truth refers to the structure of being that transcends any concrete form of existence (or any particular concept). While there are basic differences between the theologies of St. Thomas Aquinas, Bishop Butler, and Professor Tillich, each of them used a theological method that grants reason a positive role on the grounds that rational order, moral principles, and special divine revelation ultimately derive from the same source.

The Islamic tradition, similarly, has had theological questions regarding the relationship between reason and revelation. One of the most dramatic uses of reason for formulating truth in Islam is found in the Mu'tazila tradition. The Mu'tazilites criticized fellow Muslim theologians who claimed to present a theology exclusively on the authority of the *Qur'an* and the tradition (the *Hadith*). They insisted on using logical principles to affirm the uniqueness of God's unity, and, where this assertion was jeopardized by statements in the *Qur'an* or the *Hadith*, both had to be interpreted in light of logical assertions. The heavy use of reason put them very often at the opposite pole from orthodox theologians, especially on such complicated questions as the relationship of man's freedom to God's absolute determinism and the nature of the *Qur'an*—whether it was a creation of God or an attribute of God.

Lest these examples suggest that the use of reason by religious scholars of necessity leads them to argue for a universal essence that exists beyond, and as the source of, every particular religious expression, another example shows the use of logic as a valid procedure for realization of the highest truth without the assumption of a universal essence beyond all concrete expressions. This is found in the assertion of the second-century Buddhist philosopher Nagarjuna that "all things are empty." In his *Fundamentals of the Middle Way* his denial that there can be a self-existent essence as the object of human knowledge or intuition was expressed through a dialectical criticism of all positions that maintain the reality of such essences. When Nagarjuna was criticized by his opponents for assuming more reality for his argument than that of his opponents, he maintained that his use of logic was relative, not absolute, as is the case with any means of knowing. Thus, on the one hand, reason is not just a first step in knowledge to be dropped when either revelation or intuition take over; on the other hand, it does not get its certainty from a perfect deduction based on an essential premise. Rather, concepts and inferences are as useful as any other means for realizing the truth when they are recognized as being as empty of essential reality as any forms in existence.

Rationality as a Means of Ultimate Transformation

The process of rational thought can become an independent means of ultimate transformation when it is considered to be the prime or only valid source of knowledge. In the Western intellectual tradition, some philosophers, especially logicians, regard human reasoning as the most distinctive feature of human existence. They hold that the development of rational skills and clarity in thinking are necessary bases for personal relationships and socio-political decisions. Some central elements of the structure of this nontraditional religious process are (1) the emphasis on clear and distinct ideas as the power for ordering human life; (2) the prime value placed on knowing not only what is true, but *why* it is true through a logical inquiry into the necessary relations between things; (3) the attitude that concepts and logical procedures correspond to the most profound nature of reality since philosophy deals with universals and timeless realities; and (4) the innate capacity of human beings not only to attain the level of clarity of some contemporary logicians, but to develop techniques of linguistic, grammatical, and logical exploration that can explain all human experience. The late philosopher A. N. Whitehead expresses the high hope of human rational capacity in the following definition of speculative philosophy:

> Speculative philosophy is the endeavour to frame a coherent, logical, necessary system of general ideas in terms of which every element of our experience can be interpreted. By this notion of "interpretation" I mean that everything of which we are conscious, as enjoyed, perceived, willed, or thought, shall have the character of a particular instance of the general scheme. Thus the philosophical scheme should be coherent, logical, and in respect to its interpretation, applicable and adequate.[76]

Even those philosophers who regard speculative philosophical systems as a waste of intellectual effort—those within the movement called "logical positivism"—share Whitehead's assumption that human beings can become self-conscious about their most significant experiences through a logical (linguistic) analysis of experienced reality.

Within the Western religious traditions, some theologians used reason to expound the meaning of divine revelation and to help prove the validity of denominational claims. Since the eighteenth century, intellectual and social movements outside of the Jewish and Christian communities in Europe have emphasized rationality as the basic source of human freedom and improvement. In fact, the European "Enlightenment" of the eighteenth century (which is sometimes labeled "the Age of Reason") spoke of a new awakening of the human spirit through critical and analytical thought. Within this movement, those with a rationalistic outlook often criticized the dogmas, creeds, and socio-political attitudes that church or synagogue claimed were based on revelation. A rationalist attitude is expressed in an article on philosophy in the *Encyclopédie,* edited by Enlightenment spokesmen D. Diderot and J. d'Alembert:

> Reason is to the philosopher what grace is to the Christian. Grace causes the Christian to act, reason the philosopher. . . . [The philosopher] takes for true what is true, for false what is false, for doubtful what is doubtful, and for probable what is only probable. He does more, and here you have a great perfection of the philosopher: when he has no reason by which to judge, he knows how to live in suspension of judgment.[77]

Likewise, such men of letters as Voltaire (died 1778) and the Marquis de Condorcet (died 1794) strongly opposed traditional Christianity for its traditional authority, and—from their perspective—fanaticism, and sought to place reason in the center of all knowledge.

The European Enlightenment was a cultural movement led by a few intellectuals who expounded their views in light of a more narrowly philosophical expression of "rationalism" that began in the seventeenth century. As a philosophical view, rationalism assumed that a universal set of comprehending forces (an *a priori* rationality) influenced human cognition before people became conscious of it. This claim was combined with the notion that a necessary and natural correspondence exists between thought processes and reality and the idea that all concepts can be related logistically. The French philosopher Descartes (died 1650) had already argued that the three innate modes of apprehending were unlearned. These fundamental modes or "ideas" are God, mind, and physical extension. His conception is important because it considers how human beings can know the true nature of things. If fundamental ideas exist in prereflective consciousness and are equally available to all people through the exercise of thought, then human beings have access to ultimate transformation through the perfection of a natural means—rationality.

An even more specific statement about how reason could be used to develop a deductive system that would account for all phenomena was given by the Dutch philosopher Spinoza. The source of everything, of cause itself, said Spinoza, was "God"; however, his notion of God was radically different from that derived from personal faith; "God" was, rather, absolutely infinite being, or "substance consisting of infinite attributes." Thus, "God" was already the expression of all true ideas and "a true idea must necessarily first of all exist in us as a natural instrument."[78] Spinoza then explains an important part of the method for apprehending "God":

> Now it is clear that the mind apprehends itself better in proportion as it understands a greater number of natural objects; it follows, therefore, that this portion of the method will be more perfect in proportion as the mind attains to the comprehension of a greater number of objects, and that it will be absolutely perfect when the mind gains a knowledge of the absolutely perfect being or becomes conscious thereof.[79]

Perfect comprehension of "God," including the mind, is then possible with reason. The goal would be to express the comprehension in a mathematical system so complete that it would account for all possible units of thought and the laws that govern thought. Also, the German philosophers Leibnitz (1646–1716) and Kant (1724–1804) continued to wrestle with the application of reason to human perplexities and affirmed in different ways that unclouded understanding could and should provide the norms for true cognition as well as ethical decisions.

In the twentieth century, the school of "logical positivism" has sought to grasp cognitively "those things of abiding importance" that have made rational and discursive processes of thought into a means of ultimate awareness. Represented by such philosophers as R. Carnap and A. J. Ayer, this school makes two fundamental assumptions about the nature of reality and its relation to human comprehension: (1) discursive thought (including the abstract languages of mathematics and algebra) is the primary or even sole means for articulating thought, and (2) feeling is whatever human beings express that cannot be projected into discursive language and then empirically verified. Any formulation of thought that attempts to give information must follow the norms of validity that apply to science. The accurate rules for true knowledge depend on the development of a scientific grammar. All statements that convey knowledge do so because they have only a literal meaning; such a statement is a proposition that can be judged true or false. A proposition that conveys knowledge must convey information that can be verified or refuted—otherwise it is a pseudo-proposition. This means that many traditional religious statements or metaphysical claims, such as "God is love," or "all people have the Buddha-nature," or "the *Tao* is in many forms," are pseudo-propositions, i.e., meaningless statements because they do not contain information that can be verified or refuted by empirical or rational criteria. At best, they are like exclamations or emotional gestures. For the logical positivists, human cognition is essentially scientific thought, which combines the development of rational skills with a principle of physical verification (another mode of human apprehension that will be discussed in Chapter 12).

The forms and uses of language or of symbolism, rather than being *sources* of knowledge, are the foci of contemporary thinkers for whom rationality is the dominant or central means of ultimate transformation. Logicians and philosophically oriented semanticists and linguists recognize that the analysis of human thought require further empirical study of widely scattered data. At present, a central issue is whether or not there is a common universal rationality. If not, perhaps the differences in grammatical rules among various language families imply different uses of such notions as necessity or obligation. Likewise, shouldn't logicians recognize different principles of validity for different types of cultural experience? If so, the claim of magical power made by members of nonliterate societies would be just as valid in that cultural context as a professor's claim to logical deduction in a university course on logic. Similarly, would it be possible to devise a "universal calculus" in the form of a metalanguage or a symbol system that could be used to talk about *all* different languages and the meanings available through them. Such a metalanguage might bring about a more perfect comprehension of human existence. Some have even raised questions as to whether it would be possible to find ways of communicating with beings from outer space or minds that lack conventional physical, mental, or emotional attributes. Many linguistic philosophers recognize the existence of nondiscursive or nonrational modes of being or awareness but believe that these modes can be named and their expression related to more general concepts. Such general concepts would not only give human beings insight into what has been known, but into what *can* be known.

SELECTED READINGS

*S. K. Langer, *Philosophy in a New Key,* Chapters 3, 4, and 5. In these chapters, especially in Chapter 4, "Discursive Forms and Presentational Forms," the kind of meaning available through conceptual abstractions and the logical relationships of concepts is analyzed.

*F. S. C. Northrop, *The Meeting of East and West* (New York: Macmillan, 1960). See especially Chapters 7 and 8. The theoretic character of Western knowledge is described as central to the forms and values of Western civilization.

The use of reason for knowing truth by Western philosophers such as Spinoza, Locke, or Leibnitz is seen in readily available translations of their works, or in books of readings in the philosophy of religion. For example, see N. Smart, ed., *Historical Selections in the Philosophy of Religion* (New York: Harper, 1962).

*B. Russell, *Mysticism and Logic and Other Essays* (New York: Longmans, Green, 1925). Essay I, "Mysticism and Logic," Essay 3, "A Free Man's Worship," and Essay 4, "The Study of Mathematics," are popular articles that declare the importance of perceiving necessary relationships between classes of things and using laws of thought to determine man's choices.

For an introduction to contemporary analyses of the relationship between religious language (mainly Western) and the use of language and logic for learning truth see E. Cell, ed., *Religion and Contemporary Western Culture,* Section 5, "Religion and Philosophy," which includes readings from E. Brunner, P. Tillich, and J. Wisdom; *I. T. Ramsey, *Religious Language* (New York: Harper, 1961); and W. A. Christian, *Meaning and Truth in Religion* (Princeton, N.J.: Princeton University Press, 1964).

K. N. Jayatilleke, *Early Buddhist Theory of Knowledge* (London: George Allan & Unwin, 1963). See especially Chapter 6, "Analysis and Meaning." An authoritative discussion of the importance of ideational classification and logical analysis in early Buddhism.

S. Bagchi, *Inductive Reasoning: A Study of Tarka and Its Role in Indian Logic* (Calcutta: Calcutta Oriental Press, 1953). An in-depth survey of the use of reason in Indian philosophy.

For an introduction to the role of reason in Chinese philosophy, see *Fung Yu-lan, *A Short History of Chinese Philosophy,* translated by D. Bodde (New York: Macmillan, 1948), especially Chapters 23, 24, and 28; *Fung Yu-lan, *The Spirit of Chinese Philosophy,* translated by E. R. Hughes (Boston: Beacon, 1947), Chapters 9 and 10; and Wing-tsit Chan, ed., *A Source Book in Chinese Philosophy* (Princeton, N.J.: Princeton University Press, 1963), Chapters 32–34 and Chapter 42.

*M. White, ed., *The Age of Analysis* (New York: New American Library, 1955). This brief anthology of twentieth century philosophers clearly indicates the role of reason in the analysis of human experience.

Two books present some basic analyses and arguments of the logical positivists: R. Carnap, *Logical Syntax of Language* (New York: Humanities Press, 1937), and *A. J. Ayer, *Language, Truth, and Logic* (New York: Dover, 1936).

J. W. Weilgart, *The Language of Space* (Decorah, Iowa: Cosmic Communication, 1962). A formulation of a "cosmic symbol system" based on an examination of human languages and a simple intuitive logic called "aUI." A reader and aUI-English vocabulary are included.

The Power of Rationality

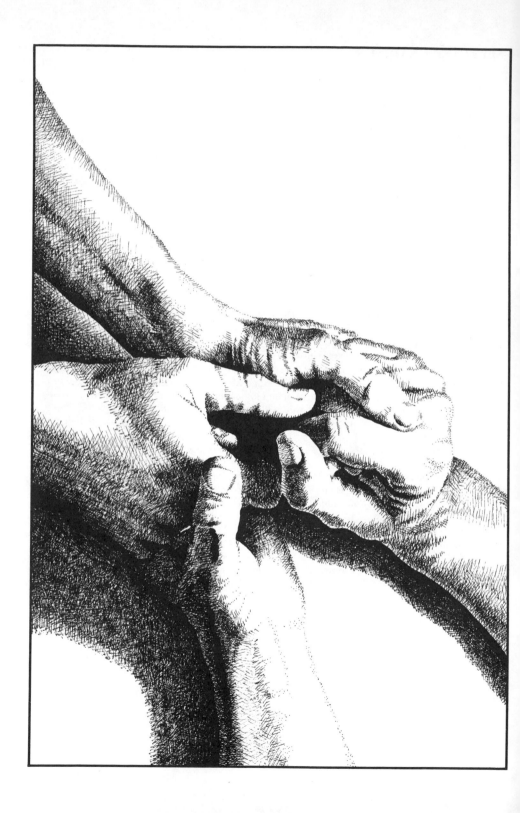

11.

The Religious Significance of
Fulfilling Human Relationships

Why consider the religious function of human relationships? Given the definition of religion as a means of ultimate transformation, interpersonal relationships form a dimension of life to which any traditional religious orientation must relate. Moreover, for those who regard spontaneity, intimacy, and self-fulfillment through interpersonal relations as central to their being, human relations are at the core of their spiritual life. Many people, however, take interpersonal relationships for granted; they are unaware of the power and significance of their encounters with others.

Human relationships define everyone's capacity for good and evil. The development of the human personality requires a relationship with others at some point in life. We define our individual uniqueness in terms of the contrast between us and those who influence us significantly. At the same time, our awareness of the world and our way of functioning within it come in large part from models set by those significant others—the immediate family, other members of the extended family circle, peers, a close friend, or teacher. Although people learn about themselves and grow from many experiences—even the most negative human relationships—human interaction can become a religious encounter when a dynamic and living exchange with another leads to self-discovery. In the experience of a sensitive touch, the warmth of companionship, or the feeling of being really understood, many people are aware of an intrinsic healing effect. Growing, sensitive caring, sharing relationships that are deep and meaningful give people something to live for and the courage to seek excellence. Such experiences may even provide the will to live under otherwise intolerable circumstances.

An awareness of the complexity and importance of human relationships means that each encounter poses innumerable problems but also offers opportunities for personal growth in unexpected dimensions of life. In every relationship, there are tensions between expectation and reality. For example, a lonely man tries to buy friends and ends up with none, a little girl prays for her sick father who eventually dies, or a husband and wife try but fail to make each other over. Common reactions to such disappointments include suspicion, distrust, withdrawal from the possibility of future encounter, and even the development of neurosis and psychosis.

An awareness of the discrepancy between human ideals and the reality of human relationships can, however, have the positive effect of encouraging people to make greater efforts to achieve their ideals. An ideal can spur individuals to grow beyond their present capabilities. For example, among certain American Indian tribes, adolescent boys are sent to fast and meditate in a wilderness cave. When one of them is inspired by a vision, the elders of the tribe prophesy that he will become a great chief, whereupon the boy rises to the occasion and cultivates the virtues of courage, patience, and concern for his people. Another example is Theodore Roosevelt, who believed that by acting as if he had complete mastery over his fears of danger he would eventually be able to master them. In both cases, the tension between ideals and self-awareness was resolved in a kind of transformation. Strength and courage replaced weakness and fear; a hope of greatness helped to stimulate the development of a new self-identity. Transformation may occur as a result of appeals to transcendent or divine sources or may result from efforts to improve human relationships. In both cases, the transformation of a person's ideals into concrete behavior often removes the pain of broken relationships, allays fears of rejection, loneliness, and insecurity, and paves the way for more meaningful encounters both within existing relationships and in future ones.

This chapter will examine the role of human relationships within organized and traditional religious structures as one form of ultimate transformation in everyday life. It will also discuss the ways in which personal creative interaction can assume ultimate significance outside of traditional religious structures as, for example, in a psychotherapeutic encounter group or through a depth awareness of everyday relationships.

Human Relationships Within Traditional Religion

A concern for human relationships characterizes all traditional religious structures. It is found generally and abundantly in the teachings of the major religious traditions that advocate love of neighbor, compassion for all beings, or showing kindness to those in need. It is seen in the counsel and advice given to people by priests, ministers, and spiritual teachers. It is expressed through both personal relationships and symbolic gestures at especially important moments in a person's life, for example at a Jewish bar mitzvah, a Christian confirmation, a Hindu sacred thread ceremony *(upanayana)*, marriage, or a funeral or cremation. Its source is the personal discovery of oneself as a child or servant of God.

Traditionally, two important functions of a priesthood organized to minister to the lay community have been the performance of regular devotional and sacramental services for the community primarily and some form of pastoral care for individuals. Worship services constitute the collective means whereby large numbers of believers come into relation with divinity through the leadership of an officiant and, through that relationship, understand that they have a significant relationship with each other. Worship services include both the somber piety of a high Catholic mass and group communion in a hogan during a Navaho peyote ceremony. In either case, the relationship is not simply between people. Because the priest or "road chief" acts as a medium through which human beings come into more intimate contact with divinity, a person has a new interpersonal relation through participation in the transcendent power that frees people from past sins and self-destructive tendencies. Of course, the religious service is more than a social function and the priest is more than a leader because the relationship among the people, and between them and the leader, takes on a sacred character. The symbolic acts of the priest and the experience of the believer are the means through which transcendent reality (divinity) is manifested (see Chapter 6).

Likewise, a worship service that focuses on personal awareness of a holy presence without the special services of a priest evokes a new awareness of personal value and self-confidence. For example, those who openly witness to their faith at a "fundamentalist" tent meeting, feel an overpowering (divine) presence, swoon, recover, begin to "speak in tongues," and gain a new sense of personal worth. Another kind of awareness may emerge during the silent, nondirective service of a Quaker meeting. In both cases, people gain a sense of ultimate value by experiencing divine power within their lives.

Similarly, the field of "pastoral care" can be seen as an extension of the priest's mediation between God and human beings. Among the pastoral duties of the Roman Catholic priest are hearing the confessions of penitents and comforting the gravely sick in the rite of supreme unction. Pastoral care is also expressed in the efforts of a Chippewa Indian shaman to perform a healing ceremony for a sick tribesman by building a "shake lodge" to call healing spirits into the body of the sick person. It is seen in the care for young people and their training in the way of the Lord, in the *Tao,* or in the Buddha's path to spiritual freedom. It is found in the special ministries to jails, reformatories, and mental hospitals.

Pastoral concern, one of the major historical developments of ministry in Christianity, is known in traditional terms as the "cure of souls." The efforts of the early church were directed toward sustaining people through the vicissitudes of life in this world, which all believed was swiftly coming to an end. Later, during the era of persecutions (180–306 A.D.), more emphasis was placed on reconciling troubled persons to God and the church and codifying major sins and their appropriate penalties. Once Christianity became a legal religion under Constantine the Great, the church grew more concerned with guiding people to behave according to the norms of the newly formed Christian culture. By the medieval period, pastoral care was part of a well defined sacramental system designed to treat all maladies besetting any segment of common life. During the Renaissance and Reformation, there was an increased emphasis on individuality. Although the church opposed some of the rationalistic and skeptical attitudes of the European Enlightenment, the influence of scientific, economic, and political forces on "Christian nurture" in the eighteenth and nineteenth centuries eventually led to a greater acceptance of individual convictions and value systems. Today, pastoral care is administered in conjunction with, and in some cases is subordinate to, the more highly developed nonreligious helping professions of medicine, psychology, and psychiatry.[80]

Out of this historical context have grown the four general Christian pastoral functions of healing, sustaining, guiding and reconciling.[81] Mental and physical healing may include such acts as annointing sacred places or body afflictions with holy water or oil, healing through contacts with religious relics, the laying on of hands and prayers by charismatic persons, exorcism, or psychotherapeutic and encounter group techniques administered by the clergy. Sustaining, which is mostly employed during times of personal crisis, involves averting an individual's disintegration, giving consolation and emotional support, consolidation of existing personal resources, and redemption in the eyes of God and the church despite whatever has happened. Guiding, on the other hand, serves more of a counseling than crisis-oriented function. It may entail listening, giving advice, and encouraging the making of decisions. Finally, reconciliation restores strayed or lost souls to the community of the church. Its chief means are forgiveness for wrongdoing and the assignment of a penance. Although each function has a particular emphasis, they collectively stress the importance of human relationships for the continued existence of organized religion and the spiritual well-being of individuals.

Another important facet of human relationships within traditional religious structures is the training of novitiates and the maintenance of monastic communities. Of great significance in many Asian traditions, although less so in the West, is the relationship between spiritual teacher (guru, *acarya, murshid, roshi*) and disciple. Of all obligations recognized by religious Hindus, for example, the *guru padasraya,* or servile veneration of the spiritual teacher, is considered the most important and compulsory. In exchange for the household maintenance, systematic begging, and personal devotion of the disciple, the guru bestows esoteric teaching and spiritual power upon the disciple.

Perhaps the most important expression of the concern for human relationships within traditional religious structures lies in the values of kindness, patience, and compassion taught by the founders or chief spokesmen of the tradition. The Buddha, for example, preached the *dhamma* (truth, law) for more than forty years after his enlightenment so that all sentient beings might be set free from suffering. Many Buddhist teachers instruct followers that friendly relationships with others are part of the virtuous path. One of them, the Tibetan Sa-skya Pandita (1182–1251), who combined a monastic life with that of an international diplomat, said:

> Gentleness conquers the gentle
> gentleness conquers the fierce
> gentleness accomplishes everything
>   gentleness is sharpness
>   the wise men say.[82]

A famous aphorism in the Confucian *Analects* indicates the practical implications of knowing the nature of things, the *Tao:*

> Tsekung asked, "Is there one single word that can serve as a principle of conduct for life?" Confucius replied, "Perhaps the word 'reciprocity' *(shu)* will do. Do not do unto others what you do not want others to do unto you."[83]

Jesus preached "Do unto others as you would have them do unto you" at one point in his life, and said "Father forgive them for they know not what they do" as he was being crucified.

The Mahayana scriptures express the Buddhist goal of the bodhisattva (enlightenment-being), who combines a transcendent inner awareness with a concern for others. The bodhisattva combines highest wisdom with compassion and seeks enlightenment not for his own sake but for the sake of others. The concern for others was part of the great vow of the bodhisattva, which shows the nature of enlightenment, unselfishly promising to remain in the world of suffering until all sentient beings down to the most tortured creature in hell have been liberated. By integrating wisdom with compassion, he participates in the flux of existence without attachment to it and thus exists without pain. The attitude of the bodhisattva is clear in the following lyric poetry from the manual ''Setting Forth in the Practice of Enlightenment'':

> I am medicine for the sick & weary
> may I be their physician & their nurse
> > until disease appears no more
> may I strike down the anguish of thirst & hunger
> > with rains of food & drink
> may I be food & drink to them
> > in famine & disaster
> may I be an inexhaustible treasure
> > for those in need
> may I be their servant
> > to give them all they desire
> my body : my pleasure : my merit
> > now & forever
> > everywhere
> > > I care nothing about them
> > > I cast them aside
> > > > to accomplish the aims of beings. [84]

These examples of care for other persons within the traditional religions show that significant human relationships result from a more basic reality (for example God, *Tao,* or the Buddha-nature). The relationship between oneself and others has profound significance because it is an expression of transcendent reality or God's will. Within a traditional religion, human relationships are expressions for, or adjuncts to, other means for ultimate transformation because they are seen as a vehicle for a more basic source of change outside of, or beyond, the strictly human situation.

Fulfilling Human Relationships as a Nontranscendent Ultimate

While human relationships within the context of these traditional structures have provided a vehicle for a transcendent ultimate reality to transform lives, many contemporary sources regard recent developments like psychotherapy or sensitivity-encounter techniques as more powerful means of personality transformation. Because there is no appeal to some transcendent source, they argue, the individuals involved in such a therapeutic relationship must recognize their responsibility in promoting mental health, growth, and change. Moreover, proponents see the therapeutic relationship as the source of the ultimate dimension of human experience. Ultimate transformation occurs because of the power inherent in human encounter, not because God or an eternal cosmic order is involved in a human relationship. Some basic forms of contemporary therapeutic techniques have been, and are being, used within traditional religious structures in the West. Some therapists, however, suggest that personality therapies will eventually replace traditional religious institutions because transformation can be accomplished by human encounter alone. O. H. Mowrer, for example, holds that therapy groups will replace the Christian church:

> I think there is a good possibility that these groups represent the emerging form of the church of the twenty-first century. They will very likely differ from conventional Catholic and Protestant churches in that they will not be specifically christocentric, nor will they be explicitly theistic (compare Confucianism and Buddhism). But they will, I think, be *profoundly religious*. . . . The term "religion," in its literal derivation, has no necessary relation to "theology." The former term comes from the Latin root *ligare,* which means connection, and *re-ligare,* from which our term "religion" comes, means reconnection. And this, more than perhaps anything else, is what the small-groups movement is concerned with: the reconnection, reintegration, reconciliation of lost, lonely, isolated, alienated, estranged persons back into a loving, concerned, and orderly fellowship or group of some sort. [85]

The ultimate character of personality development through psychotherapy is also noted by a leader of the "humanist" movement in psychology, Dr. A. Maslow. In a radio interview about the nature of a healthy society, he maintained that it is possible to find ultimate values by directing attention to the healthiest aspects of human life:

> In general, the consequences of psychotherapy are moves toward better values. The person in successful therapy generally comes out a better citizen, a better husband, a better wife—certainly a better person. He is more perceptive and more spontaneous— this practically always happens. These results are achieved through self-knowledge— the main path to discovering within ourselves the best values for all mankind. The more clearly we know these values, the more easily, spontaneously, effortlessly we can grope toward them. [86]

To suggest that creative human relationships within a therapeutic setting can be a source of personality transformation is not to claim that all human relationships are therapeutic. Some human relationships are too casual or superficial to promote any lasting change. Others are so destructive that they damage the individual, possibly preventing healthy relationships in the future. Neither type contributes to a person's fundamental health.

Some types of therapeutic relationships are not intended to be a means of ultimate transformation. Many psychologists do not place ultimate value on their work. Orthodox Freudian techniques of psychoanalysis, as well as contemporary behavior modification procedures, for example, envision the goal of therapy as adjustment to the normal functioning of society. For Freud, success was conceived as liberating a person from the neurotic daily behavior resulting from forgotten feelings, fears, anxieties, and control systems of his past. Such liberation required the conscious awareness of repressed feelings in past experiences and of the ways the repressed feelings were still determining a patient's reactions to other people. The goal was to free the conscious, rational ego so that patients could control their own actions in comfortable and socially acceptable ways. The behaviorists have felt that modification of behavior by retraining—without reference to other (unconscious) determinants—was sufficient evidence of cure if the patient could return to work. In both cases, the goal of therapy is not the transformation of a person's selfhood in personal relationships, but the elimination of socially unacceptable or personally painful symptoms. The patient-therapist relationship is incidental to the therapeutic goal and does not focus on inner change of the patient in relation to others. Thus, these techniques do not develop human relationships for the purpose of achieving ultimate transformation.

One important element in Freudian therapy, however, is basic to the development of therapies in the humanist movement in psychology—this is the evocation of deep feelings in the patient, which are ostensibly directed toward the therapist, but—according to Freud's interpretation—represent unresolved sexual and aggressive conflicts between the patient and his or her parents. This projection, known as "transference," onto the therapist of the patient's feelings, is interpreted as the patient's way of avoiding various unresolved unconscious material that emerges during sessions. Such projections are exposed through therapy as illusions since the therapist is not the patient's parent. In this sense, the therapeutic relationship is a means of transformation but it lacks an ultimate context because it only deals with unresolved conflicts between the patient and authority figures. It does not necessarily engage the entire psyche of the patient, nor does resolution of such conflicts call for the therapist to do more than uphold the role of therapist. Revelation of the therapist's personal identity is insignificant; of greater importance is the maintenance of a strictly professional therapist-patient relationship. Some followers of Freud and some behaviorists do, nevertheless, make ultimate claims with regard to the effectiveness of their procedures. Rather than focusing on the transforming power of human relationships, or on a transformation of "the whole person," they emphasize the changes in behavior brought about by following a scientific method.

The Growth-Motivated Therapeutic Relationship

In more recent developments of the humanistic movement, the therapeutic relationship and human relationships in general are considered situations that may be able to bring about individual personality transformation. One of the most influential therapists and a man who focused almost totally on the character of the therapeutic relationship was Carl Rogers. Emphasizing that the therapist-client relationship needed a very permissive, nondirective, and accepting atmosphere, Rogers proposed six basic points as necessary and sufficient conditions for therapeutic personality change:[87] (1) There must be a relationship, that is, some kind of psychological contact between two people. (2) The patient must recognize some kind of incongruence between his or her self-perceptions and the behavior that is causing anxiety. (3) Within the therapeutic relationship, the therapist must be genuinely and freely himself or herself—in other words, integrated to the extent that the therapist's self-image and behavior are congruent (even if this congruency reveals that the therapist is not a perfect human being.) (4) The therapist must place no conditions on the relationship, such as "I like you only if thus and so," but must make an attempt to accept unconditionally and in a positive manner all aspects of the client's behavior whether it is deficiency- or growth-oriented. (5) The therapist should try to develop an empathetic understanding of the client's inner world of meaning, come to know that inner world *as if* the therapist were the client—without ever losing the "as if" condition—and communicate this understanding to the client. (6) To some minimal degree, the patient needs to acknowledge this empathetic understanding. Under these conditions, says Rogers, constructive personality change is certain, and he emphasizes that any warm, accepting, and open person can fulfill the therapeutic role, suggesting that professional diagnosis and training are not only unnecessary, but can be detrimental to the degree that they foster a dependent attitude toward the therapist as "the expert" and prevent the client from developing inner resources for solving problems.

The general attitude toward the power of human relationship that emerged as a result of the work of psychologists like Rogers does not emphasize scientific determinism or theistic metaphysics; it stresses the importance of a positive humanistic approach to the possibilities life holds for each person and the search for means that will actualize these potentials. The goal is not only to produce fully functioning people, but to create a psychologically healthy culture. The total person is felt to be more important than the symptoms. By appealing to the best in a person through love and approval, a profoundly creative power can be released. Psychological forces are seen as the most influential power in the development of a value orientation.

While people need the aid and support of others to function well in a healthy culture, knowledge of self is crucial. Such personal traits as honesty, sincerity, and courage are necessary for self understanding if individuals are to deal effectively with the inner forces of their lives, which are normally hidden by habits and social customs. They must learn to trust themselves in order to be free and spontaneous with others. Thus, it is only through self-knowledge that effective reconciliation can take place between people in a normally alienated and fragmented society.

Although the psycho-therapeutic process is an effective means for learning about oneself, its early development was slow because it was not readily available to many and for a long time emphasized a primarily verbal interchange between two people in a clinic or office setting. This situation changed rapidly with the development of group-therapy techniques such as psycho-drama, family oriented groups, and the multiple-therapist approach. At present, almost every individual therapy system has been conducted on a group basis. With the flowering of the humanistic movement in American psychology during the early 1960s, therapists were challenged from within their own ranks and by their clients, to discover new ways of effectively communicating. The result was the emergence of techniques designed to facilitate nonverbal forms of communication through touch, attentive looking, silence, intuition and an emphasis on the here and now. The new movement initiated changed in many spheres. In some cases, the changes were small but nevertheless significant. For example, the word "therapy" was dropped from group work in favor of any other less deficiency-oriented terms. On a larger scale, "growth centers," such as Esalen in Big Sur, California, sprang up all over the United States emphasizing that the same techniques (plus some new ones) that had made sick people well could also make well people better.

Along with Carl Rogers, some other therapists like Fritz Perls, Ida Rolf, and William Schultz have widely implemented these techniques in order to transform people's lives in a healthy and total way. Rogers, for instance, in his *Freedom To Learn,* proposes a practical plan for educational revolution even in the classroom. He advocates the use of the intensive group experience, otherwise known as sensitivity training, "T" group, or the encounter workshop, as the most effective means yet discovered for facilitating constructive learning, growth, and change—in individuals or groups:

> The intensive group or "workshop" group usually consists of ten to fifteen persons and a facilitator or leader. It is relatively unstructured, providing a climate of maximum freedom for personal expression, exploration of feelings, and interpersonal communication. Emphasis is upon the interactions among the group members, in an atmosphere which encourages each to drop his defenses and façades and thus enables him to relate directly and openly to other members of the group—the "basic encounter." Individuals come to know themselves more fully than is possible in the usual working and social relationships; the climate of openness, risktaking, and honesty generates trust, which enables the person to recognize and change self-defeating attitudes, test out and adopt more innovative and constructive behaviors, and subsequently to relate more adequately and effectively to others in his everyday life situation.[88]

While William Shultz is well-known for his effectiveness in leading encounter groups at a popular level, and Ida Rolf for developing techniques of intensive therapeutic body massage, the late Fritz Perls developed group techniques to their height as a constructive tool within his Gestalt therapy. The following is a brief account by a neurophysiologist of a group session with Perls where "the hot seat" is used. This is a vacant chair next to Perls which is used by a person who wants to work with him:

> I got into the hot seat again, this time about the death of my mother. I had some unfinished business . . . having to do with guilt about her death. . . . I had spent 7 years working to keep her alive and then at the end, when the cancer finally killed her through a respiratory death, I blamed myself for having kept her alive by artificial means so long.
> I got into the hot seat and Fritz said, "Okay, go back to your mother's death." I went back to that particular day and began to hear her dying, became frightened, and came back to the group. Fritz said, "Go back." I went back again and started going through the fear, the grief, and the guilt connected with the doctors, with my own part in it. I examined very carefully the whole (sequence) having to do with her death. I cried. I became extremely fearful, got into a panic, then I cried with grief again. Three

times Fritz put me through it and finally he said, "Okay, you haven't quite finished with that but you have dealt with most of it." He let me off the hot seat.

I spent a total of two weeks and one weekend in his workshops and learned very much about myself and about others and about his technique. I was impressed with the fact that he could tune in on where one was and then program one to move even further into the space that one was reluctant to go into. I found that as long as one was willing to allow him to program one and to go ahead into whatever it was, then Fritz was happy and one made progress.[89]

Perls' handwritten and original epigraph to his *Gestalt Therapy Verbatim,* encapsulates the entire process most aptly:

To suffer one's death
and to be reborn
is not easy[90]

These glimpses into the goals and techniques of encounter workshops will perhaps indicate a few of the institutional forms that a concern with human relationships has taken. They express, from the standpoint of the therapist, a possible means of ultimate transformation in the psychotherapeutic setting.

One of the goals of group therapy has been to make group members sensitive to personal relationships and the way they comport themselves with others in their daily life. The advocates of this means of ultimate transformation suggest that people sometimes do not realize the full significance of their relationships with co-workers, neighbors, the man who delivers the mail, the old woman who passes by every day, and so many others. They claim that seemingly minor encounters can have far-reaching effects. A brief glance, sneer, or smile, can cause joy or tragedy. Every human encounter offers a chance to learn something new about oneself and others. Likewise, often people not only miss the chance to grow, but perpetuate and worsen many avoidable problems in their relationships through distortions of themselves and fear of others.

To be fully human from this perspective, means to take responsibility for the influence of one's behavior on others. Unresolved problems in one's personal life, for instance, often cause one to have negative perceptions of others. Excessive rigidity and self-control and continual criticism of self or others often disguise inner hostility. Such patterns create tension in most relationships and prevent warmth and trust from developing. The sensitive person can become aware of them and take responsibility for changing undesirable patterns or unsatisfying relationships.

To be a fully functioning person in a relationship means to be able to experience oneself fully through another, to discover that other, and to share a sense of direction and mutual enjoyment. At the same time, becoming a fully functioning person entails exploring and developing one's ability to relate on a deep and sensitive emotional level and to love other people. It means to give love, to be loved in return, and to have grown more fully human because of the experience. To actualize these possibilities is—from this perspective—the highest goal of life and the deepest awareness of true joy in existence.

SELECTED READINGS

W. A. Clebsch and C. R. Jaekle, *Pastoral Care in Historical Perspective* (New York: Harper, 1964). Useful information on the history and functions of the Christian pastoral care movement with extensive examples of eminent theologians discussing various aspects of the topic.

*E. Fromm, *Psychoanalysis and Religion* (New Haven, Conn.: Yale University Press, 1950). A series of five lectures, including "The Psychoanalyst as 'Physician of the Soul'." He distinguishes the humanistic psychoanalytic therapy from both behavioral adjustment therapy and institutional religious practice.

R. A. Harper, *Psychoanalysis and Psychotherapy; Thirty-six Systems* (Englewood Cliffs, N.J.: Prentice-Hall, 1959). A brief but informative collection of sketches covering most of the major psychotherapeutic systems in America prior to the rise of the humanistic movement. See especially Chapter 9, "Group Psychotherapies."

*R. B. Levy, *I Can Only Touch You Now* (Englewood Cliffs, N.J.: Prentice-Hall 1973). Humanistic encounter movement philosophy emphasizing the here and now, peaks, valleys, and plateaus of feeling, the paradox of control, the magic of touch, and a concluding appendix on useful techniques anyone can practice.

*A. Maslow, *Religions, Values, and Peak-Experiences* (New York: Viking, 1964). Author advocates finding the sacred in ordinary experience and regards this as the lesson to be learned from all true mystics.

*R. May, *Man's Search For Himself* (New York: New American Library, 1953). An advocate of humanistic psychology discusses techniques for integrating oneself by getting in touch with one's feelings, perceiving goals, and recovering a relationship with one's subconscious.

*F. Perls, R. Hefferline, and P. Goodman, *Gestalt Therapy* (New York: Delta, 1951). Theory and application of Gestalt therapy before it became nationally known. *F. Perls, *Gestalt Therapy Verbatim,* compiled and edited by J. O. Stevens (Lafayette, Calif.: Real People Press, 1969). Verbatim accounts of intensive workshops and dreamwork seminars conducted by Perls at Esalen from 1966 to 1968.

C. R. Rogers, *Freedom to Learn* (Columbus, Ohio: Chas. E. Merrill, 1969). Advocates a humanistically oriented approach to the educational process, particularly the training of scientists, by focusing on the person and his values. Contains interesting revolutionary tactics for renovating the educational process using the intensive encounter group experience.

F. J. Streng, C. L. Lloyd, Jr., J. T. Allen, *Ways of Being Religious.* Chapter 5, "Attaining an Integrated Self through Creative Interaction," provides readings in advocacy, interpretation, and critique of humanistic psychotherapy as a means of ultimate transformation.

J. White, ed., *What is Meditation?* (Garden City, N.Y.: Anchor Press/Doubleday, 1974). A selection of readings from current authors in East and West on the meaning and techniques of meditation with emphasis on the relationship of personality integration to spiritual practice.

12

The Power of Artistic Creativity

The Religious Importance of Beauty

Beauty has religious significance because whatever is beautiful is a perfect expression of what is. Beauty, in this sense, is different from prettiness or attractiveness—these can be deceptive. With this description of beauty, we cannot say, "Beauty is only skin deep," but prettiness or attractiveness can be only skin deep. Something that is pretty, appealing, or pleasurable does not necessarily have religious meaning. Rather, the beauty that is found in various forms of art is an expression of truth; lines, colors, rhythm, sound, and space are all potential means of revealing the most profound dimension of existence.

This chapter will neither describe the history of artistic styles nor discuss the theory of aesthetics in a systematic way. It will focus on only one aspect of the problem of understanding artistic production—the capacity of the artistic process to expose the religious dimension in life. Of course, art has other important functions and there are different conceptions of how ultimate truth is expressed in sensuous forms.

The religious importance of art becomes clear when people see that art is an intrinsic part of being human. Art, in this sense, is not the luxury of a few sophisticated connoisseurs nor the activity of a few technically disciplined artists. At the heart of artistic effort is the concern to expose and express what it means to be human at its most profound level. That is, art is the incarnation of a meaning-producing human being. Art does not attempt to imitate the world of natural phenomena; it interprets these phenomena as they stream into the vortex of human meaning. Artistic activity—from this perspective—is the purest form of being self-consciously human. Through artistic creativity people structure their universe, not simply by putting together lines, form, and space, but by putting them together in a way that is *significant to them*. What is embodied in oils or water colors in painting or in sound waves in music is the construction of meaning arising from the inner tension between the life of the artist or perceiver of art and the factors of sensuous experience (space, line, color) available to nomal human awareness. Thus, the "meaning" of an art object is not found only in interpretive statements about it, nor in a projection of the artist's concept of human experience or the cosmos; the meaning of art lies in the intuitive and the aesthetic effort to be aware of the nature of existence. The religious significance of art, then, resides in the activity of the artist and the perceiver of art through which both parties generate meaning and significance from the sources of their being-in-existence.

What do we mean when we say that spiritual truth is expressed in beauty? Are there differences in the way that beautiful things express truth? Without attempting to exhaust this question in a few pages, this chapter will discuss three ways in which religious meaning is expressed in concrete art forms. These are: (1) liturgical art as visual theology, (2) works of art that express an awareness of the real, or essential, qualities of life using nonreligious subject matter, and (3) the expression of religious truth through the process of creating perfect form in life.

Liturgical Art as Visual Theology

For purposes of this discussion, the phrase "liturgical art" will designate that art which consciously seeks to express the content of a religious tradition. In most cases, aesthetic sensitivity is an adjunct element for expressing the mythical and ritual powers of ultimate transformation. Liturgical art depicts the content of myths, such as gods, saviors, and saints, and plays an important role in the architecture of holy places. Two elements in such religious art articulate truth. The first is the *symbolic* expression of theological content, and the second is theological expression through different artistic *styles*.

Liturgical art, like theology, is the expression of the infinite through the use of finite form. It is more suggestive or symbolic than it is descriptive or diagrammatic. This must be kept in mind, for example, when one approaches animal-headed gods of multiple-armed deities in ancient Egyptian or Indian religions. The religious artist strives, nevertheless, to express in the most perfect way possible the content of a religious tradition. Therefore, vagueness in expression is a defect in art. The artist seeks to express something he or she knows and "to know something" means to have assimilated its true being. The religious purpose is to express the true being in perfect form. In this context, religious artists seek to lose their individuality and to become the medium for God's self-expression, using identifiable symbols from a religious tradition. In India, for example, the art manuals suggest that the artist eliminate distracting influences through yoga and thereby visualize perfectly the divine power—even its terrible, supernatural characteristics. Art, like other forms of revelation, is said to have a divine origin. What is revealed by the true artist in every religious tradition is not a repetition of what anyone can see, nor an idealized world as one might wish, but the way things are in their elemental character.

Various art forms have been used to express eternal truth. The drama and dance in primitive societies were clearly religious forms. Much ancient drama was directed toward the exposure of divine activity. The dance was the imitation of a god's movement; in repeating the divine actions, power was released. Dancing in a circle or in a long, serpentine line dramatized the divine actions of creation or the battle between the powers of life and the dark forces of nature. The movements and verbal expression in archaic drama and dance were based on formal elements revealed not only in these art forms but also in myths and other religious rituals. Here one could dance a prayer.

Similarly, the images and architecture of contemporary world religions that express the infinite through particular forms that reflect different theologies. In

Christian theology, for example, the focus is on Jesus Christ. The images of Jesus teaching, healing, dying on the cross, "lying in the manger," or simply of the cross or the empty tomb are central to the expression of God's revelation. In Hinduism, on the contrary, there is a use of *many* images and forms to express the infinity of the divine. A multitude of myths and stories provides the background for many different images of the divine in Hindu temples and shrines. The "otherness" of God is portrayed also through various suggestions of the "nonnatural": multiple arms or many eyes, or skin that is gold or dark blue. Perhaps the unique Hindu quality is best expressed in the image of the union of opposites in the combination of gods and goddesses (for example, Shiva and Shakti).

At the opposite pole of anthropomorphic iconography is Islamic art. Here the infinite is described in arabesque design, which is found on mosques and tombs and on common household objects. The design is a continuation of a given pattern, whether abstract or figurative, which generates new variations of the same original elements into infinity. Any design, then, is only a small, visible part of a complete, infinite whole. The design, whether it is on a mosque or a small wooden box, expresses the relationship of that particular point in existence to the infinite, and "dissolves" that particular "thing" into infinite lines, curves, and rhythms of divine energy. The designs, then, are not static, but radiating forces of the infinite.

While there are many similar images, symbols, and architectural forms within a given religious tradition, it is also important to note that different groups within the Christian, Hindu, and Buddhists traditions articulate different insights into the meaning of a religious vision at different times and places. The difference in style is clearly evident when we compare the heavy, expressionistic lines of George Rouault's forms, the ethereal quality of William Blake's works, and the rich, material forms of Michelangelo's painting. The distinction can be seen even when the subject matter is the same. El Greco's "Resurrection," for example, is a mystical, nontemporal expression of this event in comparison with Tintoretto's painting of the same name, in which the resurrection is portrayed as a fact more real than the trees and grass and animals that serve as a background.

Similarly, in Buddhism, the Buddha may be shown in various ways—as an active, dynamic savior of the world or as an ascetic in meditation and nonworldly contemplation; there is also a difference in the style of expression. The Gandharan art of second century A.D. India, for example, shifts from a concrete, materialized human form to a spiritualized and formalized expression of a transmundane Buddha. Likewise, standard hand gestures *(mudras)* in the images of the Buddha symbolize various activities such as teaching or contemplation. Thus, both the form and the style used in religious art portray a vision of ultimate reality.

Nontraditional Religious Subject Matter

Religious power is found not only in art that depicts the content of a specific religious tradition, but by some people in landscape paintings, still-life scenes, clothing designs, house construction, the Japanese tea ceremony, and some modern novels and drama. Such an understanding of the religious function of art is found in Western scholars like Paul Tillich and Jacques Maritain, and in Eastern scholars such as Ananda K. Coomaraswamy and D. T. Suzuki. This understanding holds that *any* aesthetic performance, regardless of explicit content, arises from the pressures of life's experiences, which are grounded in ultimate reality. The artist and observer participate in this ultimate ground or spiritual essence when they are sensitive to beauty.

In this context, art is a means for revealing a reality that transcends the concrete experience of aesthetic enjoyment. Art becomes the symbolic construction in time and space of eternal archetypes or spiritual essences. To learn the truth of existence means to know the inner side of things. A person cannot recognize the inner side of things, however, unless there is a corresponding pattern within the depths of his inner self. The structure, rhythm, and coherence produced in a work of art become the medium through which an individual's inner logic or personal existence interprets the logic of the cosmos. When the observer of an art object perceives something about himself or herself and the meaning of human life in the artist's forms, colors, or sounds, the observer's awareness is transformed to this pattern of meaning. Such an awareness can sometimes be translated into conceptual beliefs and metaphysical statements, which may happen when a person talks about art; however, the conceptual proposition cannot take the place of the power or immediacy of perception expressed by the work of art.

One means whereby artistic form incites an awareness of basic reality is in the identification of a "pure form" with a specific meaning. This is an expressionistic style of art in which there is no attempt to imitate the natural form of an object, but rather to depict its fundamental qualities through standard forms or images. Expressionism is seen, for instance, in the art of the American Indians on the north Pacific coast. Different animals and birds are portrayed by focusing on particular shapes of eyes, beaks, or tails; these features are regarded as the essential characteristics of that animal. The symbols have fixed associations.

In contemporary Western society, also, typical forms are used to convey meaning. A lute expresses music, a book education, a lion strength, a fox cunning, a machine the dehumanization of man. Also, there are motifs or symbolic activities in short stories, novels, and drama—for example, the young person leaving home for the first time, the initiation into a new world, the hero or heroine who conquers with cunning and strength, or the uncontrollable factors of life that provide surprises and often reveal a person's true character.

In another process whereby the essential nature of things is shown through nontraditional religious artistic forms, the artist "becomes in spirit" the reality or essence presented. A classical notion among oriental artists, for example, is that once the spirit is understood, the form creates itself. A painter who can "get into" the spirit of the plant, mountain, or seascape to be painted becomes that object. This sense of going beyond the outward form also underlies the Japanese notion of *yugen,* the intuitive sense of the profound, remote, and mysterious. It is exemplified, for example, in the *Noh* theatre, where the moments of nonaction spontaneously reveal what gesture or sound cannot convey. Dancing, singing, and gestures are imitations performed by the body, but the moments of nonaction reveal "emptiness" (that is, the way things are). Perhaps the best known aesthetic expression of spiritual reality in a common activity is the Japanese Zen tea ceremony,[91] in which ordinary activities like pouring tea and drinking it manifest reality. The exterior and interior of the tea hut and the garden, as well as the actions themselves, reveal to the sensitive observer the selflessness, peace, and spontaneous power said by the Buddhists to express the true nature of things.

Art can reveal the basic structure of things in a third way—by intensifying the latent structures of life within the observer. This takes place when a reader of a novel or an observer of an art object recognizes a significant portrayal of the most profound experience in human life. In *The Fall*, for example, Camus portrays human freedom and guilt, both of which people endure through their limited, but real, human capacity. For centuries, tragedies such as *Oedipus Rex* and *Hamlet* have produced insights into human existence. For some artists and viewers, modern abstract painting techniques disclose the elemental modes of matter, emphasizing the matter-of-factness of existence and the dissolution of traditional forms and syntheses of meaning. While much of modern art denies the traditional patterns of sacred meaning, it declares that human beings have the freedom and power to create a world out of the original material they possess by virtue of existence.

Art as the Process of Living

A third way of looking at the religious dimension in artistic effort is to view aesthetic form as a dynamic process in life. In this context, the most profound significance of art lies neither in visualizing the theology of a religious tradition nor in exposing the "pure form," essence, or universal pattern of existence. Rather, art is the aesthetic way of doing something. It is a sensitivity to form, interrelationships, and rhythm. Life is perfected in the process of ordering one's existence according to the natural, spontaneous forces that constitute the rhythm of one's particular effort. In this sense, the farmer who plows straight furrows and judges correctly just when to plant so that the crops can be harvested at a particular time is an artist, and so is the merchant who builds up trade through attractive advertising, sets prices according to true quality, and is sensitive to the tastes and needs of people. The notion of art as the process of living is related to the second way of exposing spiritual reality through nontraditional subject matter, wherein the artist, actor, or performer embodies the essential nature of life. Here, however, art is the functioning of any individual in such a way as to convey the proper rhythm or form of the activity involved.

For the past thousand years in Japan, and longer in traditional Chinese culture, a profound concern for aesthetic expression marks the common, everyday lives of people. In China, the deepest meaning was seen in relation to natural beauty and human perfectibility. Much Chinese poetry has dealt with everyday experiences and activities. An appreciation of common experiences, for example, is sensed in a short poem by Li Po (701–62 A.D.), "In the Mountains on a Summer Day":

Gently I stir a white feather fan,
With open shirt sitting in a green wood.
I take off my cap and hang it on a jutting stone;
A wind from the pine-trees trickles on my bare head.[92]

Especially among cultured Chinese, there has been little concern about a future life or transcendent reality. Rather, the intention was to live happily, which meant "wisely," and to enjoy the rhythm, order, mystery, and surprise of life in everyday activities. In creating moods of peace, harmony, or loneliness, the Chinese landscape artist, as well as the poet, sought to stimulate the mind and ennoble the spirit for the improvement of the human being. In cultivating an aesthetic sensitivity, the Chinese produced a sense of the rhythmical relationships of things and enhanced their capability to enjoy the immediate things of life.

The concern for rhythmical vitality was equally important in Japan. The appreciation of nature is evident not only in the formal religious expression of Shinto, but also in the cultivation of gardens, the imagery found in poetry, and the subject matter of ink line-drawings. Since the days of the Heian court (ninth to twelfth centuries A.D.), when refinement was of great importance, a concern to cultivate taste in the perfect expression of beauty has filtered down through the military classes to the peasantry. At present, one of Japan's new religions focuses on the aesthetic as the truest expression of religion. The first precept of this religion, PL Kyodan (perfect liberty order), is that "life is art."[93] To fulfill one's potential constitutes artistic creativity, which is held to be the most profound religious statement.

To understand art as a dynamic process rather than simply as an object of perception is to see that art is a capacity shared, to some extent, by everyone. To experience meaning in concrete forms is, largely, to experience concrete life as a *human being*. Thus, the artist is not a different species of animal but has a unique role in every culture to show the spiritual significance of the totality of human life rather than to perform one task well, such as farming or teaching. The artist can embody the elemental forces of humanity that seek spiritual expression. Thus, the energy and patterns of the American square dance, or the blues sung by blacks in the cotton fields, or the rhythmical movements of a policeman directing traffic in Rome show that people can get meaning from their movements and relationships. Nevertheless, the artist is most often the one who embodies the surge of creative possibilities. The artist reveals—say those who view aesthetic production as a means of ultimate transformation—a depth dimension in portraying the comedy and tragedy of our common humanity. With aesthetic sensitivity, skill, and expression, the artist is able to pose the questions of what it means to be human—questions that all people ask to some extent but that have exceptional power through artistic media.

Artists in their performances or works embody the human urge to give meaning to experience, and, thus, their lives are caught up in the question of what it means to be human. Of course, most artists are not systematic theorists. On the contrary, they express meaning through modes of experience other than rational and systematic discursive thought. The artist's power of creativity, however, often transcends the individual personality of the artist. Vincent van Gogh, to take one well-known example, felt driven by a creative power that was more than his conscious self. What this power is, or the goal toward which the artist strives, is difficult to name. Albert Hofstadter, in *Truth and Art,* suggests that in the creative process artists do not know exactly what the goal is, nor what they want to say. The reality they wish to express takes form during the process of creation; it is not preconceived. Artists reveal truth to the extent that the creative forms they adopt truly derive from the relationship between their natural capacities and the realities they perceive. Only then is the symbol true to the experience of life.

SELECTED READINGS

G. van der Leeuw, *Sacred and Profane Beauty: The Holy in Art,* translated by D. E. Green (New York: Holt, 1963, first published 1932). An eloquent discussion of the religious significance of dance, drama, rhetoric, the pictorial arts, architecture, and music, concluding with a general Christian theological aesthetic. Still one of the best statements on art as a sacred act. The book deals predominantly with the art of archaic society, the ancient Near East, and Europe.

Two readily available collections of essays on the expression of truth and reality through Western art are J. B. Vickery, ed., *Myth and Literature* (Lincoln: University of Nebraska Press, 1966), and E. Cell, ed., *Religion and Contemporary Western Culture.* In the former collection see especially Section 2, "Myth and Literature"; in the latter, Section 3, "Religion and Modern Art," and Section 4, "Religion and Modern Literature."

For an introduction to a variety of philosophical analyses of the truth expressed in aesthetic experience, the following are suggested: *S. K. Langer, *Philosophy in a New Key,* Chapter 9, "The Genesis of Artistic Import"; *F S. C. Northrop, *The Meeting of East and West,* Chapter 9, "The Traditional Culture of the Orient," and Chapter 10, "The Meaning of Eastern Civilization"; P. Wheelwright, *Metaphor and Reality* (Bloomington: Indiana University Press, 1962); A. Hofstadter, *Truth and Art* (New York: Columbia University Press, 1965); J. Hospers, *Meaning and Truth in the Arts* (Chapel Hill: University of North Carolina Press, 1946).

The importance of expressing Christian faith through pictorial and literary art has been recognized in recent decades. The following books will introduce the reader to some of the theological and aesthetic problems involved: J. W. Dixon, *Nature and Grace in Art* (Chapel Hill: University of North Carolina Press, 1964); R. Hazelton, *A Theological Approach to Art* (Nashville, Tenn.; Abingdon, 1967); N. A. Scott, *The Broken Center: Studies in the Theological Horizon of Modern Literature* (New Haven, Conn.: Yale University Press, 1966); A. N. Wilder, *Theology and Modern Literature* (Cambridge, Mass.: Harvard University Press, 1958).

For an introduction to the presentation of truth through art in non-Western cultures, the following books are readily available: *A. K. Coomaraswamy, *The Dance of Shiva: On Indian Art and Culture (New York: Noonday, 1957); *A. K. Coomaraswamy, *The Transformation of Nature in Art* (New York: Dover, 1934); Lin Yutang, *The Chinese Theory of Art: Translations from the Masters of Chinese Art* (New York: Putnam, 1967); *L. Warner, *The Enduring Art of Japan* (New York: Grove, 1952); *F. Boaz, *Primitive Art* (New York: Dover, 1955).

See J. Campbell, *Masks of God: Creative Mythology* (New York: Viking, 1968), as an expression of the self-consciousness of poetic creativity as a way to know personally and socially the ultimate nature of life.

13.

The Religious Significance of Physical Existence

Most of us agree that human life is part of a physical world. People see trees, ground, and sky, and everyone experiences life as an "I" moving about from one place to another. This direct perception of the world, however, is interpreted in light of the experiences and accounts of the world other people give us. For example, while many people experience the world as a relatively level surface, most Westerners regard the world as round or elliptical. Likewise, one's image of the world reflects not only spatial extension but time. People are conscious of being (in the present moment), and they know that they have been. By feeling related to a past, they experience time as both continuity and change but at the same time they are aware that they are different from their past.

Since the prehistoric dawn of self-awareness, human beings have been confronted with the profound existential experience of recognizing the reality of their personal, physical presence in the world. People have physical sensations and experience life in terms of now or then, here or there. This existential experience helps prompt such questions as "Who am I?" "Why am I in this world?" "What is this world, *really*?" "What is life all about?" and "Where do I fit into it?"

In asking these questions, people show an awareness of their physical existence. Answers to questions about the physical dimensions of life have a significant impact on a person's self-identity and image of being in the world. Immediate sensitivities to, and symbolic models of, time and space provide an important part of the human experience. One's definition of "fact" involves immediate sensations, an integrated organization of past experience, and information gained from what one believes to be reliable authority. For example, only a handful of astronauts have seen the roundness of the world; the rest of modern society believes that the earth is round and that the earth moves around the sun.

Various analogies have been used to form a cosmological picture of the way things are. Such models or images reflect different views of what the human race is and how people came to know their place in the order of things. Some of the best known models for human understanding of this world picture the world as a product of a transcendent maker or creator, or, in a biological image, as a product of a cosmic egg or seed, or as a whirlpool in one of the eddies of a huge stream of energy. The cosmological images that people use, however, are not pictures arbitrarily chosen, nor are they universally self-evident. They present an orientation to life, a set of assumptions and ways of interpreting existence that molds people's understanding of themselves. The human images of the physical world are, then, a power. They are an organizing force drawn from past experience that provides a pattern for future experience. Thus, a cosmology is a set of notions about the universe that also patterns our perceptions of the potential of the universe.

Among the great religious traditions, most have had more than one cosmology and different schools or branches of a religious tradition have chosen one cosmology or another. Most people use more than one cosmology to handle the variety of their experiences. This is highlighted by the contemporary concern within Christianity to demythologize the narrative of the New Testament gospels. The effort to translate the imagery of a Near Eastern cosmology common at the beginning of the Christian era into that of a twentieth-century Western culture poses several problems, however. There is a major shift in orientation. The gospels record human experience in terms of a three-level universe in which God is in heaven, man lives in the world, and the Son of God is sent into the world to redeem people from their sins. In contemporary science, existence is conceived of as energy, which has an inherent capacity to bring forth new phenomena, such as animate matter from inanimate matter. Contemporary scientists see a continuity extending from protein molecules, to energy exchanges in chemical transactions, to mammals, and finally to human life. During the past century, many scientists hav understood human life as a product of physical forces resulting from natural selection or chance mutations. The early Christian and contemporary scientific cosmologies provide different systems of self-definition and contrasting patterns of direction for future experience and further understanding of human life.

Time, like spatial extension, can be understood according to different models. Among the Swahili-speaking Bantu people in Africa, for example, time is not divided into (infinite) past, present, and (infinite) future, as in the modern West; it exists either as present (*sasa*) or as unlimited past *(zamani)*. What modern Westerners call "infinite future" is a return to the unlimited past for the Bantu. Events in *sasa* "move backward" into the *zamani*. [94]

Time can also be defined in terms of "original time" when the world began and the earliest or noblest ancestors, or divine beings, lived in the physical world. The Christian calendar used in the West, for example, designates time in relation to a sacred event, the birth of Jesus Christ. Other religious communities, like the Jews, Muslims, and Buddhists, also base their calendars on sacred events.

In a modern industrialized society, time is most often regarded as a mechanically segmented quantity of duration symbolized by the office clock. In this context, time has very little personal significance, since it is the record of an impersonal physical mechanism of identical consecutive moments. Occasionally, however, events such as birth, puberty, marriage, and death raise deeply disturbing questions: "When do I really start or stop existing?" "Did I or any part of me exist before birth or after death?" "Why exist at all?" "Who or what is finally responsible for what is?" "In which imagery can I find the most profound awareness of who I am?" "Must I choose one image or another, or can there be a reconciliation among several?" "Can human beings live with only one world-view and still do justice to the uniqueness of the individual person and the variety of human experiences?" These are some of the questions that arise when people reflect on their temporal-physical existence.

In forming a world-view, at least two religious issues need to be considered. The first issue concerns existence before birth and after death. It is sometimes phrased as two questions: Where do we come from and where are we going? These questions, from a religious perspective, are closely related. They reflect the fact that human existence is not an isolated phenomenon but part of a larger whole. In recognizing the facts of birth and death, many people within and outside organized religions seek to relate their direct physical-temporal awareness to some more lasting reality. A person's self-image is partly based on a recognition of the source of existence and its projected consequences.

The second issue involves the relationship between personal decision making and the nature of the universe. Is there order in the universe, and, if so, what relationship is there between that order and my actions? The recognition of a relationship between individual action and the universal order of things poses problems of morality. The specific way in which one deals with these issues—even the claim that these are foolish questions—provides some symbols of self-identity and eliminates others.

This chapter will deal with the impact of various cosmologies on individuals who are attempting to understand the reality of their physical presence in the world. Such cosmologies are found both inside and outside of the framework of traditionally defined religious structures. In either case, they can participate in ultimately transforming processes. Where they provide the vehicle for symbolizing everyday experience within a religious process based on a transcendent power, they are auxiliary elements in that process. They provide the imagery through which the interaction of the transcendent power and the physical-temporal world is understood. Most of the cosmologies discussed below serve an adjunct function of providing a picture of the world for a more comprehensive process of transformation. The last two sections, however, discuss contemporary scientific views of the world. There, the concern with historical and physical existence expresses a religious significance independent of a transcendent power. These sections analyze the contemporary Western concern with historical conditioning and technology as means of ultimate transformation.

Some people may find that more than one cosmology has functional religious significance for them. For different people, and even within the same person, various world views can provide an ordering force that transforms human experience from chaos to order, from confusion and weakness to understanding and control. Therefore, different types of cosmologies or world-views are significant within ultimately transforming processes; even a focus on the physical world, if it leads to the development of skills for controlling human life—as in some contemporary scientific endeavors—can become a means for ultimate transformation.

The World as God's Creation and Time as Revelation of God's Purpose

The first world-view to consider is the awareness of existence as the creation of an eternal God. Here human existence is not the natural product of an impersonal force, but the stage on which people express their obedience or disobedience to God's will. Such a view is represented by the prophetic tradition in Judaism, by Christian orthodoxy following the fourth-century theologian St. Augustine, and by the orthodox (Sunni) tradition in Islam. In this view, humanity lives not in a series of equally important (or unimportant) time segments but in response to unique manifestations of God's will and love in human history. Thus, present existence is dependent on ultimate reality, with which the passing moment is never to be confused.

Within this frame of reference, time and the physical world began with God's creative act and they remain meaningful only in relation to his ultimate purpose. As God's creation, time and the physical world were once full of possibilities for human happiness. But mankind's ancestors misused their opportunity to enjoy God's creation, and thus humanity experiences turmoil and suffering. Nevertheless, God uses a few people (like the prophets), certain historical events, and some societies as the media for revealing his will and love through which all people can live in at least limited happiness. The special moments of revelation, for example, God's gift of the Torah (law) and the prophetic tongue to interpret it properly, the incarnation of the divine word in Jesus Christ, or the recitation *(Qur'an)* of God's will to Muhammed, signify a qualitatively different moment than can be found in the natural world. Special revelation illuminates the true order of existence and its ultimate goal of fulfillment.

In the three Western religions of revelation, the moment of revelation is closely connected to the hope of an eventual fulfillment of God's purpose. This hoped-for goal can be expected either in this world or after death, although the ultimate realization comes at the end of time—when the world is no more. Human beings, together with the rest of creation, find their ultimate purpose and reality in following the laws of God. In Christianity and Islam, people depend on God's mercy and love; those who respond to him are brought into a blessed situation (heaven) that transcends the anxieties, pains, and sins of this existence. It would be presumptious for people to find meaning as a result of their own efforts; human beings can only wait and depend on God's pleasure. God, as the radically unconditioned total reality, is the "wholly other"; his mysteries surround temporal existence both in the beginning and at the end of the age.

The World as the Eternal Rhythm of Primal Energy

Another world-view sees human beings as part of a dynamic nature. Concrete experiences of life, natural phenomena, a person's self-awareness in relation to others in everyday events—all these hold ultimate reality, the potential of bliss, the power of "God." Here, the whole cosmos has the potential for expressing the divine order of things, the terrible-blissful power that brings all things into existence. The divine reality is seen in such common elements as water, fire, or human intellectual and political achievements. Such a cosmology is found in the Shinto apprehension of the divine *(kami)* in natural phenomena. It is also in the ancient Vedic awareness that the world is the appearance in many forms of the divine energy, Brahman, as controlled by the cosmic order *(rita)*. Similarly, the Chinese Confucian writer Tung Chung-shu (ca. 179–104 B.C.) sees human life as part of a totally interrelated cosmic order:

> The vital forces of Heaven and earth join to form a unity, divide to become the yin and yang, separate into the four seasons, and range themselves into the five agents. "Agent" in this case means activity. Each of the activities is different, therefore we speak of them as the five activities. The five activities are the five agents. In the order of their succession they give birth to one another, while in a different order they overcome each other. Therefore in ruling, if one violates this order, there will be chaos, but if one follows it, all will be well governed.[95]

This view can be classified with those cited in Chapter 7 as living harmoniously with cosmic law.

The view of human life as part of a cosmic order is consistent with both polytheism (many personal extraordinary powers) and monism (an impersonal universal power). Human beings are seen to live with all other existing beings in a vast community of forces and are expected to fulfill their natures and values by conforming to the inner necessity of the whole. Those who live in the flow of the eternal rhythm realize the most profound level of awareness; they are "blessed."

Human beings can get knowledge of eternal rhythm by looking at the sequential patterns of change in the natural and social worlds. Although the rhythm is too profound and mysterious for any simple conceptual formulation, people can know it directly because they participate in it—if they remain sensitive to its expression. This eternal power, as manifested in the concrete phenomena of life, provides answers to the most perplexing questions of the human situation. Sometimes special divination techniques have been used to reveal the mysterious universal rhythm. For example, the ancient Chinese classic *I Ching* (book of changes) was—according to those who gained advice from it—a special lens through which people could perceive their proper relationship to the ever-changing social and physical rhythm of the universe. Once individuals know where they are in relation to the whole, they can make appropriate personal decisions for attaining success in a particular situation. Those who are deeply aware of life know that the common experiences of day and night, the change of seasons, and relations between people reflect the natural rhythm of life. Those who perceive existence as successive beginnings and endings have a quite different view of their place in the cosmos from those who see humanity solely as God's creation.

One of the key religious implications of the notion that humanity is an integral part of the cosmos is that the terms "divine" and "natural" can be used simultaneously in reference to experienced phenomena. Nature is not a dead mechanism. The sun, rivers, mountains, and trees are divine in that their life force, the dynamics of their growth, movement, or stability, derives from the inherent order of cosmic energy. In this context, the world is the place to find spiritual fulfillment. Human participation in the cosmic rhythm of nature makes physical existence the normal place for spiritual attainment. A person's central religious concern is not to learn the unique revelation of God's will but to express spontaneously the natural order and rhythm of life. Human beings can be comfortable in this world and do not seek a transworldly existence. They can enjoy the manifestations of divine energy (which they are) in relation to all other things.

Eternal Patterns and the Everyday World

A third way in which people address themselves to the fact of existence is to regard the everyday world as a process of continual deterioration. At the same time, a few concrete actions can establish the "real world" when these actions are seen as repetitions of eternal, universal patterns. These patterns are known either through sacred myths (stories of divine actions) or by abstracting universal principles from everyday processes and events. In the mythical experience (see Chapter 6), the eternal patterns are considered more real than the changing flow of moment-by-moment experiences. In fact, *change* threatens the continuation of the eternal patterns. Some people have maintained a transtemporal and spatial pattern by repeating a ritual act.

The symbolic construction of a person's cosmos through ritual action is seen in a wide variety of expressions, such as the religious dances found in nonliterate societies, the rites of Osiris in ancient Egypt, the building of the Vedic fire altar in ancient India, the setting up of Roman altars to the *Soter* (savior) who guaranteed peace and prosperity, and the medieval interpretation of the Eucharist within Roman Catholic Christianity. This orientation distinguishes between divine realms and human realms; human activity is valid only insofar as it duplicates and re-forms human existence in the divine pattern. Through the ritual, a structure and order are given to chaos; value is infused into the fleeting, unstable moments of time.

Together with ritual activities and sacred symbols, certain mental activity has given stability and consistency to human experience. This activity is the use of logical principles and distinct concepts by which people analyze and organize their awareness into a meaningful system (see Chapter 10). The Western philosophical heritage provides many examples of attempts to find an eternal universal pattern or law that would account for many diverse and fleeting human experiences. Already in ancient Greece, the philosopher Plato asserted that there is a realm of eternal ideas more real than the experienced forms of human life. There is a gulf between the realm of universal, eternal abstraction and the concrete "things" of life. This bifurcation between the eternal idea and its refracted images known in everyday awareness was taken up by the Neo-Platonists when they defined humanity as a combination of spirit and material existence. The spirit, as the perfect aspect, was thought to be held down by material forces. The concrete forms of life were regarded as deviations from pure, divine reality. This attitude continued in different attempts at systematic reflection, so that one basic position in Western philosophy is that abstractions, universal laws, or principles are the tools by which people know the truth. If human beings can know the "pure ideas" or principles that are abstracted from concrete data, then they can *control* nature so that it becomes the servant of the spirit. Thus, the concern of the eighteenth and nineteenth century philosophers and scientists to learn the universal and eternal laws of nature was, in part, an attempt to overcome the ambiguous and unstable human physical situation.

Another expression of the phenomenal world as less than real, but directly established by eternal reality, is found in the Hindu devotional awareness of the world as God's "play" *(lila)*. In this perspective, all existence—the sun, moon, or a religious thought— is seen to be God's activity manifest in concrete events and things. The events of human life can reflect and suggest the divine reality of Vishnu, Shiva, or the great goddess Shakti. The continuing creation of the world, for example, is the cosmic dance of Shiva, just as the continual process of maturing, decay, and death is the relentless activity of the goddess Kali, one of the many forms of Shakti. While all life's activities are divine expressions, they are regarded as limited moments of divine exposure. As the Lord Krishna says in the *Bhagavad-gita,* the everyday realm of action *(karma)* is to be transcended by being absorbed in Krishna: "From the realm of Brahma downwards, all worlds are subject to return to rebirth, but on reaching Me . . . there is no return to birth again." (VIII, 16) Thus, the world, which is divine expression, is ultimately an illusive delight from which people must separate themselves if they are to return to the divine essence.

Experienced Existence—an Ambiguous Fabrication

Another orientation to man's awareness of time and space considers this world as illusion. The flux of time and physical things confuses the perception of what is ultimately real. As long as people are subject to these and believe that they reveal the true nature of things, they can never know who or where they are. Indeed, from this perspective, to ask where one is is to delude oneself because the question implies that there is a real context of time and space. The answer can be powerful, however, because it forms people's images of the world and binds them to false expectations. The view of the world as an illusion is found in such Indian systems of thought as Jainism, Advaita Vedanta, and Samkhya-yoga, and in Theravada Buddhism as expressed in the Abhidhamma literature. In these systems, concrete things are, by definition, constructed, impermanent, and nonuniversal and, thus, cannot be regarded as appropriate tools for expressing the truth.

A related but in many ways quite distinct position is found in the thought of the Chinese Taoist philosopher Chuang-tzu, the Buddhist philosopher Nagarjuna, the Zen Buddhist teacher Hui-neng, or the existential philosopher Karl Jaspers. Here time and space are relatively real conditions of human existence, but without any *intrinsic* positive or negative value. Human existence has no absolute meaning found in universal patterns of divine pronouncements, nor is change meaningless as it was in the third sub-type described above. These Taoist, Buddhist, and existential thinkers define happiness differently and prescribe different methods for attaining truth but share a common concern for living life spontaneously in light of the fluidity of all existing situations. This means a detachment from concrete material forms on the one hand and, on the other, an appreciation of the experiences that anyone can have in any concrete moment. Thus, sensitivity to time and conditions is crucial if people wish to realize their potential as human beings, so long as the immediacy of this sensitivity is *not* transformed and crystallized into absolute, universal, abstract principles.

Historical Study as a Method for Understanding Human Life

There are various approaches to the meaning of time in traditional religious expressions, but in the West a special technique, called historical study, has been used to investigate human existence. At its base, historical study assumes that the particular events of man's existence significantly convey some measure of reality. If human beings want to know who they are, they have to take seriously both the historical context in which they live and the past with which they feel some continuity.

While sensitivity to the concrete historical conditions of life may seem an obvious necessity to some readers, it is not found in all people either in the past or in the present. For example, a well-known American industrialist of the early twentieth century claimed that "history is bunk." Those who hold this view do not regard the history and culture of others as intrinsically significant to their self-awareness. The past simply represents a realm of spent energies, immature activities in the development of humanity, and preliminary stages in technology. For someone dominated by a concern for industrial production, time is a measure for marking off the quantity of manufactured things or the number of man-hours related to a rate of production.

During the nineteenth century, historical study came into full bloom. It did not begin with the assumption that history was the revelation of God's grace; rather, its aim was to get facts about human activity. The past was interpreted in terms of *human* effort. The concern with concreteness and particularity was aimed at freedom from any doctrine, faith, or philosophical presupposition. The object was to examine the complex set of conditions in which a historical phenomenon took place and then to understand it by reconstructing the phenomenon emerging in the temporal process.

If historians were to interpret a human phenomenon in its historical context, however, they had to assume that there were patterns of continuity and order that prevented life from being chaotic or arbitrary. Various models of the process of continuity and change have been used. Some of the most famous are Hegel's notion that history is the unfolding of the Spirit through a dialectical expression of opposites emerging in a new synthesis; Giambattista Vico's notion that history developed much as an organism in nature; and Wilhelm Dilthey's notion of the creative capability of man to produce culture, philosophy, and religion, which are manifested in patterns of meaning first in individuals and eventually in institutions. This last approach emphasizes that the historian deals with *human* phenomena rather than with eternal principles or simply physical phenomena. It requires an interpretive technique that exposes the human capacity to make free choices, rather than universal principles or causal factors that account for specific historical forms.

The distinction between explaining life in terms of physical, inanimate forces and in terms of human decisions is a very important one when human historical concreteness is used as a basis for interpreting who or what humanity really is. Understanding the human world, claims Dilthey, requires concepts usually regarded as unnecessary in explaining the physical world: intention, will, decision. The process whereby the historian grasps the meaning of human existence requires sensitivity to data as a field of *human* activity. Historical data are not just objective facts to be related as pieces of a puzzle outside the observer. Rather, historians must become sensitive to their humanness in order to interpret life as a human event rather than as a natural, mechanical process. In order to interpret the data correctly, they must be aware of the questions people ask. In Dilthey's notion of understanding, then, the questions of an historian participate in the interpretation of data; at the same time, the historian must appeal to empirical data available to every historian.

The Scientific View

Just as historical studies called into question mythical and "sacred history" interpretations of human existence, so the empirical sciences developed during the last three centuries have questioned the understanding of the physical world and human life that was thought to be derived from divine authority. Scientific knowledge does not simply supply people with new information; it provides them with a world-view in terms of its methods and imagery.

The scientific view does not represent the first human effort to take account of the concrete characteristics of human experience. This has been the intention of every cosmology. The scientific method is distinguished by its intentions to define the world in terms of empirically measurable forces and conditions that produce given consequences, and to limit self-consciously the understanding of life to these identifiable factors and processes. The scientific effort that began with the European Renaissance and developed in the eighteenth-century Enlightenment challenged the earlier view that "natural knowledge" and "revealed truth" were two ways of knowing. From the scientific perspective, there were *not* two realms of reality: God and creation. Empirical data alone exposed the creative process.

This reformulation of the nature of existence requires a new method for knowing the truth. No longer are there two sources for human understanding of life, with empirical analysis taking second place to a body of revelation preserved by a religious institution. The truth about life has been available to all people at all times in the natural processes. Perhaps even more importantly, from a religious point of view, is the affirmation that human beings can understand themselves by objective empirical studies, without divine revelation. People interpret humanity as a process of becoming, which not only controls them, but which they can control in part. Some contemporary scientists feel that the deepest human meaning does not lie in something given in the historical past or expressed in mythical forms; it is something to be discovered empirically. The careful analysis and verification of scientific hypotheses can advance human understanding, say such scientists, by developing new realms of awareness, concepts, and procedures. Such a development will extend the horizons of predictability and control, thus opening new worlds of discovery.

The effort to form a better world is dramatically evident in visionary scientist R. Buckminster Fuller's huge computer-fed game, "How Do We Make the World Work?" In this learning game, teams of players win by making humanity a continuing success at the earliest moment possible:

> The general-systems-theory controls of the game will be predicated upon employing within a closed system the world's continually updated total resource information in closely specified network complexes designed to facilitate attainment, at the earliest possible date by every human being, of complete enjoyment of the total planet earth, through the individual's optional traveling, tarrying, or dwelling here and there. This world-around freedom of living, work, study, and enjoyment must be accomplished without any one individual interfering with another and without any individual being physically or economically advantaged at the cost of another.[96]

Although many adherents of traditional religions would be skeptical about the possibility of providing "complete enjoyment" for everyone, those who claim ultimate power for the technological revolution urge people to have courage and patience and to make a great effort. Human beings, they insist, will be able to change their biological and cultural capacities. In *Technological Man: The Myth and Reality,* V. C. Ferkiss writes:

> Humanity today is on the threshold of self-transfiguration, of attaining new powers over itself and its environment that can alter its nature as fundamental as walking upright or the use of tools. No aspect of man's existence can escape being revolutionized by this fundamental fact—all his self-consciousness that we call culture, his patterns of interaction that we call society, his very biological structure itself. . . . [A] complex of events has altered the nature of man, the complex of discoveries and powers that we glibly speak of as modern technology.[97]

Scientists and others holding these views raise many basic religious and philosophical questions about human freedom and identity. The questions are ancient, but they are now formulated with a sensitivity to physical control of self-images, values, and consciousness.

In the West and parts of the world that have been influenced by the West, the scientific view has, to a large measure, assumed the force of final (religious) authority. Scientific analysis provides the imagery for explaining life, human personality, and social expressions. While most scientists deny that the empirical study of the world and the processes of life is religion, this procedure for discovering truth functions religiously by providing the concepts for the scientist's map of the universe. Paradoxically, the religious function that the scientific view has assumed for some modern men makes it accessible to the hazard of dogmatism that it sought to overcome.

Some scientists and theologians would deny that scientific analysis and traditional religious activity have anything in common. They are, they say, two separate activities that need not be in conflict. The procedures in a chemistry or physics laboratory contrast with the activities that go on in a church, mosque, or Zen monastery. Sometimes the two realms have been kept separate by some representatives of each, who relegate the other realm either to inconsequential discovery or to superstition. And the believer is then often left with the schizophrenia of using one world-view most days a week and a different one on holy days.

Today, however, some exponents of both science and traditional religion hold that a different stance is possible. Some contemporary leaders of religious traditions recognize the influence and contribution of the scientific world-view in articulating the relationship between traditional religious claims and other expressions of life or energy. Also, some contemporary scientists, as they attempt to reveal the cosmic order, do not feel required to assert an absolute, unchanging "natural order," into which everything is fitted and do not explain the depth and complexity of nature as the result of an exclusively naturalistic process. For these exponents, new potentialities and possibilities for change appear to increase indefinitely as more areas of human life are investigated at deeper levels. The natural laws, which at one time were held to be universally true, are seen to apply to only a limited range or dimension of human life. Thus, the scientist needs more than one theory of light, of energy, of the life processes to account for the data now at hand. Whereas the traditional methods of religious activity and those of empirical science differ radically in technique, these efforts at perceiving truth appear to overlap in the experience and imagery of many contemporary people.

To the extent that the scientific method focuses exclusively on the physical world and scientists envision the nature of existence only in terms of physical forces, this mode of human awareness has become a means of ultimate transformation. For those who place the physical aspects of existence in a context of other religious structures, the scientific mode of human awareness is an auxiliary means of approaching the ultimate dimension of human life. In both cases, however, sensitivity to one's actual presence in the world has a profound impact on the individual and the community. It provides a way of understanding everyday experiences and an implicit standard—though not necessarily the only one—of what is valuable and true. A cosmology that values concrete physical life encourages efforts to control the physical aspects of human experience.

SELECTED READINGS

The religious significance of the way people view the world is explained in W. B. Kristensen, *The Meaning of Religion,* Part I, "Cosmology," and in *G. van der Leeuw, *Religion in Essence and Manifestation,* Part IV, "The World." These important phenomenological studies deal predominantly with religions of the Near East.

A more general discussion of the importance of cosmic imagery, with emphasis on linear and cyclic world processes to contrast the Judaeo-Christian-Muslim orientation with archaic and Eastern religions, is found in W. L. King, *Introduction to Religion,* rev. ed., Chapter 8, "Cosmogonies and Cataclysms: The Mythos of World Beginnings and Endings."

A more comprehensive discussion of the variety of cosmologies in human history is found in two studies by S. G. F. Brandon: *Time and Mankind* (New York: Hutchinson, 1951), and *History, Time and Deity* (New York: Barnes & Noble, 1965).

M. K. Munitz, *Theories of the Universe* (New York: Free Press, 1957). A volume of selected readings from Western sources on cosmology from Babylonian culture to modern science, for the general reader.

H. Corbin et al., *Man and Time,* papers from the *Eranos* Yearbooks, vol. 3 (New York: Pantheon, 1957). A collection of papers on the imagery of time by specialists in different religious and cultural traditions.

An introduction to the importance of historical study for understanding human life can be found in the selections in P. Gardiner, ed., *Theories of History* (New York: Free Press, 1959), which includes representative philosophies of history and recent views on the nature of historical knowledge and explanation; and *K. Löwith, *Meaning in History* (Chicago: University of Chicago Press, 1949), in which the theological implications of some basic Western interpretations of time are analyzed.

The nature of modern science and its contribution to human understanding of existence is discussed in I. G. Barbour, *Issues in Science and Religion* (Englewood Cliffs, N.J.: Prentice-Hall, 1966) and H. K. Schilling, *Science and Religion: An Interpretation of Two Communities* (New York: Scribner's, 1962). For both authors, "religion" means predominantly Protestant Christianity, and the central focus is on understanding the differences, together with the interrelatedness, of these two sources of human meaning. Barbour's book includes an analysis of four specific problems (e.g., determinism vs. human freedom, evolution vs. creation), and the discussion presents Christian theology and modern science as alternative languages applied to human life. Schilling's book develops the author's conviction that there is a continuous spectrum of knowledge extending from the physical sciences to religion.

For an introduction to an understanding of human life derived from neurobehavioral experiments, see J. M. R. Delgado, *Physical Control of the Mind: Toward a Psychocivilized Society* (New York: Harper, 1969). Also, excerpts from advocates of a scientific transformation of human life are found in F. J. Streng, C. L. Lloyd, Jr., and J. T. Allen, eds. *Ways of Being Religious,* Chapter 7, "The New Life through Technocracy."

14.

The Consequences of Understanding Religious Life

"The future of religion is extinction." So say some social scientists and cultural philosophers. By this they mean that the beliefs, values and spiritual practices of the past are no longer useful. Modernity, with its increasing rapidity of change, requires radically different perspectives and expectations from those that have had the greatest significance or power in human history. While the claim that religion will come to an end may shock some readers—and appear as self-evident to others—it serves to stimulate reflection on the approach taken in this book.

The basic thesis of this book is that the central dimension of human life is, and will remain, religious; the dynamics of religion will not become extinct. As noted in Chapter 1, religious life always involves two separate but interrelated aspects: the observable forms and the religious intention, or the external historical expression and the internal dynamics. The ways, or structural processes, in which people seek ultimate transformation have both internal and external effects. They have an impact on, and are affected by, social and historical forces of production and destruction and lead to alternative ontological claims by their adherents. These processes bring about more complete realization of the nature of things, rather than just changes in forms of religion.

In this perspective, the motivating force of religious forms partially arises from the efforts, intentions, failures, and thwarted hopes of people in their daily lives. Moreover, a religious structure that exerts ultimately transforming power is not isolated from other modes or structures of human awareness that do not. Instead, such modes of human awareness as thought patterns, aesthetic sensitivities, or social relationships function in relation to historical, psychological, economic, or other conditions. This is true whether they operate within traditional religious forms or themselves serve as ways of religious apprehension. Although one structure of ultimate transformation may predominate in an individual or community, there may also be several subordinate structures with various historical forms. Thus, any structure of ultimate transformation has elements in it that may shift from a subordinate role to a primary one. This shift may be significant enough to produce a shift in the structure itself. This kind of shift has taken place, for example, in some modern Western thinkers whose early lives reflect a structure of "a personal awareness of a holy presence" or of "sacred action" but whose later writings reflect a structure affirming human relationships or rational thought as the basic means of ultimate transformation. The fact that secondary elements in one religious process can become primary elements in another process while maintaining the function of ultimate transformation suggests that the dynamics of religious life will endure while cultural processes and historical forms of religion continue to change.

The history of religions is a record of changes. A study of history shows that the content and expression of religious awareness have changed from both external and internal pressures and to varying degrees. If one forgets that being religious involves opening new vistas of meaning, stretching (and at times tearing) the traditional forms, and also recognizing oneself in the symbols of the past, religion turns into an extinct organism or shimmers out of reach in the mirage of abstraction. The recognition of change raises the question of what religion can and should be today. If people recognize that they are on a religious frontier, they must acknowledge at least three concerns. Each concern forms the central focus of one part of this book. The concerns are: (1) the meaning of the subjective element in religious experience and the study of religion; (2) the significance of different basic or structural processes of ultimate transformation; and (3) the relevance of contemporary processes for ultimate fulfillment in life.

The Subjective Element

Faced with the possibility of accepting the notion of religious pluralism, a contemporary American often falls into an attitude of despair. In part, this is because Jewish or Christian attitudes, which are dominant in this culture, have emphasized exclusive participation in one tradition. The admission of religious pluralism is interpreted as a defection from the "teachings of the fathers." Some people have been overwhelmed with guilt at not being, say, a good Christian, simply because they have allowed the introduction of new scientific or cultural data to challenge the primary presuppositions upon which their parents' belief system rested.

Nevertheless, people today cannot avoid engagement with neighbors of other faiths; part of spiritual growth requires the consideration of alternate religious possibilities not only as interesting intellectual options, but as influences on an individual's world-view. This may even challenge the way in which people regard their existence. Indeed, the introduction of new religious possibilities may cause a personal identity crisis, but the outcome may be crucially important for further spiritual development. The choice in today's small world is not whether to engage people of other faiths or to respond to scientific discovery; it is rather whether or not to risk becoming aware of one's own religiousness in light of several cultural traditions. It is a question of whether or not to permit a deepening of religious experience from different sources, both past and present.

The situation becomes more complex when the individual is called upon to play the dual roles of religious adherent and objective student of religion, because the roles often seem antagonistic to each other. What is one to do on becoming sensitive to the value of a life-orientation that one did not know existed as a serious option? The scholar is confronted with an inner struggle of values between personal religious beliefs and objective methods of study. Some of the most obvious reactions to the conflict are defensive and negative. Sometimes religious beliefs, instead of being reexamined, are simply cast aside as inferior to the more up-to-date methods of "objective" research. On other occasions, the objective study of religion is rejected in its entirety as impious and irreligious and the original and unexamined belief system is exalted as better simply because all other arguments have been dismissed from the field without serious consideration.

A third nonintegrating response might be to carry on the roles of both researcher and believer in isolation from one another. The result is a lack of any relationship between one's religious experience and one's work. Eventually, a double standard may develop where one's belief system does not guide one's actions and one's actions do not uphold or substantiate one's articulated beliefs.

The concern in Part I to review various approaches to the study of religious life suggests that people do not understand religious phenomena as wholly external entities. Individuals' perception of the origins, functions, or meaning of religious life are conditioned by their concerns about it. It is important therefore to become aware of the questions and answers of scholars and devotees. Such an examination illuminates some of the issues involved in the two roles and suggests how the differences and overlapping character of analysis and participation affect the outcome of claims made by either. Likewise, an investigator of religious life can become sensitive to the conflicts of benefits that may result when personal religious beliefs are related to objective methods of study.

The exploration of various kinds of objective study and different traditional and nontraditional religious options can enhance a person's understanding of religious life and ability to make religious decisions. In the last analysis, some tension and, it is hoped, a healthy balance will remain between one's religious commitment and the development of a procedure and interpretive skills for a theoretical understanding of religious life. The latter aspect is important in the scholarly world, which needs to develop an intellectually disciplined method of understanding religious life that does not depend on the adherence of all researchers to a common belief system. Scholars need a theory about religious life, not an ideology—especially one based simply on the researcher's religious belief—and they need to be able to examine that theory from the joint perspectives of empirical study and philosophical reflection. At the same time, any serious consideration of the ultimacy of a particular expression of religion may open up the possibility of ultimate transformation in the researcher's life.

This book, then, assumes that awareness of one's beliefs can initiate a personal religious transformation; however, the direction of the transformation is determined by an individual's ability to face different possibilities. The attitude that one takes toward one's own inner struggle to understand is crucial. To the extent that one retreats into the security of an option without considering any other, one fails to rise to one's potential. The person who is able to contrast and compare different possibilities has the opportunity to choose among them or to develop a new religious awareness.

The engagement with alternate religious options, of course, always takes place in a particular cultural-historical context and may have unforeseen consequences.

For example, a scholar's descriptions of ultimate significance may contribute to learning processes that have ultimate consequences for both the scholar and others.

The Significance of Religious Pluralism

The second concern of this book that has consequences for contemporary religious life is the fact of religious pluralism. Part II briefly examined the structure and elements of different traditional ways of being religious. It emphasized the important differences in function of dominant elements within various religious traditions, such as Judaism, Buddhism, and traditional Chinese family religion. Structural analysis is also one method for recognizing significant differences of self-understanding within a religious or cultural tradition. When these differences are considered important, they play a key role in the growth of contemporary religious self-consciousness.

A person does not express a religious dimension in life in isolation from historically and culturally determined religious forms. Rather, the inner religious experience arises within—or in reaction to—the concepts and structures of these forms. In addition, consciousness of particular historical forms and social structures enables an individual within a particular religious tradition to recognize that other religious people have different creeds, cultic forms, and symbols, although he shares with them a number of identifiable religious characteristics. From a cultural standpoint, the first reaction to this discovery may be to reduce all religious reality to a form of cultural forces. Then a particular religion is seen as an "ideology," a "set of mores," or "a cultural pattern", and each one is regarded as having only relative validity. Another kind of cultural reductionism is the identification of the general meaning of religion with particular historical forms; the different religions are then regarded as self-contained, separate cultural entities having no inter-relationships. In this view, Hinduism is only for South Asians and Buddhism only for East Asians. Other religions are regarded as just so many separate, unchanging systems of views, morals, and cultic acts—curious, but dead, objects of study.

A quite different reaction, however, recognizes that other human beings are (at least apparently) equally moral, devout, intelligent, and religiously sensitive as oneself, despite quite different religious views, and equally able to find happiness and peace and to perceive profound meaning. When the spiritual insights and possibilities of others are seen to expose some of the dynamic character and tensions of one's own means of ultimate transformation, then the recognition of religious pluralism raises interesting personal questions. Why not participate in the joys and freedom witnessed to by a different religion? Is it possible to learn about a religious tradition without joining a community of devotees? Does an eclectic appreciation of different religious options destroy the ultimacy claimed in each religious tradition or mode of religious awareness?

A careful study of other religious people reveals that they, like oneself, are sometimes frustrated, sometimes successful; they wrestle with meaning and attempt to transcend the limitations of their systems. Reformations and reinterpretations are part of the dynamics of every historical religious tradition. Certainly each historical tradition contains a norm, or a body of norms, setting the limits of orthodoxy, but there are also profound differences within a religion, as indicated by the different structures found in any single tradition. To understand a religious tradition means, in part, to perceive the religious tensions and ambiguities between and within human beings who seek new horizons of meaning. Sometimes people within a tradition find surprises when they study it that require changes in their questions as well as their answers.

The attempt by some devout believers to understand a person living in another religious tradition for religious or theological reasons is a new development in the religious self-consciousness of modern Western society. Up to the present time, the predominant theological view in the West has been that it is the institutional religious authorities who, by stressing continuity with former symbols, have determined the limits whereby ultimate truth can be known. Or, at best, other religious traditions have been regarded as weak reflections and different statements of the truth of one's own religion. Even traditions like Hinduism and Buddhism, which emphasize that people can best be religious in the way and at the level appropriate to them, recognize that the truth perceived by the spiritually mature differs from that perceived by the masses.

The awareness that religious commitment need not be limited by ethnic or linguistic background challenges one to examine the theological and religious forms of other cultures. Many people are exploring value-systems that their parents had never heard of in their youth. They are exploring without assuming that wholesale conversion is necessary for understanding or that they must abandon their religious heritage to enter into another's.

Although people should be willing to explore the values and forms of other religious traditions, they should not assume that all religions are really the same because they have some common elements. To overlook the differences between religious claims and religious structures is often to fail to see the intention of a particular, historical expression.

The recognition that a person's ultimate commitment is one of many culturally conditioned expressions within a context of religious pluralism avoids two kinds of interpretive shortsightedness. The first is that all religions must eventually fuse into one powerful religious system, the form of which will be identical with that of a past or present religious expression. In this view, everyone would be forced to adhere to a single religion or ideology, accept one creed, and perform prescribed rituals. The other short-sighted view is the notion that the consideration of various religious possibilities will necessarily end in chaos, confusion, and the degeneration of all values. Both types of reductionistic thinking tend to overlook the humanity of people whose values differ from one's own. Unfortunately, human history records countless people who have tried to destroy all foreign influences and foreigners. Both views also inhibit the efforts of individuals or religious communities to develop new insight about the meaning of religion for themselves or others. The consideration of various religious options does not mean the rejection of all previous commitments; people who are overwhelmed by the ambiguity of human experience may become fearful and withdraw into a defensive stance of decision-less drifting, thus losing their former sense of commitment. However, people can be helped to realize their full potential despite the initial difficulties such growth presents. By its nature, growth is a liberating and enlightening experience.

Among the implications of religious pluralism for contemporary religious self-consciousness are: (1) a religion need not be regarded as an inherited ideological system available only to those within that cultural tradition; (2) religious traditions allow significant internal differences and change in response to new historical situations; and (3) a person's religious commitment to one historical tradition can be enhanced by the incorporation of some values and practices found elsewhere.

One need not judge another person's faith as false just because one is committed to, and finds significance in, a given religious tradition. A more profound awareness of religious possibility can grow as one's own faith permits one to love another person—including the differences from, as well as similarities with, oneself. By trying to understand new discoveries while using ancient religious symbols, modern people can seek new definitions and concepts of what religion *might be*. This involves an openness to experimentation with new religious forms, techniques, and concepts that have been unknown, neglected, or denounced in the past.

Possibilities of Contemporary Transformation

The third focus of this book is on the relevance of contemporary forms of transformation; all spheres of life can provide a possibility of ultimate transformation. Any learning experience, as in classrooms, committees, political meetings, or artistic creation, can develop insight, receptivity, and fuller human relationships. Religious elements pervade dimensions of human existence beyond those culturally and historically associated with religion. The investigator should be aware of today's emerging possibilities for ultimate transformation, even though they appear to be quite different from traditional religious forms. Thus, Part III focused on five "modes of human awareness" that have become means of ultimate transformation for some people.

The recognition that new kinds of religious life are emerging today implies that the study of religion is not limited to certain traditional sorts of human expression labeled "religion." It raises questions about the inner dynamics of life. It also indicates that, today as in other times, there is an ultimate context of human awareness and commitment that is not limited by the specific cultural definitions of religion that are used to expose that context. To recognize this ultimate context, one must be aware of the ultimate dynamics of one's own life and be willing to consider others' experiences of transformation.

In becoming sensitive to the dynamics of ultimate transformation in a variety of processes and forms, the investigator may also cultivate an awareness of one or more evaluational processes in which he or she participates. One characteristic of any symbol or concept is that it carries a normative force; what it signifies is considered real. Concepts indicate objects of consciousness, which, in being designated, take on the quality of importance. What is most important for people is what is real for them. The study of religion and all it signifies may itself become a means of ultimate transformation for some people. This does not mean that the academic study of religion will or should become the one universal religion of the future. People find an ultimate dimension within many different religious traditions and outside of formal religious institutions. The study of other religious forms need not lead to the rejection of one's own tradition (it may even make one more aware of the richness of that tradition), but it can enlarge one's range of religious options. In describing some of the options, this book makes no judgments as to their relative value but indicates the kinds of significance religion can have as a practical force in a person's life. Each reader must decide on the advantages and disadvantages of particular forms and processes of religious life—recognizing that some forms and processes are already influencing that decision.

Nevertheless, religious forms die when they no longer provide the direction and power for making decisions. Indeed, the great religious traditions have a history because they have met human problems differently in different times and places; their formulations and institutions change while at the same time preserving some continuity with past expression. One may feel regret and anxiety over the loss of a former structure of meaning and in the same moment experience a more profound order of reality that changes, yet deepens, a former understanding.

The accumulation of experiences over the years does not always bring spiritual maturity. To recognize this is only to admit there is no inevitable spiritual progress within the individual person or within the human race. It is to recognize that the creative power in discovery can be turned back on itself in a destructive way. For example, the concern to better oneself or to transcend one's limitations, while apparently springing from the highest motives, can turn into a struggle to control others for the benefit of oneself. Or, as many educators, psychiatrists, and theologians have warned regarding contemporary America, the development of industrial power, technological discovery, and economic prosperity—while in themselves not to be equated with evil—provide a capacity for dehumanization in the loss of self-respect and individual creativity in a mass society. Also the legacy of Western Enlightenment, freedom from absolute commitments, has provided the conditions for a situation often recognized today: a monotony of uncommitted lives.

The freedom attained by rejecting one value orientation does not necessarily mean freedom from the bondage of another value orientation that also turns out to be less than ultimate. The exchange of one idol for another is not spiritual freedom. How to avoid slipping into spiritual ignorance in the midst of the highest spiritual efforts is a continuing religious problem. The tools for a creative spiritual life may, without one's recognizing it, turn into weapons that result in spiritual death. Nevertheless, if the history of religions points to one truth, it is that the less-than-authentic (or idolatrous) ways of living will be found out by *other* people—people who themselves are subject to some sort of limitations!

To have any kind of religious commitment is to make choices among the options given in the ideas we use, the social and psychological relationships we have with other people, and the symbolic and aesthetic sensitivities we have of life. The most profound limitation is not, however, in the finite (though vast) number of possibilities in a given situation; the greatest danger often is to crystallize the status quo with religious fervor and thereby reject the dynamic, the uncontrollable, the indefinable (and undefined) character of the spiritual.

To live authentically, then, is to recognize the status quo for what it is: a set of conditions *and* the capacities to transcend this status quo. The religious forms in which human beings *have* participated and the tension within modern man's self-identity are part of the status quo. They are part of the limitations and possibilities we must consider in order to interpret who we are. In this light, understanding the religious life of man and reflecting on "the characteristics" of religious life are not just abstract problems to be approached by a few specialists in history, philosophy, or theology; they are directly related to what it means to be human.

SELECTED READINGS

The condition of contemporary Western culture is described as "post-Christian" by G. Vahanian in *The Death of God* (New York: Braziller, 1957) and *Wait Without Idols* (New York: Braziller, 1964). Both books clearly describe the difference between the assumptions expressed in present European and American culture and those of the Christian gospel.

Two books stating a religious perspective that includes the "best" in traditional religious expressions while emphasizing the capacities within human life are: *J. Dewey, *A Common Faith* (New Haven, Conn.: Yale University Press, 1934); and *R. Tagore, *The Religion of Man* (Boston: Beacon, 1931).

R. N. Bellah, ed., *Religion and Progress in Modern Asia* (New York: Free Press, 1965). A collection of papers by a variety of scholars on the influence of religious life and belief in different Asian countries. The epilogue provides an incisive analysis of the problems of defining and understanding the role of religion in contemporary Asian life.

*C. Castanada, *Journey to Ixtlan; The Lessons of Don Juan* (New York: Touchstone Books, Simon & Schuster, 1972). Explores the consequences of opening a person to a new self-awareness.

*Dom A. Graham, *The End of Religion* (New York: Harcourt, 1971). A personal statement by a Roman Catholic who sees "ultimate religion" as a person "responding to the Existence in virtue of which he himself exists" and making use of insights from the whole history of human spiritual experience.

D. Howlett, *The Fourth American Faith* (New York: Harper, 1964). Here the fourth faith, the "faith of adventure," is described over against Protestantism, Catholicism, and Judaism.

*T. Luckmann, *The Invisible Religion: The Problem of Religion in Modern Society* (New York: Macmillan, 1967). A sociologist of religion analyzes the religious significance of various social and cultural forms in Western industrial society with particular concern for those unrelated to church organizations.

R. E. L. Masters and J. Houston, *The Varieties of Psychedelic Experience* (New York: Holt, 1966). After discussing the history of psychedelic drug use and the experiences described by its users, the final chapter, entitled "Religious and Mystical Experience," explores the possibility of interpreting dimensions of some psychedelic experiences as religious.

*C. A. Reich, *The Greening of America* (New York: Random, 1970). Advocates the development of a new consciousness in America that focuses on humanistic values and projects that such a consciousness will transform American society through individual inner change.

C. Tart, ed., *Altered States of Consciousness* (New York: Wiley, 1969). One of the pioneer readers in the contemporary transpersonal movement in psychology, this work includes contributions from major authors on dreams, meditation, hypnosis, psychedelic drugs, and biofeedback.

*A. Toffler, *Future Shock* (New York: Random, 1970). A study of the impact of accelerating social, political, and technological change in the West; the author calls for a humanization of planning in social and political structures.

Notes

1. E. Cassirer, *The Philosophy of the Enlightenment,* trans. F. Koelln and J. Pettegrove (Boston: Beacon, 1951, first published 1932), p. 13.

2. "Pre-animistic Religion," *Folklore* 11 (1900), 162–82; reprinted in R. R. Marett, *The Threshhold of Religion* (London: Methuen, 1909).

3. See Chapter 5, "Mana and Taboo," in W. A. Lessa and E. Z. Vogt, eds., *Reader in Comparative Religion: An Anthropological Approach,* 2d ed. (New York: Harper, 1965), or Chapter 3, "Mana and Tabu: A Force and a Danger," in W. Howell, *The Heathens* (Garden City, N.Y.: Doubleday, 1948).

4. E. Durkheim, *The Elementary Forms of the Religious Life,* trans. J. Swain (London: George Allen and Unwin, 1915), p. 422.

5. In C. H. Kraeling, ed., *The City Invincible, Symposium on Urbanization and Cultural Development in the Ancient Near East* (Chicago: University of Chicago Press, 1960), pp. 351–66.

6. C. G. Jung, *Psychology and Religion* (New Haven, Conn.: Yale University Press, 1938), p. 98.

7. See R. N. Bellah, "Civil Religion In America," in his *Beyond Belief* (New York: Harper, 1970), pp. 168–89; and W. L. Warner, *American Life: Dream and Reality* (Chicago: University of Chicago Press, 1953).

8. T. Luckmann, *The Invisible Religion: The Problem of Religion in Modern Scoiety* (New York: Macmillan, 1967), pp. 53–56.

9. See A. L. Kroeber, *Anthropology,* rev. ed. (New York: Harcourt, 1948) and *Nature of Culture* (Chicago: University of Chicago Press, 1952).

10. C. Kluckhohn, "Myths and Rituals: A General Theory," *Harvard Theological Review* 35 (January 1942), pp. 45–79. Reprinted in W. A. Lessa and E. Z. Vogt, eds., *Reader in Comparative Religion,* pp. 144–58.

11. See L. H. Jordan, *Comparative Religion: Its Genesis and Growth* (Edinburgh: T. and T. Clark, 1905).

12. G. van der Leeuw, *Religion In Essence and Manifestation* (New York: Harper, 1963) p. 688.

13. J. Wach, *The Comparative Study of Religions,* J. M. Kitagawa, ed. (New York: Columbia University Press, 1958), p. 30.

14. *Ibid.* p. 121.

15. See W. C. Smith, *The Meaning and End of Religion* (New York: Macmillan, 1962), pp. 185–92.

16. See N. Smart, *The Science of Religion and the Sociology of Knowledge* (Princeton, N.J.: Princeton University Press, 1973), pp. 67 ff. and *The Phenomenon of Religion* (New York: Herder and Herder, 1973), pp. 62 ff.

17. N. Smart, *The Phenomenon of Religion,* p. 102.

18. *The Life of the Holy Mother Teresa of Jesus,* trans. by E. Peers (New York: Sheed and Ward, 1946) p. 121.

19. *The Pearl of Great Price: A Selection from the Revelations, Translations, and Narrations of Joseph Smith* (Salt Lake City, Utah: The Church of Jesus Christ of the Latter Day Saints, 1949), p. 50.

20. C. Isherwood, *Ramakrishna and His Disciples* (New York: Simon and Schuster, 1965), p. 66.

21. H. Van Straelen, *The Religion of Divine Wisdom: Japan's Most Powerful Religious Movement* (Kyoto: Veritas Shoin, 1957), p. 41.

22. R. Coles, "God and the Rural Poor", *Psychology Today* (January 1972), p. 36.

23. *Vedic Hymns,* trans. by H. Oldenburg (Delhi: Motilal Banarsidas, 1964, first published 1897) Part II, p. 352.

24. See R. H. Robinson, *The Buddhist Religion* (Belmont, Calif.: Dickenson, 1970), pp. 72–73, for the place of the *Tri-kaya* doctrine in Yogacara thought.

25. See L. G. Thompson, *Chinese Religion: An Introduction* (Encino, Calif.: Dickenson, 1969), pp. 34–35, for a discussion of the ancestor cult in Chinese culture.

26. Reprinted by permission of the publishers from F. Edgerton's translation of *The Bhagavad-gita,* Cambridge, Mass.: Harvard University Press. Copyright 1944 by the President and Fellows of Harvard College.

27. *The Koran Interpreted,* trans. A. J. Arberry, 2 vols. (New York: Macmillan. 1955), 2:114 (Sura XXXI).

28. J. Brough, *Selections from Classical Sanskrit Literature* (London: Luzac, 1952), p. 81. Reprinted by permission.

29. R. Jones, *The World Within* (New York: Macmillan, 1918), pp. 18–19.

30. F. S. Ferré, *Making Religion Real* (New York: Harper, 1955), pp. 51 and 54.

31. See K. Cragg, *The House of Islam, 2d ed. (Encino, Calif.: Dickenson, 1975), Chapter 1, "Lord of the Worlds."*

32. *J.* Neusner, *The Way of Torah,* 2d ed. (Encino, Calif.: Dickenson, 1974), p. 18.

33. *The Documents of Vatican II,* Walter Abbott, S. J., ed., trans. Msgr. Joseph Gallagher (New York: Guild Press, 1966), p. 143.

34. R. B. Pandey, "Hindu Sacraments (Samskaras)," in *The Eternal Heritage of India,* rev. ed., 4 vols. (Calcutta: The Ramakrishna Mission, 1967), 2:406.

35. E. Erikson, "Ontogeny of Ritualization," in R. M. Loewenstein et al, eds., *A General Psychology: Essays in Honor of Heinz Hartmann* (New York: International University Press, 1966), p. 603.

36. See H. B. Earhart, *Japanese Religion,* 2d ed. (Encino, Calif.: Dickenson, 1974), especially pp. 5–6, 72–73, and 110–12; H. B. Earhart, ed., *Religion in the Japanese Experience,* pp. 9–19; and T. J. Hopkins, *The Hindu Religious Tradition* (Encino, Calif.: Dickenson, 1971), pp. 11–19.

37. See *Sunday Missal Prayerbook and Hymnal* (New York: Catholic Book Publishing Co., n.d.), p. 45.

38. An excellent Roman Catholic explanation of the unique character of sacred symbolic acts is found in V. Warnach, "Symbol and Reality in the Eucharist, in P. Benoit, R. E. Murphy, and B. van Jersel, eds., *The Breaking of Bread,* vol. 40 of the series Concilium: Theology in the Age of Renewal (New York: Paulist Press, 1969), especially pp. 95–100.

39. See T. J. Hopkins, *The Hindu Religious Tradition,* Chapter 2, "The Creative Power of the Sacrifice," and pp. 111–117 for a discussion of *mantras* in Vedic sacrifice and Hindu worship *(puja).*

40. Trans. by S. Beyer in S. Beyer, ed., *The Buddhist Experience: Sources and Interpretations* (Encino, Calif.: Dickenson, 1974), p. 56. See pp. 46–64 and 116–153 for excerpts from various sources that assume the power of special words and actions in the Buddhist tradition.

41. See K. Cragg, *The House of Islam,* 2d ed., Chapter 3.

42. *The New Testament in Modern English,* trans. J. B. Phillips (New York: Macmillan, 1958), pp. 327–28.

43. *The Sacred Pipe,* recorded and ed. by J. E. Brown (Baltimore, Md.: Penguin, 1971, first published 1953), p. 92.

44. See J. Neusner, ed., *The Life of Torah: Readings in the Jewish Religious Experience* (Encino, Calif.: Dickenson, 1974). Part VII, "Torah as a Way of Life: The Sanctification of Time," includes excerpts from litugical manuals and explanations of the religious significance of Jewish festivals, feasts, and the "higher holy days."

45. S. Radhakrishnan, *The Hindu View of Life* (London: George Allen & Unwin, 1961, first published 1927), p. 55.

46. From the *Central Harmony (Chung yung),* trans. by Lin Yutang, in Lin Yutang, ed., *The Wisdom of Confucius* (New York: Modern Library, 1938), p. 105.

47. From *The Mencius,* trans. by B. Watson, in *Sources of Chinese Tradition,* comp. by W. T. de Bary, Wing-tsit Chan, and B. Watson (New York: Columbia University Press, 1960), pp. 105–106.

48. See F. M. Conford, *From Religion to Philosophy: A Study in the Origins of Western Speculations* (New York: Harper, 1957, first published 1912), pp. 43 ff.; and J. E. Harrison, *Themis: A Study of the Social Origins of Greek Religion* (Cambridge, England: Cambridge University Press, 1927), especially pp. 483 ff.

49. From *The Meditations of Emperor Marcus Antonius,* trans. by A. S. L. Farquharson (Oxford: Clarendon Press, 1944), p. 81.

50. D. S. Muzzey, *Ethics as Religion* (New York: Simon & Schuster, 1951), pp. 2–3.

51. Trans. by Lin Yutang in Lin Yutang, ed., *The Wisdom of Confucius,* p. 229.

52. See L. G. Thompson, *Chinese Religion: An Introduction,* 2d ed. (Encino, Calif: Dickenson, 1975), Chapter 3; and L. G. Thompson, ed., *The Chinese Way in Religion* (Encino, Calif.: Dickenson, 1973), Chapters 3, 4, 6, 18, 20, and 21.

53. C. K. Yang, *Religion in Chinese Society* (Berkeley and Los Angeles: University of California Press, 1961), p. 36.

54. *Laws of Manu,* trans. by G. Buehler in Sacred Books of the East Series, vol. 25 (Oxford University Press, 1886), pp. 30–31.

55. See T. J. Hopkins, *The Hindu Religious Tradition,* pp. 73–84.

56. See J. Neusner, ed., *The Life of Torah,* Part V, "Torah as a Way of Life: The Joy of the Commandments."

57. See K. Cragg, *The House of Islam,* 2d ed., chapters 4 and 5.

58. See L. G. Thompson, ed., *The Chinese Way in Religion,* Chapters 3 and 6, and L. G. Thompson, *Chinese Religion,* 2d ed., Chapter 1.

59. From the *Digha-nikaya* (collection of long discourses) in S. Beyer, ed., *The Buddhist Experience,* p. 83. See also the other excerpts in Chapter 5, "The Stages on the Path."

60. See T. J. Hopkins, *The Hindu Religious Tradition,* pp. 67–69 for a brief discussion of "the eightfold yoga."

61. See Vyasa's text of and commentary on the first seven verses of the *Yoga Sutras* in *Yoga Philosophy of Patanjali,* with commentary by Swami Hariharananda Acarya, trans. by P. N. Mukerji (Calcutta: Calcutta University Press, 1963), pp. 1–30.

62. Sri Auribindo, *A Practical Guide to Integral Yoga* (Pondicherry: Sri Auribindo Ashram, 1965), p. 26.

63. From the *Katha Upanishad* II.1.1,2, 4, 5, in *The Principal Upanishads,* trans. by S. Radhakrishnan (New York: Harper, 1953), pp. 630–32.

64. See the excerpts in S. Beyer, ed., *The Buddhist Experience,* Chapter 2, "Personal Morality".

65. From *Jaina Sutras,* trans. by H. Jacobi in Sacred Books of the East Series, vol. 22 (Oxford: Oxford University Press, 1884), Part I, pp. 79, 80.

66. *The Perfection of Wisdom in Eight Thousand Lines,* trans. by E. Conze (Bolinas, Calif., Four Seasons Foundation, 1973), p. 98. Italics added.

67. From Hui-k'ai, *The Gateless Barrier,* trans. by S. Beyer, in S. Beyer, ed., *The Buddhist Experience,* p. 268; see also other examples of *koans* on pp. 261–69.

68. Trans. by Lin Yutang, in Lin Yutang, ed., *The Wisdom of Lao-tzu* (New York: Modern Library, 1948), pp. 106–107.

69. See J. White, ed., *Frontiers of Consciousness; The Meeting Ground Between Inner and Outer Reality* (New York: Julian Press, 1974), pp. 9–18, or White's *Highest State of Consciousness* (New York: Doubleday, 1972), for an extended discussion of these states

from a psychological point of view. Compare the discussion in N. Smart, *Reasons and Faiths* (New York: Humanities Press, 1958), on the relation between particular religious practices and different religious goals.

70. See R. H. Robinson, *The Buddhist Religion,* pp. 15–20 on the content and interpretation of the Buddha's enlightenment.

71. See excerpts from Buddhist literature on the highest experience of insights in Buddhism in S. Beyer, ed., *The Buddhist Experience,* Chapter 9.

72. K. Nielson, "Ethics Without Religion," in P. Kierty, ed., *Moral Problems in Contemporary Society: Essays in Humanistic Ethics* (Englewood Cliffs, N.J.: Prentice Hall, 1969), p. 21.

73. J. Huxley, "Transhumanism," in *New Bottles for New Wine: Essays by Julian Huxley* (London: Chatto and Windus, 1959), pp. 13–14. See also his book, *Religion Without Revelation* (New York: New American Library, 1957), especially Chapter 9, "Evolutionary Humanism as a Developed Religion."

74. A. Camus, *Resistance, Rebellion, and Death,* trans. by J. O'Brien (New York: Knopf, 1970), p. 93.

75. J. H. Cone, *Black Theology and Black Power* (New York: Seabury Press, 1969), p. 7.

76. A. N. Whitehead, *Process and Reality: An Essay in Cosmology,* (New York: Humanities Press, 1929), p. 4.

77. In F. le Van Baumer, ed., *Main Currents in Western Thought* (New York: Knopf, 1934), pp. 374–75.

78. B. de Spinoza, "The Treatise on the Improvement of the Understanding," in T. V. Smith, and M. Greene, eds., *Philosophers Speak for Themselves: From Descartes to Locke* (Chicago: University of Chicago Press, 1940), p. 246.

79. *Ibid.,* p. 247.

80. W. A. Clebsch and C. R. Jaekle, *Pastoral Care in Historical Perspective* (New York: Harper, 1964), p. 13.

81. *Ibid.,* Part III.

82. From "The Treasury of Precious Sayings," in S. Beyer, ed., *The Buddhist Experience,* p. 25.

83. From Lin Yutang, ed., *The Wisdom of Confucius,* p. 186.

84. From S. Beyer, ed., *The Buddhist Experience,* pp. 40–41.

85. O. H. Mowrer, "The Problem of Good and Evil Empirically Considered, with Reference to Psychological and Social Adjustment," *Zygon: Journal of Religion and Science* 4, no. 4 (December 1969): 12.

86. A. Maslow, "Eupsychia—The Good Society," *Journal of Humanistic Psychology* 1, no. 2 (Fall 1961): 8.

87. See C. R. Rogers, "The Necessary and Sufficient Conditions of Therapeutic Personality Change," *Journal of Consulting Psychology* 21 (1957): 95–103.

88. C. R. Rogers, *Freedom to Learn,* (Columbus, Ohio: Merrill, 1969), pp. 304–305.

89. From J. C. Lilly, *The Center of the Cyclone: An Autobiography of Inner Space* (New York: Bantam, 1973), pp. 103–104.

90. F. Perls, *Gestalt Therapy Verbatim,* comp. and ed., J. O. Stevens (Lafayette, Calif.: Real People Press, 1969), frontispiece.

91. See Okakura Kakuzo, *The Book of Tea* (Rutland, Vt.: Tuttle, 1906), for an exposition and advocacy of "teaism" as an expression of the Japanese art of life.

92. Trans. by A. Waley, *Translations from the Chinese* (New York: Knopf, 1941), p. 121.

93. See H. N. McFarland, *The Rush Hour of the Gods* (New York: Macmillan, 1967), Chapter 6, "PL Kyodan: An Epicurean Movement."

94. J. S. Mbiti, *African Religions and Philosophies* (Garden City, N.Y.: Doubleday, 1970), pp. 27–29.

95. From *Ch'un-ch'iu fan-lu* [deep significance of the *Spring and Autumn Annals*], trans. by B. Watson, in *Sources of Chinese Tradition,* comp. by W. T. de Bary, Wing-tsit Chan, and B. Watson, p. 218. For further explanation of ancient Chinese cosmology, see L. G. Thompson, *Chinese Religion.* 2d ed., Chapter 1; and L. G. Thompson, ed., *The Chinese Way in Religion,* Chapter 6.

96. R. B. Fuller, *Utopia or Oblivion* (New York: Bantam, 1969), p. 159.

97. V. C. Ferkiss, *Technological Man: The Myth and Reality* (New York: Braziller, 1969), pp. 17, 19.

Index

Evil, 43, 105, 133, 155
Evolution, 25–27, 29, 32, 42, 43, 48, 49, 54, 114, 129, 176
Experience, transcendent, 16, 26, 37, 54, 62, 68, 71–80, 83, 88, 113, 118, 121

Faith, 62, 63, 66, 69, 79, 80, 114, 118, 122, 124, 149, 182, 190, 191
Feeling, 13, 26, 28, 42, 72, 78, 80, 83, 88, 114, 118, 126, 152, 155, 161. *See also* Emotion; Religion, subjective experience of
Ferkiss, V. C., 184
Ferré, Nels, 78
Frazer, James G., 28, 29, 30
Freedom:
  political, 137–140
  spiritual, 113–123
Freud, Sigmund, 39–41, 46, 160, 161
Fuller, R. Buckminster, 184
Function of religion, social, 37–50
Funeral rites, 45, 84

God:
  action of, 71, 72, 83, 89, 90, 122, 168, 178
  communion with, 77–80, 99, 156
  experience of, 42, 58, 59, 71–80, 99, 118
  notion (concept) of, 12, 27, 28, 30, 31, 43, 53, 54, 76, 77, 147–149, 151
  revelation of, 25, 59, 71, 86, 87, 91, 93, 146, 168
  will of, 80, 100, 105, 132–135, 159, 178
Goodness, 12, 99, 131, 132, 133, 155
Greece, data from ancient, 135, 136

"High being," 31
Hinduism, data from, 71, 73, 75, 77, 78, 80, 84, 89, 91, 94, 103, 104, 106, 107, 108, 115–117, 119, 121, 123, 147, 158, 168, 169, 178, 181
History, study of, 182, 183. *See also* Study of religion, historical
Holy Presence (Holiness), 71–80, 99, 113, 128, 157
Human relationship, religious significance of, 126, 127, 128, 155–164

Ideals, 155, 156
Identity, personal, 44, 46
Image(s), divine, 67, 68, 83, 92, 93, 95, 96, 122, 168, 169
Initiation, 44, 46, 47, 54, 57

Insight, spiritual, 6, 8, 15, 16, 69, 113–124, 192
Institutions, religious, 37, 38, 44, 45, 66
Intention, religious, 15, 17, 22, 58, 147, 189, 193
Interpretation of religion, 9, 14, 21, 25, 43, 59, 60. *See also* Understanding religion, problem of
Islam, data from, 76, 80, 90, 91, 100, 105, 133, 134, 147, 169, 178

Jainism, 117, 118, 123
James, E. O., 41
James, William, 39
Japanese religion, data from, 72, 79, 170–172, 178
Jen, 106, 107, 133
Jones, Rufus, 78
Joy, 6, 25, 79, 80, 113, 115–124, 128, 164
Judaism, data from, 73, 75, 80, 83, 90, 95, 100, 105, 133, 134, 135, 147, 178
Jung, Carl, 39, 41, 42
Justice, 105–107, 131, 133, 137–140

Karma, 104, 116
Kluckhohn, Clyde, 41, 47
Kristensen, W. Brede, 58, 59
Kroeber, Alfred L., 46, 47

Language, religious use of, 26, 27, 44
Law, moral, 100–107, 128, 131
van der Leeuw, Gerardus, 59, 60, 75
Levi-Strauss, Claude, 29, 48, 49, 60
Levy–Bruhl, Lucien, 28
Li, 102
Liturgical art, 168, 169
Logical thinking, 27, 31. *See also* Reason, interpreting life through
Luckmann, Thomas, 45, 46

Magic, 28, 29, 30, 47, 146, 152
Malinowski, Bronislaw, 29
Mana (power), 27, 28, 60, 73, 104, 107
Marett, R. R., 28, 30
Mark Antony, Emperor, 101
Master, spiritual, 114, 120, 121, 124, 156, 158
May, Rollo, 42
Meaning, general construction of, 48, 49, 56, 66, 86, 90, 114, 118, 128, 144, 146, 167, 172, 192

Meaning, religious, 10–14, 17, 25, 32, 37, 43, 56, 58, 60–66, 68, 83–85, 123, 126–129, 147, 172, 183, 192, 193
Means of ultimate transformation, 7, 12, 17, 18, 66, 67, 69, 127, 131, 138, 149, 151, 152, 155, 164, 172, 177, 185, 189, 192, 195
Meditation, spiritual, 67, 71, 91, 114–120. *See also* Contemplation, spiritual; Discipline, spiritual
Melanesian religion, data from, 73, 89, 104
Mode of human awareness, 12, 61, 62, 131, 143, 146, 189, 194
Modern society, religion in, 4, 5, 9, 126–129, 189–196
Moral order, eternal, 99–107, 132, 178–180
Methodology for studying religion, 25, 30, 63
Miki, 72
Mueller, F. Max, 26, 53
Muzzey, D. S., 101
Myth-making, 64, 85–91
Mythology, 25, 26, 31, 47–49, 53, 55, 64, 86–91, 118, 168, 169, 180, 183

Nagarjuna, 149, 181
Naming (giving something a name), 26, 27, 28, 85, 86, 90, 143
Neusner, Jacob, 83
Nirvana, 63, 119, 121, 128
Nonliterate society, religion of, 26, 27, 28, 29, 31, 32, 47, 48, 61, 66, 76, 152
Nonreligious, 4, 5, 7

Objective study of religion. *See* Study of religion, objective
Origin of religion. *See* Religion, origin of
Otto, Rudolf, 58, 59, 63, 75

Pastoral care, 156–158
Pattern, social, 44, 46
Pettazzoni, Raffaele, 31
Perls, Fritz, 163, 164
Personal dimension of religion, 1–3
Phenomenology of religion. *See* Study of religion, phenomenological
Philosophy, 114, 119, 127, 136, 143, 145, 146, 149–152, 180, 181
Physical existence, religious significance of, 126, 175–185. *See also* World, religious views of
Piaget, Jean, 48

Plato, 136, 180
Pluralism, religious, 190–194
Power, spiritual, 8, 9, 11, 12, 15, 72–75, 78, 83, 88, 90–93, 158
Praise to God, 77, 78, 79, 132
Prayer, 30, 63, 67, 73, 77, 78, 88, 132, 168
Prehistoric religion. *See* Religion, origin of
Priest, 93, 94, 104, 156, 157
Primitive religion. *See* Nonliterate society, religion of
Process of ultimate transformation, 8, 11, 12, 16, 67–69, 126, 127, 138, 151, 159, 164, 167, 172, 177, 184, 189, 190
Processes of human awareness, 17, 37, 127, 183, 189
Processes, types of religious, 12, 13, 17, 68, 192
Psychotherapy, 159–164
Punishment, 44, 133
Purification, religious, 92, 93, 117, 119

Ramakrishna, Sri, 71
Reality, 67, 71, 72, 76, 85, 86, 95, 119, 120, 143, 144, 155, 159, 170, 171, 178, 183, 194
Reason, interpreting life through, 20, 53, 114, 117, 126–129, 143–152, 180
Religion:
    definition of, 1–9, 17, 29, 62, 63, 66, 194. *See also* Means of ultimate transformation
    dimensions of, 1–7, 16
    inner dynamics of, 3, 16, 17, 37, 189, 190, 194. *See also* Dynamic character of religion
    nature of, 63, 64. *See also* Ultimate dimension of life
    origins of, 25–33, 53
    purpose (aim) of, 27, 29, 30
    social scientific study of, 10, 20–50
    study of, 9–18. *See also* Study of religion
    subjective experience of, 13–18, 28, 41, 190–192. *See also* Personal dimension of religion
Religions, history of, 27, 31, 32, 53. *See also* Study of religions, historical
Religious life. *See* Religion
Religious quality, 62, 63, 64. *See also* Ultimate dimension of life
Religious tradition, 2, 9, 11, 15, 67, 68, 92, 107–109, 129, 168, 192, 193, 195. *See also* Traditional religion